MAVERICK MAYOR

To Johanna Egan Yorty: Born Johanna Egan in Clonmel, Ireland, September 27, 1880; died in Los Angeles, California, at the age of 81 on January 18, 1962. She was the wife of Frank Patrick Yorty, whom she married in Lincoln, Nebraska, where she reared her family. She was the mother of Samuel William Yorty and Kathleen and Enid. She moved to Los Angeles in 1928.

She was a woman whose greatest desire and determination was for her children to be well-educated; who lived by the conviction "If you really want something enough and put forth the effort, you can achieve it," and that "Whatever happens, happens for a reason, time proving this to be so." She was a woman whose belief in God was unswerving, based on the contention that "God does not burden us with things we cannot handle."

She started a long career in real estate soon after coming to Los Angeles and became a successful business woman through foresight and ingenuity. Her children spiritedly claimed for her "The luck of the Irish," yet she remained, in their words, "First of all a home-maker." Her ambition for her family was foremost in a life characterized by a happy disposition, hard work, excellent health and "generosity to a fault". She was a woman who remembered the little things which are important to people, especially for her three grandchildren and five great-grandchildren.

Johanna Egan Yorty was cherished and respected by the many who came to know her in the district in the heart of Los Angeles where she resided, worked, devoted herself to her family, and loved and served her fellowmen in humility and understanding.

Books by Ed Ainsworth

POT LUCK

EAGLES FLY WEST

CALIFORNIA JUBILEE

BILL MAGEE'S WESTERN BARBECUE COOKBOOK

DEATH CUES THE PAGEANT

PAINTERS OF THE DESERT

THE CALIFORNIA I LOVE
  (*By Leo Carrillo with Ed Ainsworth*)

BECKONING DESERT

GOLDEN CHECKERBOARD

ERNIE PYLE'S SOUTHWEST
  (*Editor*)

MAVERICK MAYOR

A Biography of Sam Yorty of Los Angeles

by Ed Ainsworth

Doubleday & Company, Inc.

Garden City, New York

1966

Library of Congress Catalog Card Number 66–19531

Dedicated to
The women in Sam Yorty's life

His mother
  Johanna Egan Yorty

His wife
  Betty Hensel Yorty

His guide
  The Spirit of Liberty

INTRODUCTION

On a certain hot evening in late spring—it was Wednesday, May 31, 1961—I was driving west across eastern Arizona between Gallup, New Mexico, and Tucson, headed home to California with my younger son-in-law, Dr. Jerome Lengyel, with whom I had been down in Texas where he was taking his State Board examinations in Veterinary Medicine.

"This," I remarked, "is Election Day for Mayor in Los Angeles because yesterday—Tuesday, the normal date—was Memorial Day and they couldn't have it then. I think Sam Yorty is going to lick the hell out of Norris Poulson."

My son-in-law looked at me out of the corner of his eye as if the Oracle of Delphi suddenly had predicted a World Series triumph for the New York Mets.

"How come you think he can do it?" Dr. Lengyel inquired. "Who ever heard of him?"

As a strong Democrat himself, Dr. Lengyel had expected me as a supposedly impregnable Republican to tout the fortunes of Poulson, the Republican, rather than Yorty, the Democrat.

"It's got nothing to do with partisan politics," I hastened to assure him. "I know Sam's been a loser lots of times but he loves a fight and he's sure had one this time—all the political pros are backing Poulson but Sam has managed to 'come over' with the voters on TV. And California voters are funny—they don't care how they're registered, they just do whatever they damn please. You watch, Sam's going to win."

Sure enough, next morning the Tucson paper had the story that Sam had walloped Poulson. I was delighted at the correctness of my prediction. And Dr. Lengyel regarded me as a Grade A prophet.

To tell the truth, Sam and I both are considered mavericks. It's easy for me to know how he thinks. I've known him since he was a young, eager, idealistic Assemblyman way back in 1936. I have watched him through victory and defeat—particularly defeat—and become more and more convinced that he possesses the rare and almost mystic quality of political leadership. He radiates a charm which communicates itself not only in person but on television. He arouses strong feelings. Many love him. Some detest him. Few are neutral.

His seeming-impetuosity keeps him continually in the forefront of battles on a multiplicity of subjects. Actually, he is almost never impetuous. His moves are well-studied and calculated, even though they may appear on the surface to be spontaneous. His mind is so quick, he is so accustomed to dealing with a dozen or a hundred problems simultaneously that he confounds his opponents by the depth of his knowledge on the particular topic under discussion at the moment.

Sam has been much in the public eye. Yet he is virtually unknown as an individual. This is the situation I have set forth to correct. Just as I felt that hot evening in May 1961 when I guessed Sam was going to win and become Mayor of Los Angeles, so now do I feel that people would like to know what kind of human being he is.

Political pitch man or genuine statesman? Petulant fraud or sound thinker? Hypocrite or true friend?

Sam Yorty has been called all of these.

He is in his second term as Mayor of America's third largest city after having overwhelmingly defeated U. S. Representative James Roosevelt, son of the former President. The nation is acutely aware of him due to his appearances on TV, his imagination in tackling problems common to all great American cities, his bitter clashes with California's Governor Brown over the handling of the Watts Negro riots in Los Angeles in August 1965, and his growing reputation as a political leader who never pulls his punches on any issue.

This book is not intended to be a definitive work on the City of Los Angeles or on urbanization in America. It is, rather, the attempt to describe a man against the backdrop of his great City.

What is Sam really like?

Let me try to tell you.

Ed Ainsworth

Los Angeles
December 1, 1965

CHAPTER I

Any man who reads beyond the second paragraph
of the Los Angeles City Charter would be out of his
mind to run for Mayor.

SAM YORTY

At exactly 11:47 P.M. Sam knew for sure he was elected.
Mayor Sam!

Everybody called him "Sam," friend and foe alike.

Last-Chance Sam, Hard-Luck Sam, Grab-Bag Sam, Do-or-Die
Sam, Come-from-Behind Sam, Loud-Mouth Sam they labeled
him during the campaign. But always "Sam."

By morning, all Los Angeles was saying, "Well, I'll be damned!"
and muttering unbelievingly about him as the newspapers, TV
commentators, and radio newscasters rather dazedly reported his
victory that incredible first day of June 1961.

"Sam elected mayor?"

The startled exclamations, in a mounting and almost-deafening
sound wave arose from the smelly docks at San Pedro to the fancy
film mansions of Encino and from the concrete banks of the Arroyo
Seco to the chaparral hills of Palos Verdes, and battered against
the white tower of the City Hall, a bewildered and conquered
bastion.

Samuel William Yorty? Who was he, really? People who had
ignored the long-shot tried to dig into their memories. Yes, Sam
had been in the Legislature, way back; later in Congress; and had
run unsuccessfully for United States Senator. Then he had been
out of sight for seven years, just practicing law. Hardly anybody
had heard of him during all that time.

Suddenly there he was, a maverick Democrat announcing for
mayor against the powerfully entrenched "downtown" Republican

1

machine of Norris Poulson, the incumbent, in a nominally "non-partisan" election. Poulson, supported by the "regulars" was considered a certainty for another term. The metropolitan newspapers, with the locally powerful and usually invincible *Times* leading the chorus, proclaimed the necessity of Poulson's re-election, and thundered against Sam for daring to think he could unseat the mayor. Mayor Poulson began mapping the program he planned after his expected triumph. Business went on as usual in City Hall where tranquillity was a watchword, and discord was not tolerated.

Toward the end of the campaign, it must be admitted, a few twinges beset some of the more astute political observers, particularly when George Putnam, KTTV news commentator who had been a most effective advocate of Yorty's candidacy intensified his strong efforts.

Sam had taken to TV, with a full awareness of his own effectiveness there and remembering the success of Kennedy, the underdog in the TV debates with Nixon in the presidential race a few months before. It was indeed his natural medium. His powerful, calm voice dissected the city's somewhat muddled affairs with delicate precision; his intelligent youthful face with the extremely wideset eyes looked candidly from the screen; his frequent and spontaneous interjections of humor were devastatingly direct.

His simple, sparse, colloquial words went radar-straight to the point. His spontaneous candor disdained all detours. His directness and clarity frightened the fuzzy and disconcerted the devious. His pungent phrases invigorated his supporters and gained an ever-widening following.

Still, nobody took his chances very seriously, even when Norris Poulson got laryngitis and sounded, croakingly on TV, like an elderly voice of doom predicting plague and pestilence if the voters listened to Sam's wiles. Sam just kept on plugging away about trash collection, tax reduction, charter reform, minority rights and such simple things, appealing to housewives. He was, indeed, accused of "campaigning from the top of a trash barrel."

When the votes were counted, there was no doubt about who won. Sam was 16,000 ballots to the good in a turnout of more than 500,000 voters; 273,701 to 257,073. But the persistent question remained: Who is Sam, this vigorous fifty-one-year-old human being, the unknown quantity, the enigma?

Assemblyman? Congressman? Unsuccessful candidate on previous occasions? Granted! A political freak? An opportunist? A

2

happenstance? Nobody could really answer those last ones. Nobody, that is, but Sam Yorty, new Mayor of the City of Los Angeles. Welling up in his memory that morning of the first day of June must have been images and impressions of his own past life forever enmeshed in his brain and heart:

A little boy eight years old selling newspapers on the blizzard-swept streets of Lincoln, Nebraska . . . The names of "William Jennings Bryan" and "Woodrow Wilson" engraved in his consciousness from hero-worshiping repetition . . . A high school lad writing for a favorite teacher about his dawning political ambition . . . Shattering tragedies in the home, discord, unhappiness . . . Wanderlust . . . Los Angeles . . . Odd jobs . . . The Great Depression . . . Poverty, both observed and experienced . . . The cruelty of political despotism . . . Rebellion . . . Political ambition . . . Success in a first campaign . . . Happy marriage . . . World War II . . . Blood . . . The Pacific cauldron . . . Planes . . . Politics again . . . New success . . . Contention . . . The beginning of a lifelong struggle with Communism . . . Washington . . . Defeat . . . Seeming oblivion . . . An abiding faith in a personal destiny.

These things were unknown outside the Yorty family. Sam never thrusts his personal life upon the public; he guarded his privacy then as he does now. The rough-and-tumble brawling antagonist in the political arena is a quiet home-loving man who seeks seclusion whenever he can. Yet the complex personality of this political figure is the end-product, the culmination of all the seemingly providential circumstances which have gone into the shaping of his character.

The resoluteness with which Sam Yorty embarked upon the manifold aims of his administration soon brought him attention far beyond the bounds of Los Angeles itself. The remark began to be heard in the East, the Middle West, and the South that "something is happening in Los Angeles." Before long, the name "Sam Yorty" was being heard in New York, Chicago, Boston, Philadelphia, Dallas, Houston, Atlanta, Cleveland, and other metropolitan areas as mayors and city administrators carried the word of the Southern California megalopolis, the super-city, being urged along toward new goals by its unorthodox chief executive. Within two years after his election Sam Yorty was featured, in this connection, on the cover of *Time* magazine, May 10, 1963.

Even amid controversies and feuds on local issues, Los Angeles itself was becoming aware of the extraordinary nature of its indefatigable mayor. The people saw him plunge headlong into attempts to thrust Los Angeles toward whole new concepts of municipal procedure. Up to the time Sam took office most advances in Los Angeles of any notable nature had been due to the efforts of the business community rather than to city administrations. Initiation of programs had rarely come from mayors or City Council. As a result the creation of such civic assets as the Los Angeles Memorial Coliseum, the County Museum, the Hollywood Bowl, the Plaza Restoration Project at the birthplace of the city, the Art Museum and the Music Center—even the concerted effort to control smog—had come from the ideas and work of citizens rather than from the leaders in government. Sam Yorty began to change this type of thinking. Trying to look ahead for the future good of the city, he embarked as the executive leader on the creation of a Master Plan for Los Angeles, something it had never had; total revision of the antiquated charter, abolition of destructive zoning in residential areas, delving into minority problems, discovering the causes of poverty and remedies for racial discrimination, a sound approach to rapid transit in the midst of the city's choking traffic jams and a more aggressive program of smog control which was under county and state jurisdiction.

In the midst of these unprecedented activities he still, however, remained blurred and obscured as an individual to most citizens. Some were keenly aware, as they had been from the start, of the "real" Sam Yorty. These included not only his old-time friends and associates but also Negroes and the down-trodden who sensed his genuine lifelong concern for them and their rights. The Negroes, in fact, contributed greatly to his initial victory at the polls. The close ties between Sam Yorty and the Negro community became closer as he made good on his pledges to introduce members of minority races, including those from the tremendous Mexican-American population, into active governmental structure surrounding him. He appointed Negroes to his own staff for the first time in the political life of the city. He appointed others to municipal commissions and advisory boards. He helped create an atmosphere of inter-racial goodwill in which Negroes were elected to the City Council.

These continuing manifestations of the Yorty philosophy of translating civil rights beliefs into practical reality became of overwhelming importance in the August 1965 Watts riots in Los

4

Angeles, which were touched off by an incident involving California State Highway Patrolmen who chased an allegedly drunken Negro from county territory into Los Angeles City. The ensuing altercation flamed into the fatal riots. During the tense days of the rioting and looting, Mayor Yorty and blunt, courageous Police Chief William H. Parker emerged as the firm and unyielding advocates of law enforcement. They stood fast amid hysteria and criticism and provided, in the long run, the only bulwarks to whom Negroes as well as whites could turn in the confusion and inconsistencies of other officials, particularly on the state level. The bulk of the Negroes were as intent as anyone else to suppress the lawless element in their ranks.

Governor Edmund G. Brown of California vacillated in regard to Chief Parker and this created uncertainty and doubt. In addition, the governor, touring abroad when the riots occurred, exclaimed plaintively in Rome on his hurried way home:

"Terrible—unbelievable—absolutely beyond my comprehension."

Meanwhile, Mayor Yorty on the home front necessarily confronted the riot situation as being within the realm of his comprehension. While Governor Brown was expressing consternation seven thousand miles away, Mayor Yorty was dealing with the necessities of the moment, unflinchingly supporting Chief Parker and the police. He even found it mandatory in behalf of law enforcement, in the midst of the violence, to denounce the tactics of Reverend Martin Luther King who had come to Los Angeles and, after a four-hour conference with the mayor, demanded the removal of Chief Parker, who was credited throughout the nation with "running the best police department in the United States."

"I had entertained Reverend Mr. King before when he was here as a guest of the city," said Mayor Yorty. "But when he indulged in inflammatory statements and attacked our Police Chief who is internationally respected, I had no choice but to take him on. He should, instead, have been urging his own people, as I did, to join in putting down the criminal element responsible for the riots."

This stern admonition, coming as it did from a man who was known by instinct and tradition as the unwavering friend of the Negro people, gained instant national attention. During the riot period tens of thousands of letters of commendation poured in on Mayor Yorty. A few were violently denunciatory. More than 90 percent, however, praised the Mayor for his vigorous and consistent stand for law enforcement and his statement that anarchy and rioting by persons of *any* color would not be tolerated.

5

Mayor Yorty took this stand at the outset of the tragic upheaval with characteristic disregard of whether it would be "popular." In his entire career he had adhered to this principle: he spoke out for what he considered right. Sometimes he broke with his associates because of this trait. If he felt he could no longer conscientiously "go along," he said so, and explained why. This had been dramatically illustrated again just before Sam's election when, in the presidential race of 1960, he had refused to support John F. Kennedy and come out strongly for Richard M. Nixon who actually carried California by about 35,000 votes. These so-called defections earned him the title of "maverick" in the Democratic party.

In Los Angeles, however, his independence of mind during his first term began to impress itself favorably upon the community consciousness. A few discerning citizens were becoming vaguely aware that for the first time the city with the abbreviated name—"Los Angeles"—had found in the man with the abbreviated name—"Sam"—someone who at last comprehended it and could confidently guide into an illimitable future. Los Angeles—actually El Pueblo de Nuestra Señora la Reina de Los Angeles de Porciuncula—never had been understood. It did not even have the distinction of having had a notable book written about it. Observers had dealt with it piecemeal, by segments, in facets. Writers dwelt upon Hollywood, on the freakishness of Los Angeles' overwhelming size, on its provinciality, on its crudeness, on its dearth of culture, on its lack of cohesion and its failure to develop a "community spirit."

It was, they said, just an overgrown mess, with freeways; some suburbs in search of a city.

Sam's feeling was totally different. He always saw something deeper. He loved the city. Its very vastness uplifted him. He could recall his first impression of it when he arrived as a youth from his small Midwestern home town. It was an exciting city even then, with its pulsating "downtown" and the suburbs billowing out toward the sea and crawling up the mountains. Main Street with its peep shows and burlesques was tawdry, of course, but behind Main Street was a story of Spanish daring and Mexican pastoral life and American conquest. The dilapidated and unlovely Plaza still whispered of gay days beyond recall when dons and señoritas paraded on warm lazy evenings and the scent of climbing roses was in the air from the gardens of old adobes and a pleading bell from the Old Plaza Church sought to entice revelers from bull-and-bear fights into the taper-scented atmosphere before the altar.

From the first, Sam sensed the drama inherent in a city with a twin cultural heritage dating from Rome via Spain on one hand and from England via Magna Carta on the other. He was unmoved by the distant traditions and pretensions of Boston and Philadelphia. Instinctively, he was more impressed by the infinitely richer cultural mulch to be found in the southwestern part of the American continent from which had sprung civilization in Alta California. In the 1500s in Mexico—Los Angeles' mother country—there had been universities and printing presses and salons and composers and literature many decades before there was a Plymouth Rock or a Jamestown squatting in muddy wildernesses.

The fandango in the Southwest had long preceded the Salem witch burnings.

True, El Pueblo de Nuestra Señora la Reina de Los Angeles de Porciuncula—the Porciuncula part referred to a favorite meditation retreat of Saint Francis in Italy—had been founded only in 1781, the last year of the War of the Revolution on the other side of the continent. But, under Roman-Spanish procedure, Los Angeles in concept at least, was a *city* from the very moment of that evening of September 4, 1781, when the little band of foot-weary settlers set up their first rude shelters near the present Plaza, and the community was designated as a *pueblo*, or town. This distinguished it, set it firmly apart from the other two Spanish colonial settlement procedures, the *presidio*, or fort, and the mission, or ecclesiastical adjunct of the royal rule.

This "city" concept, though, was strictly theoretical. Sam hated to admit it, even to himself, but Los Angeles when he took office 180 years after the founding—figuring from 1781 to 1961—was still in the category its critics ascribed to it. It was big, it was sprawling, it was clamorous, it was rich, it was glittering but it lacked cohesion, unity, stature, maturity, the essential almost-indefinable qualities of a true great city.

Could one man remedy this?

Could he pull divergent elements together, mold, heal wounds, inspire great dreams, initiate, carry through, uplift, solidify, bring order from aimlessness, set goals and reach meaningfully for the horizon of tomorrow?

Sam knew, from five elected terms in public office, that even in its simplest terms, the job of a man chosen to lead a city must be overwhelming.

The view from inside City Hall, looking out, is astoundingly different for any mayor from that of the casual observer on the outside looking in. To a man like Sam Yorty, compounded of

7

philosophic reflection as well as political ambition, it also is terrifying in its implications of responsibility to individual men and women. Out there, stretching for miles, radiating in every direction is a sea of faces; or perhaps a faceless sea. Yet somehow all the faces must be brought into focus, be recognized as individual human beings.

The composite citizen is a blur. This blur is made of the young and the old, the rich and the poor, the good and the bad, the ambitious and the lazy, the pious and the criminal. A perpetual clamor arises over differences of opinions. Selfish interest contends with community altruism.

How does a mayor, charged with the duty of leading for the common good amid babel, look compassionately at the millions of faces so he can really see them, choose proper aides, lay down guidelines for government, conduct the enormously complicated fiscal affairs of a metropolis, sleep, eat, make speeches, meet visiting dignitaries, lay cornerstones, support the laws and the police, protect minorities, fight unwarranted accusations, and keep his sanity?

These bewildering demands in the middle of the twentieth century were besetting all mayors concurrently in all cities. Metropolitan areas were groping for the right answers. The importance of the entire matter was underscored when Congress set up a new cabinet post to deal with Urban Affairs, recognizing its vital role for the future.

In Los Angeles, when Sam Yorty took office, the general responsibilities of his task were multiplied manyfold by those peculiar circumstances which for almost two centuries had made the community an incomprehensible puzzle.

Los Angeles needed a leader. It was poised for accomplishment. Yet it was confused, uncertain, lacking in direction.

Millions of citizens looked questioningly toward Sam Yorty, and he looked back trying to fathom their most pressing composite needs. Neither knew for sure at that precise instant when Mayor Sam took his oath what was going to happen in the days, the weeks, the months and the years ahead.

Would this man who had been tempered by so many defeats, who said humbly that he meditated at a fixed time each morning for spiritual guidance, who held such high ambitions for his city, be able to attain his purposes?

Sam could only say he was going to try.

8

CHAPTER II

People in foreign countries are well acquainted with only two Southern California landmarks, Hollywood and Disneyland. Outside of these, Los Angeles is the least known metropolitan area.

SAM YORTY

Even in this modern day when everything is analyzed to death, Los Angeles, with its polyglot millions sprawled across the Southern California hills and valleys has remained incomprehensible to most of the world. It is discussed in learned circles as a possible testing ground for daring new experiments in "metropolitan government" but as a city it is curiously unknown in its essential elements.

From pueblo to metropolis, indeed, it has set an international record by remaining an enigma for almost two centuries.

Rome, Paris, London, New York from their founding filled a purpose, followed a pattern, conformed to expectations. They became cities in the traditional sense. More and more people gravitated to them for the normal urban reasons—security, a market place, convenience, companionship, economics.

On the contrary, Los Angeles was built on a thermometer and a mirage as its twin foundations.

No earthly reason existed in the beginning to expect that it would ever become more than a small, lazy settlement on the bank of a dry arroyo which sometimes generated enough erratic flow to merit the dubious title of "river." Water was so scarce that it was hawked door to door in casks to the few residents. Shimmering heat waves on the nearby sands sometimes generated the visions of lakes, but these mirages vanished into nothingness with the sunset. The only real asset to which Los Angeles consistently could point was a climate day-in-and-day-out considerably warmer

9

than that on the other side of the continent. For decade after decade the community placidly accepted its apparent destiny of remaining as a sunny outpost in the desert, where men of little ambition sat under the trees of the Plaza and permitted life to flow gently by. Money was so scarce that vegetables and chickens became common currency, and a gold coin was more of a curiosity than legal tender. News of the outside world filtered in so slowly that its impact was deadened by staleness.

Los Angeles' expectation of never amounting to anything seemingly was based on sound grounds. Every big city in history shared the common attribute of having been located on a major river for a water supply. Romulus and Remus even after being suckled on wolf milk were engineers enough to establish Rome on the Tiber so the other citizens could have water. Paris emerged on the dependable Seine. London accepted the life-giving Thames River as a necessary feature of its landscape. New York made doubly sure by inserting its most salient segment on Manhattan between the Hudson and the East rivers.

Los Angeles merely squatted beside its dusty arroyo and, when things got bad enough, prayed for rain. Even the ocean was 20 miles from the pueblo and, at that, offered no harbor for supply ships. Any vessel brave enough to attempt access to Los Angeles was compelled to anchor in heavy swells offshore at San Pedro and convey its cargo by lighter to the inhospitable strand for transportation by ox-cart to the pueblo. To accent Los Angeles' precarious rural status, the ascendancy of San Francisco on its magnificent harbor to the north caught the attention of the world. "San Francisco" became a synonym for "excitement" and "wealth." The Gold Rush and subsequent events served to create the impression that California, in essence, consisted of the city by the Golden Gate. Los Angeles' drovers meekly herded tired bulls and cows 450 miles to San Francisco to feed the never-satisfied appetite of its grandiloquent neighbor, and looked with astonishment on mirrored bars and aristocratic restaurants gleaming with white napery and bedecked waiters.

San Francisco could boast militant and sophisticated daily newspapers before lowly Los Angeles in 1851 greeted its first little bilingual weekly, *La Estrella* (*The Star*) printed in both Spanish and English for the benefit of the few who could read. No prophets existed to forecast any essential change in the relative roles of the two communities, so different at the time that it never occurred to anybody to compare them.

Los Angeles, it is true, attained the formal status of an incorporated community April 4, 1850, during the formative period when California was moving toward its entrance into the Union as a state on September 9 of that same year. The first census takers had difficulty finding a sparse 1610 population amid the willows and weeds in the new "city." At that, it was suspected some visiting Indians and a few stray dogs were thrown in to swell the count.

As if an isolated situation and a lack of water were not sufficient deterrents to growth in themselves, drought and smallpox and the blighting side-effects of the Civil War combined during the first two decades after Los Angeles' incorporation to stunt its progress still further. Violently pro-Southern sentiments dominated the community and in some cases had to be curbed by a show of military force.

When Los Angeles finally did begin to emerge from its torpor, the chief causes included the completion of transcontinental rail service and the growing of oranges in the temperate climate for shipment to the East. Now, too, the sunshine began to exert an almost-magnetic attraction for cold-benumbed Americans from other parts of the country. A vanguard of lungers and asthmatics wrote back home such enthusiastic encomiums that "Los Angeles" suddenly became a symbol for sunshine and health.

These magic words attracted real estate promoters in the middle 1880s, and there ensued a frenzied laying out of new towns, mostly along the railroad lines, and the indiscriminate sale of town lots amid the raucous cries of imported pitch men and the handing out of prizes to lucky buyers. The railroads added to the razzle dazzle by offering cutthroat rates from the Middle West—at one time it cost only $1 to travel from Kansas City to Los Angeles—and a vast horde of beguiled potential millionaires risked cinders in their eyes to hasten to the Promised Land.

Since then, the city has been known primarily for its climate and, later for Hollywood.

The role of Hollywood has been both magnified and distorted in efforts to explain its part in the image which Los Angeles presents to the world. Hollywood became from the outside view the glamour capital of creation. But locally it remained just one more suburb. Yet Los Angeles was given perhaps the greatest exploitation medium in history because of the fascinated and yearning glances cast in this direction from all over the world due to the Mary Pickfords, Rudolph Valentinos, Clara Bows, Clark Gables, Greta Garbos, Tom Mixs, Gary Coopers, and Ingrid Bergmans. Los Angeles has had a difficult time trying to reconcile its ordinary existence as a big American city, with problems common to them all, and its celluloid reputation as a frivolous Babylon made up of perpetual love affairs and swimming pools filled with abundant mammaries and tanned male torsos.

If Los Angeles was indeed built at first on a thermometer and a mirage, a strip of movie film formed its third foundation.

All the other vital, significant and relevant factors in its phenomenal population rise have been, for the most part, ignored or brushed aside. Los Angeles does have its own innate and distinguishable character as have all other major cities in the world. Few, though, have bothered to try to seek it out. Some of its characteristics and fundamental elements have been present from the days of its founding as a pueblo. Everything was so defiant of analysis, however, there seemed no reasonable way to discern patterns in municipal evolution.

Any "trends" of growth in the city itself were difficult to trace because of the erratic nature of the time elements and the motivating causes. Los Angeles, although seemingly a steady example of forward movement in population and wealth from about 1885, actually was galvanized by differing stimuli during the entire period. It jumped. It jerked. It sidled. Always, though, newcomers were arriving.

In the years from 1885 until 1910, the community had been known as a haven for the "open shop," or anti-union sentiment, which resulted in an economic climate favorable to moneyed people who wanted relatively cheap and manageable labor. Ironworkers, printers, telegraphers, trolley car operators, garbage collectors, elevator operators, stevedores, oil field crews, carpenters, and many others flocked West because they were willing to work for a little less money just for the privilege of living in the pleasant atmosphere of Los Angeles.

The situation was comparable almost to the near-idyllic existence of serfs with a kind and indulgent Lord of the Manor. But Los Angeles found that despite its relative isolation geographically it could not remain an island in the tempestuous economic seas, tossed and torn by upheavals over Unions vs. Open Shop. General

12

Harrison Gray Otis, himself a printer from the age of eleven, and the thunderous publisher of the Los Angeles *Times* had led the Open Shop forces belligerently and unyielding for decades.

On October 1, 1910, the Los Angeles Times was dynamited by union wreckers, with a toll of twenty killed, many injured and the plant left in smoking debris. From that moment, whether it fully realized it or not, Los Angeles found itself caught up in the rush of the twentieth century on the same basis as any other American big city. Its days of isolation from the general municipal complexities of the age were ended. It was thrust into the present and into competitive existence in a manner it had not known before.

By degrees, then, it discovered that it was being propelled because of location and circumstance into a growingly important role on the American scene. As it gained film-making supremacy over New York it suddenly found itself linked pyrotechnically to an incandescent skyrocket known as Hollywood. Investment capital and prestige multiplied together. The success of the film industry in Hollywood was attributable both to the favorable climate which permitted almost year-round shooting in the outdoors, and the unsurpassed variety of locations and backgrounds available in Southern California. Cecil B. De Mille, D. W. Griffith, Jesse Lasky, Sam Goldwyn, and the other producers simply found they could function more efficiently in Los Angeles than they could in New Jersey and New York City where the "shooting weather" and the light were so unpredictable.

Discovery of oil on a pastoral knoll called Signal Hill at Long Beach launched an unprecedented petroleum boom coincident with the arrival of the 1920s and new flocks of settlers from Iowa to North Carolina. Signal Hill and Kern County gushers to the north of Los Angeles touched off twentieth-century "black gold" rushes far more important money-wise in the realm of subsequent financial speculation than California's original Gold Rush of 1849. Gasoline, of course, would have been brought to the Los Angeles area anyway, but its presence in such unprecedented quantities so close at hand contributed to the kind of gypsy life which made Southern California by far the greatest center of automobiles in the world. Mobility came to Los Angeles with the internal combustion engine.

Then later as in all cases of reckless dissipation of natural resources, the wildly competitive pumping of subsea petroleum deposits led to the almost overwhelming problems of land subsidence which had to be met and conquered at Long Beach and Terminal Island.

The world suddenly woke up to San Pedro Harbor and the timid little new Long Beach Harbor. Commerce flourished in a manner never before known in Southern California all because the people of Los Angeles had possessed the vision to make their own harbor when they did not have one provided for them by nature as in the case of San Francisco. They simply ran a "shoe-string" incorporation strip down from the city proper to the harbor area twenty miles away and annexed it so they could boast of having their own port even if, at first, it was like walking a tight-rope to get to it.

With riches came sophistication. New York brokerage houses recognized Spring Street in Los Angeles as a new "Financial District." Gambling in stocks became a contagious Western fever. Even the interlude of the Great Depression could only slow, not halt, the upward spiral of Los Angeles.

World War II brought sobering decisions, an aircraft-production industry which aided materially in saving the United States in its mortal crisis, and bewildering social and economic changes. At the war's outset Los Angeles was fearful of capture by the enemy or internal collapse due to the theory that it might become "expendable" because of its isolation on the West Coast so far away from the national capital, and the teeming East. But, paradoxically, it built up almost uncomprehendingly through its war effort the foundations of its future phenomenal expansion. The aircraft industry, the electronics plants and the activities relating to thermonuclear power and the approaching space exploration era all had their genesis amid the stimuli of the war effort. They gave Los Angeles a reason to keep growing and a basis on which to make that growth economically successful.

The exiling of all the Japanese population to internment camps in the desert opened up their former district around First and San Pedro streets to hordes of Southern Negroes. Little Tokyo became Bronzeville as a black labor force poured in from Georgia, Louisiana, Mississippi, Alabama, and Texas. This tidal wave of the underprivileged stemmed primarily from Los Angeles' attractiveness to lower economic groups because of its ability to absorb many types of labor. The trouble, then as later, was that the "overselling" of Los Angeles as a haven for everybody created an overpowering

14

influx of people who had no job in sight and thus became the potentially unemployed and the potentially criminal. Urban immigration in its most dangerous aspects began to manifest itself to those leaders in Los Angeles who tried to look into the future. The forces for such outthrusts as the eventual riots in Watts were building up. Sam Yorty became more and more aware of this during his first term as mayor, when he necessarily came into direct confrontation with the spectre on the immediate horizon.

After the war, the Japanese quietly began taking over in their old area, and the Negro infiltration and usurpation of white neighborhoods spreading out from Central Avenue and South Broadway started, never to cease again. The Mexican-Americans, whose heroic service for the United States during the war was unsurpassed by any other ethnic group, increased on the East Side by immigration and fecundity until the Los Angeles area was second only to Mexico City itself in Mexican population.

Another phenomenon flowered. Military men who had sojourned, even briefly, in Southern California found themselves unable to resist the desire to settle there. They formed the nucleus of the great post-war wave of residents. They found jobs in the newly born electronics industry, in the booming building trades, or created new enterprises for themselves. In Los Angeles, and around Los Angeles, bean fields sprouted subdivisions, strawberry patches became "industrial parks," brush-covered hillsides were hacked into flood-vulnerable gashes of raw earth to create building pads, supermarkets invaded citrus groves, freeways transformed villages into roaring "trade centers," and anything within fifty or sixty miles of the Los Angeles City Hall considered itself a "suburb."

In population, Los Angeles saw itself rise from 576,673 in 1920, 1,238,048 in 1930, 1,504,277 in 1940, 1,970,358 in 1950 to 2,479,015 in 1960.

The responsibility of any mayor in Los Angeles is prodigious and is not realized in many parts of the country. Los Angeles at the start of 1966, with its population of approximately 2,750,000, possessed more residents than were listed in 25 states of the Union in the 1960 census. To add to the impact of these figures is the fact that the concentration of this population of diverse racial strains is such that problems normal to states are aggravated in the city. In 1940 Los Angeles County had only 75,000 Negro residents. By 1960 Los Angeles had a Negro population of 334,916—more than one-third the total in the state of California—and this had increased to about 650,000 in the county by the middle of the decade at the time of the Watts riots.

California itself with its population of almost 19,000,000 at the start of 1966 was so urbanized that 85 percent of the people were listed as living in metropolitan areas, adding to the problems faced by the mayors of Los Angeles, San Francisco, San Diego, Long Beach, Oakland, and other large centers.

The more people, the greater the muddle. Every family, every car, every additional school pupil added to the complexity of the demands on public officials. Problems had to be solved almost before they were defined as problems. Improvisation in political accomplishment became a necessity.

As Sam saw it, Mayor Poulson's fundamental weakness was in accepting the status quo, in resigning himself to a "what can we do about it?" attitude, and in refusing to look outside the front door of the City Hall. Sam, for his part, determined that his own role must be to inquire, to delve, to recognize realities, to face up to crises, to admit unpleasant situations, to set goals, and to strive mightily for a closer understanding of people, particularly discontented and desperate people.

All the classic questions confronting a metropolis were blown up in Los Angeles as if the Sorcerer's Apprentice had unleashed uncontrollable forces, which magnified themselves into devilish monsters threatening to destroy their very birthplace. Sam felt that hitherto these monsters had been combatted only with a squirt gun. He wanted to bring on the artillery. First, though, he had to identify his targets and create his arsenal.

When Sam Yorty went into his new job he was the legatee, as had been his predecessors, of the tensions, perplexities, and abnormalities of a Los Angeles afflicted with elephantiasis, the symptoms of which were traceable to conditions created years or generations before.

Among the disagreements facing Sam when he started work as Mayor was the conflict between those who believed devoutly in a traditional "downtown" for every city, including Los Angeles, and the others who espoused with equal vigor the theory that expansion in the "suburbs" was the inevitable trend of the future. This collision was aggravated by the strange circumstance that neither the downtown area nor the suburban regions conformed to the conventional pattern. Los Angeles' central section was undistinguished because of a long-standing municipal limitation of 150 foot height limit for buildings. This was imposed originally about a decade after the construction in 1902 of Los Angeles' first "skyscraper," the 13-story Continental Building at Fourth and Spring streets, because of the fear of earthquake stresses on tall structures. Later as building techniques improved and the use of scientific engineering and more steel substantially eliminated earthquake danger, another factor entered into the situation. Los Angeles' citizens became alarmed lest a multiplicity of skyscrapers might cause intolerable congestion in the downtown area, and they therefore imposed by ordinance the 150 foot height limitation. Some blame for the over-all effect of monotony undoubtedly attached to the architects of the period during which many of the buildings were being constructed. Lack of height was not the only factor in Los Angeles' unattractive downtown section.

Then, by the time better architecture was emerging, the phenomenon of Wilshire Boulevard and its so-called "Miracle Mile" materialized and utilized distinguished and modernistic architecture, so much in contrast to its downtown predecessor. The only exception until recently was the City Hall itself with its overpowering 452-foot tower, although now limitations have been officially removed. Variety in the architectural landscape thus was stifled by ordinance for many years and the whole downtown region was invested with a drab monotony.

The suburbs, for their part, were not in general mere annexations of small outposts of dwellings which gravitated naturally toward the central magnet as in most cities of the East, Middle West, and South. Instead, they were an amalgamation of once-belligerent rival municipalities which had been absorbed into the octopus-like clutches of Los Angeles during a particular period for a particular reason. The whole thing had been accomplished on the basis of trade and barter.

In the period from approximately 1910 to 1927, Los Angeles the Ambitious was in a position to dangle the most precious of commodities—water rights—before the eyes of its thirsty little neighbors who were desperate from desiccation. The new Owens River aqueduct bringing water 250 miles from the Owens Valley and actually arriving in 1913 was capable of supplying far more water than the citizenry of Los Angeles in its boundaries at the time could possibly absorb. The smaller cities, anxious to share in the bounty of this watery bonanza were faced with a realistic proposition.

Los Angeles said to them:

"If you want to get a share of our water you will have to annex."

Many of the communities were not particularly anxious to subordinate their municipal personalities and lose their entities yet they were confronted successively with crises which forced their hands. One by one they capitulated, accepting water privileges in return for surrender to the gluttonous yearning of Los Angeles for sheer size. It was inevitable under such circumstances where compulsion was so large a factor in the annexations that "civic pride" in a sense continued unabated in areas which, although technically absorbed, remained militantly individualistic within their own confines. This seemed to apply with equal truth to both the unincorporated and incorporated regions. Eagle Rock, Garvanza, Owensmouth, Palms, Venice, Highland Park, and dozens of others continued to assert their abridged independence long after they were in "the city."

Actually by the time the swallowing up was complete "Los Angeles"—a bloated monster with acute civic indigestion—was trying to digest 64 former communities within its municipal stomach.

At the time of Sam Yorty's swearing in the main question of further annexations for Los Angeles remained as a provocative and disturbing challenge, but in a somewhat different and possibly more disturbing form in 1961 than it had ever been before. Much of the metropolitan area territory which might still be considered as part of an impending megalopolis was made up of incorporated cities which by the very passage of the years had become toughened in their determination to remain as entities. They would proud of their own accomplishments and suspicious of the monstrous Los Angeles even though it had manifest in recent years no overwhelming desire to gobble them up.

A difference existed between the raw material of the 1910–27 annexations and those which could be considered potential material in the decade of the 1960s. The reason Los Angeles was surrounded by so many relatively weak neighbors in the early period was due to the frenzied real estate activity of the mid-1880s when communities were laid out by the score. The promoters sold town lots, reaped their harvest, and in many instances moved on to other lush pastures. The resulting heritage of small struggling towns made them easy prey for Los Angeles when water problems developed. By the 1960s, however, such remaining independent cities as Long Beach, Pasadena, Glendale, Burbank, Santa Monica, Arcadia, Redondo Beach, and numerous others on the perimeter of Los Angeles had become so self-sufficient with their water supplies obtained through the area-wide Metropolitan Water District that they were in a position to withstand annexation pressure if it were exerted.

By a quirk of fate, a possible incentive for new expansion—at least from the standpoint of civic pride—materialized in the very year Sam Yorty became mayor. Until 1961 Los Angeles had rested somewhat smugly upon its laurels as "the biggest city in area in the United States." Shockingly, a brazen upstart, Oklahoma City, suddenly reached out with gargantuan abandon into the prairies surrounding it and annexed such enormous tracts that it attained an area of 475.55 square miles as contrasted with astounded Los Angeles' "mere 457.95 square miles." This rambunctious act on the part of Oklahoma City apparently was stimulated by the city's selection over all other candidates in the nation as the site of the National Cowboy Hall of Fame and Western Heritage Center and its growing importance as the crossroads of East–West and North–South freeways. Regardless of causes or motivations, Los Angeles had lost its supremacy in this category and was confronted with the question whether it wished to regain it.

"Planners"—both amateur and professional—discovered that whole new concepts were needed even to define the term "annexation" in this swift age of computers and mechanization.

It was no longer a simple matter of merely acquiring territory. Involved now was the larger element of evaluating that nebulous realm known as "metropolitan government." This meant economic and sociological decisions regarding the desirability of the fusing of functions between city and county, between city and city and even the outright creation of new governmental procedures. Mayor Yorty vigorously espoused amalgamations where possible to provide equal or better services at less cost. His experience in the California Legislature and in Congress had acquainted him with these pressing questions as they affected many regions of the United States. He was in a position from his own experience and his acquaintanceship with mayors, members of the legislature, congressmen, and governors to bring to the Los Angeles scene a knowledge of many approaches to intergovernmental cooperation and consolidation of functions. Mixed in all this was the question of how big municipal or regional government should be.

California and Los Angeles already were suffering from the almost insurmountable difficulties of coping with growth problems unprecedented in the history of the world. Los Angeles had added in the two decades between 1940 and 1960 nearly 1,000,000 residents, or the equivalent of almost its entire population in 1930, just a generation previous. The newcomers to California spread themselves out into rural as well as urban areas but by far the greatest funneling of population was into the urban centers. A state with 18,000,000 residents and a Los Angeles metropolis of perhaps 7,000,000 were of such enormous proportions that they had benumbed almost all who had tried to evaluate them in the light of modern government. The demand for necessary schools, public buildings, recreational facilities, relief of indigents, rapid transit, airport expansion, smog wars, and governmental services of all kinds was so imperative that it blurred the necessity of over-all planning.

Within Los Angeles City itself, a "pattern of change" was recognized as a part of life. Change was accepted as a commonplace. Initial public astonishment over "the Miracle Mile of Wilshire Boulevard" as a new "downtown" with big department and specialty stores had given way to almost apathetic acceptance of super-shopping centers in "the Valley," around UCLA, in the Crenshaw area, at Los Angeles International Airport, and elsewhere throughout the urban sections. Primarily, the creation of Wilshire Boulevard and the other centers had not been a mere "moving away" from the traditional downtown but a deliberate and carefully planned evolution by downtown merchants to create branch operations in the most advantageous locations. This economic factor became the key to future marketing patterns in Southern California. It was inevitable that the downtown area suffered from lack of patronage and some individual stores like the Fifth Street Store disappeared amid the stress. In the eventual cycle, however, the so-called "downtown" has become, as it were, just one more shopping center itself.

Even in publicly maintained parks there was a whole movement for what might be described as "civic cores." The Coliseum, the Los Angeles County Museum, the Sports Arena, and a State Museum and a State Armory transformed the region around Exposition Park where they are located into a horror of snarled traffic and jangled nerves. As if this were not enough, some citizens advocated the placing of an underground convention center at Exposition Park. Others contended loudly that this would make an already dreadful situation utterly impossible; and they urged the use of a portion of Elysian Park near the Los Angeles River as a practical alternative.

Griffith Park, separating Hollywood and Glendale with its hilly terrain, was a focal point for golfers, star gazers visiting the Planetarium and Observatory, horseback riders, and zoo enthusiasts. Even tiny Hancock Park on Wilshire Boulevard was attaining the status of a magnet far beyond its original concept. It had started out as a gift from G. Allan Hancock, oil man and philanthropist, to preserve the tar pits which Spanish explorers had noticed on their first visit to the Los Angeles area in 1769. These later had become the source of tar for caulking the flat-topped roofs of the early-day adobe dwellings of Los Angeles, and then suddenly had startled the scientific world by yielding the preserved bones of sabretoothed tigers and mastodons which had been trapped in the pits. Now, in its latest phase Hancock Park was selected as the site of the new Los Angeles County Art Museum which moved from its old home in the parent County Museum in Exposition Park.

All these developments were focusing attention on the evolution, whether consciously or otherwise, of little civic "centers" entirely apart from normal "Civic Centers" in metropolitan areas. Los Angeles was in the process of bringing into being its own Civic Center second in size only to the great array of buildings in Washington, D.C., but the multiple use of its parks on such a scale was something new in its experience.

The city's challenge to its new mayor was not only a physical one. He assayed correctly the enormous complexity of dealing with air pollution, rapid transit, tax burdens, freeway routing, the guiding of orderly building, and the creation of new recreational facilities for people continually getting more time on their hands. He viewed this matter of leisure and its attendant demands as part of a growing municipal need. He wanted Los Angeles not only to be a beautiful and expanding city in a material sense but also for its people to have greater opportunities in many spheres to develop their own potentials culturally and artistically.

In simple words he summed up his own objective:

"I feel I am taking office freer of fetters than anybody I've ever known in my whole political experience. So I have only one obligation and that is to do a good job, get the best people I can get to help govern this city and, naturally, it is my desire to make it a shining example of real good government."

In so stating he was expressing in essence a phenomenon which since has attracted national attention. Sam Yorty has no fetters for a good reason. He has no brain trust. He has no backroom cabinet.

He has no predominant adviser. He makes his own decisions. Sam Yorty the mayor is never Sam Yorty the composite; he is just Sam Yorty the individual.

Sam's inborn tendency to look as far as possible into the future with Irish canniness and political sagacity led him to believe that Los Angeles not only was at a crossroads politically, economically, and physically, but also in the cultural sense.

The mayor began vigorously to encourage steps for a cultural awakening so that Los Angeles could move coherently to attain the ultimate from its unique potential.

Ever since the modern period of its phenomenal growth had begun, the city had been catapulting forward so rapidly that it never had time to pause and evaluate its own position in the scheme of things. Everything was action, with no time for contemplation. For the first time, coincident with the advent of Mayor Sam, Los Angeles had reached a psychological point where it was ready to become aware of its own history and heritage.

Sam Yorty was, in a sense, the catalyst in this particular situation. But he was not able to operate in a quiet vacuum. Around him swirled, as around all big-city mayors in the United States, the clamorous, physical problems of the restless metropolis, itching from a rash of unsolved dilemmas. Congestion of the three million automobiles was growing worse by the day despite the frantic efforts of freeway builders to keep them moving. Rapid transit as a partial remedy in a land where "driving to work" had become an established way of life was failing to materialize in any effective form. Air pollution was blotting out the skies as the result of automotive emanations.

Racial concentrations, predominately those of the Negroes and Mexican-Americans, were creating enormous districts where poverty in extreme forms contrasted startlingly with the general air of prosperity in Los Angeles. Los Angeles city dwellers were smarting under what they considered to be double taxation for expanded facilities being provided by the Metropolitan Water District for wide areas outside the city limits. City government itself was groaning along under a crippling system of divided authority under a charter as obsolete as horse and buggy traffic on Broadway.

Amid these problems and vexations, professional planners in various realms of government—city, county, and special districts—sought to find the key to some sort of workable metropolitan fusion. They were not encouraged by the example of Miami, Florida, which was attempting to operate under what was touted as the first "Metropolitan Government" in the United States starting in 1957, but was finding the practical impediments to the realization of its dream almost insuperable under present techniques. The Los Angeles megalopolis on the contrary was attempting tentative, step-by-step approaches in some phases of this sort of regional rule.

Amalgamation of the City of Los Angeles and the County of Los Angeles Health Departments was still being talked about when Sam Yorty took office although no decision for merger had been reached.

"The Lakewood Plan" under which the county provided a municipality with such basic services as police, fire, and health protection under a contract system had been started a decade before the Yorty era and adopted by a number of other new municipalities. Many of these new cities, one or two with populations of less than a thousand were being formed because of their ability to share in the State Sales Tax revenues which, in part, were channeled back to the cities of their origin.

All the approaches to true metropolitan rule were tentative, hesitant, lacking in the regional cohesion necessary to attain any definitive objective. Almost everyone was aware of the demanding nature of the multifarious problems facing the millions of persons crowded into the Los Angeles region, but few were capable of seeking the over-all solutions.

The city sprawled there in its awkward uncertainty in the dawning of the 1960 decade like some gigantic child yearning to walk forward with confidence, but continually falling on its face and waiting for some sure hand to lift it and guide its faltering steps. Los Angeles the Enigma was hardly capable of understanding itself. Desperately it wanted to deserve the privilege of being considered the prototype of big cities of the future.

How was it to gain the maturity which was the key to such a brand new role?

Curious onlookers watching the political drama wondered whether Mayor Sam was equal to the task of being proper tutor to the giant.

"All of us together," said Sam himself in his first inaugural address, "with the energy which springs from a fresh start, will now commence to seek new solutions to the problems which challenge us—problems which provide opportunities for us to test our talents and our resolve. Ours is an especially beautiful city, looking out on the blue Pacific whose shores touch so many lands and so many peoples. I hope the beauty of our deeds can be made to match the beauty with which God has so richly endowed us. I hope each of you, irrespective of color, creed, or station in life will feel that you are my partner in the exciting task of charting the course of one of the world's greatest cities."

CHAPTER III

When I was a child, I spake as a child, I understood
as a child, I thought as a child: but when I became a
man I put away childish things.

I CORINTHIANS XIII, 11

From the tall tower of the Los Angeles City Hall—if time ever permits—Sam Yorty can look out at the past, the present, and the future.

His own poignant personal memories are deeply embedded there amid the manifest symbols of the city itself. For exactly two-thirds of his life at the time he was elected mayor he had been nurturing his own character in this city of his choice. He was seventeen years of age when he first saw it; thirty-four years later, at fifty-one, he was its chief executive official by the expressed will of the untrammeled voters.

Often his thoughts must have dwelt upon the seemingly circuitous route by which he had arrived at his present goal. Invariably he recalled a favorite saying of his Irish mother:

"When God slams the door in your face, He always opens another one."

Many a door had been slammed in Sam Yorty's face. Sometimes it took a dreary search to find the other one. But it was always there if you hunted hard enough and long enough. Sam was realistic enough to know that on occasion he had helped slam the door in his own face. His impatience with stupidity and duplicity led him to unwise denunciations of opponents. He had a tendency to hold grudges. The cocksureness of his judgments galled some people. It was asserted he fumed over little things. He sometimes was too impatient. Combined, these attributes tripped him up occasionally.

25

He lost opportunities because of them. This slowed the realization of his political aspirations.

Sam supposed, though, this was the only way you could figure life. It took awhile to get places. For him, "getting places" was not just a fleeting or idle ambition. From his early high school days, Sam's goal was to work his way up in politics until he was in an executive position of sufficient importance to permit him to exercise all his powers in the social and economic betterment of everyone within his sphere.

He refused to call himself a reformer. He loathed being considered a "do gooder." His philosophy was more comprehensive than that. He believed he possessed certain qualities which could be employed in a catalytic fashion, in government, to contribute to human progress. His belief was that all Americans were striving to move forward along the path of "the pursuit of happiness," and that particular leaders were endowed with a kind of magnetism or universal quality which could assist in this progression. He considered himself to be one of these, as a matter of birthright.

Possessing such an outlook, he was distinctly an individualist. He depended upon his own judgment and decisions, and was ready to take the consequences for them. As a result, he found himself nearly always in conflict with conventional political contemporaries who preferred to hedge rather than to come right out in the open and say what they meant. Sam never seemed to care very much whether people agreed with him. He felt himself so close to average citizens, with all their ills and woes, that he based his intuitive judgment and political philosophy on getting the best he could for them through political means. By natural consequence, this meant getting the best for himself too. This remarkable quality of independence led him to treat party allegiance as a light matter. In this sense he became not the Democratic party's mayor or a political machine's mayor in Los Angeles, but rather a people's mayor in the true sense.

He was described by puzzled opponents and sometimes by his friends also as "the man nobody knows" because they could never figure out when Sam's independence might crop up and lead him to kick over the traces of normal party allegiance. He was called a tough operator because he refused to compromise. He did not necessarily love a fight for a fight's sake—as Franklin Delano Roosevelt said he did—but he was always precipitating himself into a fight because of his bewilderingly simple philosphy of picking out a line of action quickly and then sticking to it.

His setbacks along the way apparently never bothered him much. They were transient, fleeting, temporary. He looked at things in the long context.

"I have always had a strong sense of political destiny," he is accustomed to say candidly.

The unique thing about him, as his supporters seemed to sense, was his ability to absorb defeats and to grow stronger from them. If Sam had been a boxer he would have found himself on the canvas oftener than standing upright. Yet he never considered quitting. From the day in 1936 when he was first chosen to elective office as a California Assemblyman, until he ran for mayor in 1961, Sam was out of office more than he was in. His record of losing contests was appalling. He either was beaten or withdrew from races for city councilman, mayor, governor and United States senator.

He was accused of inordinate ambition, lack of a sense of fitness, abandoning his party, ruthlessness, vindictiveness toward his political enemies, extremism against the Communists, overweening brashness, and vanity. He lost a race for the U. S. Senate in 1940. He temporarily gave up politics to enlist in the Air Force soon after the outbreak of World War II. On his return from the Pacific where he had served on the staff of General Douglas MacArthur, he again was elected to the Assembly, and then in 1950 was chosen as a Representative in Congress from the 14th California District, and re-elected in 1952. In 1954, he was the Democratic nominee for United States Senate, but was beaten for the second time in a Senate contest.

This was another door slammed in his face, when he was forty-five. He turned to private practice of law again, waiting—not very patiently—for another door to open.

✸ ✸ ✸

Now that he was mayor he could look from the City Hall tower upon the immensity of the city rimmed by mountains and sea and reflect upon the strange and devious route by which he had come to his present position. He and his city had both changed, yet the essential affinity between them remained.

Down below where the municipal flower, the Bird of Paradise, blooms amid date palms and rubber trees just outside his own office, is the spot near Main and First streets where the first City Hall was located in a crude little adobe.

To the north, beyond the Post Office and Federal Building, is the circular Plaza close to the original spot where the pueblo was founded by royal Spanish decree. Olvera Street, clustered around the mellow old Francisco Avila adobe dwelling, is a Mexican market-thoroughfare reminiscent of the community's beginnings, giving a Latin flavor to the modern city.

Beyond the two state buildings rises Bunker Hill crowned by a few weatherbeaten gingerbread mansions, now doomed in redevelopment projects. Through that hill, in the Second and Third Street tunnels, auto traffic roars night and day.

One tunnel holds particular significance for Sam.

Through the Second Street tunnel, from the west end on a hot clear spring day in 1927, a rather scared Nebraska boy got his first view of Los Angeles after an arduous trip from his home in Lincoln via Salt Lake City.

Dominating everything as it soared toward the intensely blue sky was the shining white tower of the "New" City Hall, 452 feet high by special dispensation of Los Angeles voters who had made an exception to their height-limit ordinance. The City Hall was almost ready for its occupants, including Mayor George C. Cryer who was just as unaware at that moment of the arrival in town of one of his successors, as Sam was of the name or personality of Mr. Cryer.

Sam's first thoughts were of getting some cheap place to stay. His ready cash of about $80 seemed to be nearing the vanishing point because he had discovered that travel—even via chair car and jitney share-the-ride auto—was expensive. He walked about in a daze on Hill Street and on Broadway, overwhelmed by the hurrying masses of people, the most he had ever seen. Nobody paid any attention to him. He felt absolutely alone and alien.

Almost immediately, though, he was cheered a bit when he saw a familiar sight—two of them, in fact—within a block of each other. Newspaper offices! Familiar havens from his earliest boyhood! The third building of the Los Angeles *Times*, constructed after the union bombing of the newspaper in 1910, stood in gray stone solidity and dignity on the northeast corner of First and Broadway, with its symbolic eagle atop the tower which housed Radio KHJ and its folksy announcer, "Uncle John" Daggett. On the east side of Broadway near Second was the office of the Los Angeles *Herald,* one of the Hearst chain.

Sam looked at both offices with a feeling of reassurance, confident that in case of necessity he could find someone there to befriend him.

Now, though, carrying his one small suitcase he began looking for a modest hotel. Both First and Second streets on the inclines leading up to Bunker Hill were lined with old hotels and ugly frame boardinghouses. He trudged up Second and selected a hotel which looked dingy enough to be cheap.

In the bare room, with its faded carpet, tawdry curtains, and cheap iron bedstead he lay down to plan his future. Somewhere in Los Angeles, he knew, was a man, a native of Lincoln, who might advise him on getting a job.

He carried with him from his friends in the clothing business in Lincoln an introduction to the manager of Silverwood's at Sixth and Broadway. The leading men's clothing stores were concentrated in a small area on Broadway and Hill streets in the neighborhood of Sixth and Seventh streets. These included in addition to Silverwood's, Mullen & Bluett, Desmond's, Bullock's, and Alexander & Oviatt.

The next day Sam began making the rounds. He was tempted in his boyish enthusiasm, from the standpoint of association with a celebrity, to try to work for Mullen & Bluett because this was where Dan Tobey of Lincoln worked as a salesman during the daytime. At night Tobey was something of a sporting institution in Southern California. He was the premiere ring announcer at the fights which then were in their heyday at the old Vernon Arena, the Olympic, Hollywood Legion Stadium and—for the really big boxing contests—Wrigley Field, nominally the home of the Los Angeles Angels of the Pacific Coast League.

Sam hesitated, however, to try to capitalize on his Lincoln background by approaching such a notable figure as Tobey. Instead, he took a part-time job at Desmond's and later went to work for Alexander & Oviatt which he considered the finest men's store in Southern California. He immediately registered at Southwestern University, a long-established institution which operated at night as well as in the daytime for the convenience of aspiring law students who were compelled to work their way through school. It had graduated many notable attorneys. Sam, because of his college preparatory work, was qualified for entrance.

In between work, classes, and study he went exploring in his captivating new surroundings. Around him the lavish city spread out a never-ending array of fascinating by-ways and entertainments. In contrast to Lincoln's modest movie houses, the splendid and glittering Los Angeles theaters and film palaces presented dramatically all the great names which he had known only at a distance. Every day the opportunity casually presented itself to see some celebrity in person, to catch a glimpse of a movie star on the street, or to watch daredevils swinging from building to building as scenes for movies were shot.

At the brand-new Orpheum on upper Broadway, the home of big-time Keith vaudeville, the marquee blazoned names as local realities which had been only a faraway vision in Lincoln—Jack Benny as Master of Ceremonies, Gus Edwards presenting Ray Bolger the dancer. Rudolf Friml's operetta *The Vagabond King* was on the legitimate stage of the Biltmore. Over at the Pantages Fatty Arbuckle was featured "in person." Mary Pickford was much in the news in her own personal appearances to aid a "better homes" drive in Los Angeles. Over at the naughty Burbank on Main Street the latest burlesque featuring "a new cast" was *Under the Covers*. A young fellow named Gary Cooper was reporting nervously for work in the picture *Children of Divorce*. And the array of hit movies was seemingly endless—Wallace Beery in *Casey at the Bat* at the Million Dollar at Third and Broadway, *What Price Glory*, with Victor McLaglen and Edmund Lowe at the Cathay Circle, Lon Chaney scaring kids in *Mr. Wu* at the Forum.

As Sam wandered about he gloated in participating in a new kind of life. Everything thrilled him. He took rides in "the Big Red Cars" of the Pacific Electric to the suburbs, all unmindful that rapid transit would be one of his own major problems in the future. He gazed at the huge crowds congregating at the rush hours at the Pacific Electric Station at Sixth and Main streets to be whisked away. You could ride out to the ostrich farm in South Pasadena for postcard pictures of yourself on the big ungainly birds or gaze in horror at the squirming masses of jaws and tails at the Alligator Farm or go to the foot of the inclined railway for a ride up Mount Lowe to the famous hotel for a view of the clearly defined Los Angeles area and for a "look at Catalina" before smog had been heard of.

Despite the Burbank Follies, everything was not tawdry on Main Street. At the Goodfellows' Grotto, old-time waiters in formal coats served the best gourmet food in Los Angeles. Close to it were the cavernous depths of Holmes's Book Store where you could enter on Main Street, wander around for half a day amid thousands of volumes, both new and used, and priced from a nickel to $50, and come out on Spring Street all turned around as to your directions.

Near the old hotel where Sam had stayed on Second Street after his arrival, the Angel's Flight inclined railway led up to the elegant old mansions of Bunker Hill.

Over everything the white tower of the new City Hall presided in Alpine grandeur, looking down benignly on the hurrying citizens and beckoning some to public service and greatness. It was in startling contrast to the old red sandstone City Hall at Second and Broadway, now doomed to oblivion by its splendid successor.

Sam had no occasion just then to enter either City Hall, new or old, although from news stories and conversations he began to get an inkling of Los Angeles politics. He was a strange kid in a big city, which was totally unaware of him.

*   *   *

Homesickness came suddenly upon Sam even amid the distractions of Los Angeles. Like so many other Easterners, Midwesterners, and Southerners, he felt such sentimental urgings to return to his "home town" that it was almost a nausea. The initial excitement created in him by the "big city" still remained to a degree, but it was being challenged by boyhood recollections, given a particularly roseate hue by distance. He was still only seventeen.

His thoughts turned to favorite haunts in Lincoln, to the warm metallic smell of the stereotype room at the *Star*, to his days as leader of the Melodors and to his favorite banjo, to special friends, to his hard-working mother and his unfortunate father suffering from successive injuries. He felt rather ashamed of having written a certain note back home soon after his arrival in Los Angeles:

May 14, 1927

Dear Dad and Gramma,

   . . . Lincoln is certainly a dumb country town compared to Los Angeles. . . .

Love,
Sam

The "dumb country town" was appearing to him now in a softer light. At last he could stand it no longer. He took his slender savings and bought a chair car ticket to Lincoln. His departure from Los Angeles was on a Saturday. Weary and dirty, he arrived "home" two days later. It was as if he had become a Gulliver and returned to Lilliput. The buildings in Lincoln appeared shrunken. The streets were narrower. The people downtown seemed strangers. Everything was on a smaller scale; drab life on the downbeat.

All the sentimental images which had been uppermost in his lonely mind a few days before in Los Angeles were reduced now to their true perspective. What was home? Certainly this was not it. Where could it be? He was bewildered. A wave of doubt swept over him. He did not know its name was "growing up."

o   o   o

Within ten days after he had departed, Sam was back on the job at Alexander & Oviatt's. With him to the "big city" he had brought his mother, who for years had been separated from his father, hoping she too might move West. Eventually, Mrs. Yorty did come to Southern California to make her living managing apartment houses, married again, and remained in Los Angeles the remainder of her life.

Sam, on his return from his disappointing trip to Lincoln, saw Los Angeles in a new way. It was more than just a fascinating place to visit. Its spell was upon him forever. Nothing again would be able to induce him to leave. Somehow he felt much older. The visit had served to emphasize for him the aphorism that things are not always what they seem or as they are remembered.

Los Angeles, now that he felt himself to be a man, was true home. He knew with certainty that his fortunes, whatever they might be, were inextricably bound up with it.

CHAPTER IV

The trees in the streets are the old trees used to
living with people,
Family-trees that remember your grandfather's name.

John Brown's Body,
STEPHEN VINCENT BENÉT

Sam was committed now, in every way, to his new city while he was still only seventeen. His daily life, his ambitions, his future were bound up with it. Yet he was, in essence and in a very real sense, still the youth whose thoughts, actions, sensations, outlook on life, family ties, and inherited traits were the result of his blood lines and his boyhood environment.

* * *

On the modest store fronts of Western Ireland today the name "Yorty" is to be seen blazoning the owner of a pub or a hardware shop. Some Californians while touring Ireland believe when they encounter these signs that "Yorty" indicates Sam's father's people came from the Old Sod. This is erroneous. The ghost of that vehement political dogmatist, William Penn, the Quaker, could testify on this point. Even William Penn had a good deal to do indirectly with the spelling of the surname of the Yortys, from a legalistic standpoint.

The first "Yorty" in this country was the recipient in 1754 of an old-fashioned wordy deed in Pennsylvania including the names of the heirs of the "Fighting Quaker," Penn, who had shaped the Crown Colony which bore his name on this side of the Atlantic. Peter Jorty, the great-great-grandfather of Sam was the proud possessor of this deed to 237 acres in Lebanon Township in Lancaster County, marked at its corners by "a hickory, a hickory sapling, a black oak sapling, and a post." The only trouble was the name "Yorty" was, in a sense, wrong. Although nobody seemed to care very much.

Actually the name of a certain immigrant to America was Peter Jorty and he came from that region of Bavaria or Switzerland where the boundary lines seemed to be of small importance. When Jorty arrived in this country he was poor like practically everybody else, and he availed himself of credit at the little country stores of backwoods Pennsylvania.

After he had selected his flour and sugar and cheese and pickles he would present them at the counter and the clerk would say: "Name, please?"

Peter Jorty, being unable to pronounce the letters "J" and "T," would say "Yordy" and the clerk would write it so in the books.

After a time everybody naturally called Peter Jorty "Yordy" and he accepted it himself because that was the way he pronounced it. It was just as natural that when it came time for signing legal documents in regard to the acquisition of land the mistaken pronunciation of the name should creep in once more in the actual written description. In this way the first deed was made out to Peter "Yordy"—which was at least half right. Such variations of spelling were so common on the frontier that in later years another mistake was made and "Yorty" became the accepted form of the surname.

Thus "Yorty," instead of being Irish in this particular case, was in reality of Teutonic derivation.

But, as some of Sam's antagonists have said when they have encountered the scorching diatribes of which he is capable:

"He *must* be Irish to have a temper like that!"

Of course, they are right in a sense. Sam's Irish blood came from other sources, though. On one side Sam's lineage goes to pre-Revolutionary stock, at least four or five generations back and on the other he is only second-generation Irish. His father's grandmother, Mary Callan, whose own mother was born in Ireland was married to a descendant of the original Peter Yorty. This grandfather Sam Yorty who lived in Milwaukee was ambitious and wanted to travel. He loaded up his family in a covered wagon and traveled all the way from Milwaukee to Richardson County in the southeast corner of Nebraska. On a farm here Sam's father, Frank Yorty, grew up.

Nebraska's wide plains stretched toward the horizon and formed the boundary of the Yorty world. Sam's father lived on the edge of the little town of Lincoln, which was the site of the University of Nebraska. As he grew old enough to want to marry, he began looking around among the local girls, but found no one to his choice. It was at this time that the Irish influence in Sam's destiny began to manifest itself.

In distant Clonmel in the County of Tipperary a family named Egan began to yearn for a better life across the sea in America where so many Irish people were going in the latter part of the nineteenth century and the early part of the twentieth century. Mr. Egan was a successful landscape architect or as the term was used in Ireland, gardener, but he was still unable to provide the kind of life his ambitious children desired. His two older daughters decided they would try for America. They sailed from Dublin and went to Nebraska where one of the Egan brothers already had settled. This brother had written home of the rich soil and of the enormous amounts of land to be had for practically nothing in Nebraska. These descriptions seemed almost like fairy tales in a country where every foot of ground was precious and it was worthwhile to carry rocks and make walls to gain another fraction of an acre for crops. After the girls were in Nebraska, they too wrote enthusiastically of the new life, although omitting details about severe winters, droughts and occasional tornadoes. Their enthusiasm in turn communicated itself to the youngest daughter, Johanna, who was sixteen. At first her father and mother hesitated to permit her to make the long and hazardous journey across the Atlantic and the vast reaches of the United States, but romance across the seas helped her. Her two sisters in good Irish fashion married two brothers named Sullivan and they thus could provide a haven for Johanna. Finally her parents consented to the trip.

Johanna took passage in the steerage at Dublin. At the dock there were tears and embraces, but the girl was steadfast in her resolution. The steerage was crowded and uncomfortable and smelly, but this was considered so routine in those days that no one paid much attention. Johanna was vividly redheaded and of a vivacious temperament, excited by the prospect of her long journey and effervescent in her conversation. She attracted the attention of a very distinguished passenger who was traveling in much greater style than she. On the decks he fell into conversation with her and they would walk for hours around the ship conversing on every topic under the sun. He was Sir Arthur Conan Doyle, whose *Study in Scarlet* had introduced Sherlock Holmes—a detective, of all people!—into literature. Sherlock Holmes was to enjoy an unparalleled longevity in the sixty-eight stories dealing with him, and some of the ideas and mysteries involved in detective-story writing were conveyed to the eager young listener by the author there on the vessel in the Atlantic.

It was an experience Johanna never forgot. All during her life, as Sam Yorty recalls, she harked back to those carefree moments with the sea breeze in her red hair and the wonderfully kind English gentleman expounding murder and deductive reasoning and all the other elements which went into his successful stories.

Johanna possessed the stoicism to brush aside the discomforts and hazards of the steerage passage. When the ship docked in Philadelphia she still faced one of the most difficult legs of her journey. The old coal-burning locomotives took her on the thin line of the transcontinental railroad stretching out into the vastness of the West. In the steerage and in the hot, dusty, cindery chair cars of the railroads Johanna encountered drunken men and underwent experiences which resulted in a lifelong hatred on her part for liquor and its results.

When she finally arrived in Nebraska and was met by her sisters she discovered she was indeed in a totally new world. The great prairie lands stretched in all directions, seeming to melt into the sky itself on the far horizon. It was inevitable that in this new land where the pioneering spirit still prevailed a girl as beautiful and vivacious as Johanna Egan should have suitors immediately. Among these was the young farmer named Frank Patrick Yorty, who was such a serious worker that he supplemented his farming with draying and delivery of goods to the nearby town of Lincoln where money was a scarce article indeed. Nebraska, like the rest of the country, still remembered the panic of the early 1890s and there was discussion and controversy in the little square of Lincoln about the free coinage of silver. The magic name of William Jennings Bryan was on many lips. Johanna was unaware of the currents of American politics, but she was intrigued by the serious views of Frank Yorty. He yearned to study law, but found it impossible to consider such a thing seriously because of his age— he was about fifteen years older than Johanna—and the fact that it was necessary for him to work from dawn until dusk to make a subsistence. Still the girl was attracted to him. Before long she had accepted his shy proposal and they were married in Lincoln on May 26, 1899.

After the first flush of the honeymoon Johanna discovered she had indeed entered a serious world. The tasks around the farm seemed never-ending. From that moment in the morning when she arose to prepare breakfast, often before the sun was up, until the evening arrived with its demands for a big dinner and dishwashing and other chores afterward, she was kept busy every moment. She had been brought up in a household where she learned cooking and housework, but never to the back-breaking extent she now was enduring as a routine matter. She baked bread, churned butter, milked the cow and still tried to keep the house fresh and inviting with flowers and little domestic touches to show it was indeed a home. She bore a daughter, Kathleen, who was still a tiny child when the Yorty family underwent an ordeal which affected their future lives.

The farm was situated near a stream called Salt Creek. Most of the year this was a meandering little brook which appeared incapable of getting out of bounds. Yet, before long, Johanna Egan Yorty went through an experience which was to inscribe itself so indelibly upon her memory that for the rest of her life she would awake terrified at night envisioning again the horror of the situation. It was an experience which through retelling stamped itself also upon the memory and character of her children.

It happened one winter night that a steady cold rain began to fall in Nebraska. Day after day the downpour continued. The earth became a soggy mass. Everything was a sea of mud. The streams began to rise. Innocuous-looking Salt Creek was transformed into a threatening torrent, then a devastating river at full flood.

Crest after crest came in successive waves so swiftly that the waters were almost to the ceiling of the house within a few hours, forcing Mrs. Yorty and Kathleen to retreat to the attic. Frank Yorty realized he must try to save the horses in the barn by releasing them from their stalls, so they could try to swim to high ground. He floundered to the barn, almost being swept away by the current, and forced the horses through the main door into the swirling waters. As he started back toward the partly inundated house he observed a sudden rise in the waters and attemped to hurry. As he struggled forward with the water almost to his shoulders his foot struck a plow blade and he felt a sickening wave of pain.

He staggered into the house and onto the ladder leading through a hole in the ceiling to the attic.

His foot was gushing blood. His wife helped pull him into the attic and immediately bandaged his foot with rags to try to stop the flow of blood. Almost before she was through they were forced onto the roof. There, comforting Kathleen, they clung to the ridgepole amid a scene of desolation and terror. The muddy water surrounded them on every side. Snakes—rattlers, copperheads, and giant bullsnakes—were being swept along amid driftwood, chickens, cows, pigs, dogs, and cats. The snakes were flung against the roof and some momentarily remained until Frank Yorty pushed them off with a stick. His foot still bled so profusely that a red ooze blended into the flood waters and was carried from sight in the dirty foam on the crests.

Johanna Yorty clung there wet and horrified, holding her child and praying for rescue and trying to do what she could to ease her husband's pain. In those hours until help came in boats she formed a life-long fixation against isolated flat country where floods could wreak such destruction. She knew her dreams forever would be woven of blood and writhing snakes and cold and misery. She knew that sometime she and Kathleen and any other children she was destined to bear must find a safer life, perhaps with comforting mountains nearby for shelter in time of peril. Frontier life of this kind, she knew, was not for her. . . .

CHAPTER V

Were it left to me to decide whether we should have a government without newspapers, or newspapers without a government, I should not hesitate a moment to prefer the latter.

THOMAS JEFFERSON

If Blackstone and the Common Law shaped Sam Yorty's adult professional career, so also must Gutenberg and Benjamin Franklin have directed his awakening consciousness as a boy.

Sam has been addicted to newspapers all his life. Every day he devours the press. He has been part of the newspaper craft since he was eight years old. The smell of printer's ink and the sound of presses are part of him. Yet, contrarily enough, he had been the object of newspaper pummeling to a degree rarely suffered by his political confreres of this era. The viciousness of the attacks on him have failed, invariably, to weaken his own inborn devotion to freedom of the press although he has been deeply wounded at times by what he considered the unwarranted nature of the assaults.

The sentiment with which he regards his early newspaper experience in Lincoln is an essential element in his daily life as a man. As he spreads out the current evening and morning editions to evaluate the happenings of the city, the county, the state, the nation, and the world, the headlines and the stories conjure up childhood images he can never efface. They are inevitably interwoven with the awareness of poverty and the cruelty of life. Sam's early work was, in addition to his natural instinct to be industrious, a matter of compelling necessity. The spectre of cold and hunger always hung over the Yorty family because of a succession of misfortunes befalling the father. These grew in part out of Frank Yorty's thwarted ambition.

39

Sam's father was a slight but strong man. He was capable of doing all sorts of work, but he perpetually yearned to satisfy one burning ambition. He loved the law. In his rare moments of spare time he even tried to study it, not so much with the idea that he would be able to go into practice, but for the pure love of the subject. He possessed a rare talent for the theoretical and philosophical aspects of the law. At the time of the ruinous flood on the farm, before Sam's birth, Mr. Yorty conceived the idea that the Chicago, Burlington & Quincy Railroad, by building its track enbankments where it did, had caused the flood waters to back up and flood the Yorty place. This viewpoint was presented so strongly and with such legal impact by Mr. Yorty that the railroad was impressed. Officials of the C. B. & Q. asked:

"Who is this fellow Yorty—some country lawyer?"

The answer was in the negative, but the impression that Yorty made was perhaps even more profound when it was discovered that he was merely a farmer rather than a trained attorney. Railroad officials, in fact, were so interested in his talents that they offered to put him through law school. This was impossible for Frank Yorty because of his family obligations. It was a task just to make a bare living. During his days on the farm, Yorty had supplemented his small income by driving a delivery wagon for Rudge and Gunzell in Lincoln.

Frank Yorty, after the flood, decided to move into Lincoln to give his wife a greater feeling of security. She could not stand the thought of isolation on the farm any longer. In Lincoln, even though it was a small place, she felt much safer and at home. It was during these more tranquil days that Samuel William Yorty was born on October 1, 1909.

Sam's father decided he must branch out, make more money for his expanding family. From his delivery-wagon experience he made contacts which resulted in a brief period of comparative prosperity. He went into the contracting business, particularly painting jobs, and specialized in larger buildings.

❖   ❖   ❖

Perhaps the earliest of all Sam Yorty's memories is entwined with politics.

Sam's feet hurt. He was three and one-half years old. Above him the hum of conversation seemed to have gone on for hours. He tightened his hold on his father's hand and squirmed as he stood

[1] Four-year-old Samuel William Yorty in Lincoln, Nebraska, his birth-place.

[2] *Above left,* Yorty in student days when favorite high school teacher told him to aim at being a "statesman" instead of a politician. *(Townsend photo)*
[3] *Above right,* Amy Shively Grubb, the favorite teacher. *(Townsend photo)*

[4] *Above,* entering the Mayor's race in Los Angeles in 1961. Wife Betty, beside Sam, confesses shaking with nervousness. (*Los Angeles Herald-Examiner photo*)

[5] *At right,* the campaign was a cartoonist's delight. Pulitzer Prize winning Bruce Russell's original now hangs just outside Mayor's office in City Hall. (*Los Angeles Times*)

[6] *Above,* victorious Sam Yorty giving inauguration address at traditional site on Spring Street steps of City Hall. (*Leonard Nadel photo*)

[7] *At right,* feud over? Not quite as Mayor poses with olive branch during uncertain interlude in City Hall political war. (*Los Angeles Herald-Examiner photo*)

[8] *At left,* shown in a Fire Department helicopter against the backdrop of 452 foot City Hall tower, Yorty, a former U.S. Air Force officer, is the "travelingest" Mayor in Los Angeles history. *(Bill Bridges photo)*

[9] *Below,* Bill Yorty, only child of Mayor and Mrs. Yorty, with them during track meet when he was on the team at Los Angeles' Harvard School. *(Bill Bridges photo)*

on the sidewalk in Lincoln looking up at one of the most famous frock-coat-clad figures in America. The figure, now slightly rotund, belonged to William Jennings Bryan.

To Sam's anguished gaze Mr. Bryan seemed to overshadow the figure of Sam's own father, who stood enthralled in conversation with "the Boy Orator of the Platte." Some years had elapsed, it is true, since William Jennings Bryan had won the "Boy Orator" acclamation at the 1896 Democratic Convention in Chicago with his famous "Cross of Gold" speech, which won him the nomination for the presidency. But three defeats for the presidency had been unable to dim the reputation or still the organ-like voice which had entranced so many millions of Americans at conventions and on the Chautauqua circuit.

Bryan, at this time just after the election of Woodrow Wilson to the presidency in 1912, was fifty-two and much mauled by fate and defeat. Still, at this moment in the early part of 1913 when he was talking to Sam's father, his star was in the ascendancy again. It was known he was going to be Secretary of State in Wilson's Cabinet. Frank Yorty was proud to be talking to the great man, one of his idols, who was dear in fact to nearly all Nebraskans because of his long residence there and his editorship of the Omaha *World-Herald,* and of *The Commoner,* a weekly political publication.

Now, Sam was unimpressed by oratory, editorship, or even the sartorial elegance of Mr. Bryan in the tailor-made frock coat which hung down to the Bryan knees. Sam was so uncomfortable that all he wanted was for his father to quit talking and take him home. He pulled at his father's coattails and finally Mr. Yorty looked down and recognized that Sam had to be taken on his way immediately or else be regarded as a public nuisance on the streets of Lincoln. Father Yorty made his apologies to Mr. Bryan and hurriedly departed.

This might have been considered a rather discouraging introduction to political subjects except for the fact that as he grew a little older Sam began to take an intense interest in the highly dramatized political discussions which took place in his home. His first real dawning consciousness of politics began to be manifest just at the time Woodrow Wilson was running for a second term in 1916. On the living-room table of the Yortys' next to the Holy Bible was *The Democratic Text Book.* At the top were three lines saying:

Beneath these was the scholarly face of Woodrow Wilson.

All the conversations about Bryan and Wilson and the other great figures of the Democratic party at the time made a deep impression on Sam during his grade and high school years. He participated in the politics of the day even though he still was years too young to consider casting his first vote. Politics was a constant and natural subject in the family. Later, too, Sam's favorite teacher—in the ninth grade—entered into the situation by giving him a new concept of the direction his political aspirations could take. The teacher, Amy Shively Grubb, whose husband Dr. George Albert Grubb was Dean of the University of Nebraska Dental School, was, to Sam, the ideal mentor in the kind of things he liked. She had an instinctive sense of the capabilities of her students and in Sam she apparently saw something special. Once Sam and the other students of Mrs. Grubb were requested to write a paper on the hopes for their future careers. It took Sam very little time to decide on his own subject. He sat down and wrote out the reasons why he aspired to be a politician. The theme was full of the names of the current heroes of whom he had heard in the family and on the streets of Lincoln. He handed in his paper and waited for a grade from Mrs. Grubb. When the paper came back, it contained something more important than a grade.

Mrs. Grubb had scratched out Sam's word "politician" and in its place had put "statesman" as the goal to which he should aspire. Coming as it did from a teacher whom he loved so much the emphasis on the one word made a tremendous impression on Sam. From then on he was conscious of the fact that anyone could aspire to be a politician but it took a special spiritual aspiration to be a statesman. That was the way Mrs. Grubb had put it.

Political aspirations though were on a distant horizon. Always the immediate problem with Sam due to the family's "hard times" was to try to make some money and to save a little of it.

* * *

When Sam was still very small his father was awarded a painting contract on a big hotel and was jubilant because it represented the largest contract he had ever been able to obtain. He personally supervised the work and went onto the scaffolds with the painting crew.

One day he was on a scaffold three stories up when he slipped and fell. He plunged to the ground and hit his back on a paint can. His injuries were so serious that he was taken to the hospital and was compelled to remain there for more than a year. During this period young Sam, at an age when impressions were etched on his mind, saw the agony of his mother trying to meet the everlasting bills coming in from the hospital. The small savings which the family had been able to amass were exhausted very soon. The family home at 1410 Rose Street in University Place in a fine neighborhood proved to be more than Mrs. Yorty could maintain. It was necessary to move to a cheaper home.

Mrs. Yorty, of course, went to work to try to support her family of two daughters and Sam and also to pay as much as possible toward the medical bills. Sam heard her crying in the night and he determined to try to do something to help. He was barely eight years old when he decided that he must contribute something to the family income now that his father was unable to work.

In Lincoln at the time were two newspapers, the *Star*, a Democratic newspaper, evening and Sunday, and the *Journal*, which was Republican. Even at the age of eight Sam was loyal to the Democratic party from having heard so many political discussions in the home. He decided that he would try to get a job on the *Star*. He was permitted by the circulation manager, O. E. Jerner, who later became Postmaster of Lincoln, to try his hand at selling newspapers. The corner assigned to Sam was Eleventh Street and N. Jerner told him that the toughest part of the job was the weather.

"The newspaper comes out every day, you know," Jerner said to the boy, "and it has to be sold to people. Sometimes it will be cold and sometimes it will be hot, sometimes rainy and other times it will be snowing, but in the newspaper business we have to be on the job all the time. Do you think you can do it?"

Sam nodded. From that moment he resolved that he never would let the weather interfere with his duties and that he would never let the *Star* down. His devotion to duty was so extraordinary, in fact, that Jerner was impressed. He watched the youngster and before long permitted him to have a paper route, although he was extremely young for this responsibility.

Lincoln still was a community without too many frills. Parts of town had streets which remained unpaved in the tradition of the

43

frontier. When the weather was bad the mud was deep and it was almost impossible to travel except on foot or horseback. Sam lacked a horse, so he necessarily made his rounds on foot. In the first winter after he obtained his paper route the worst blizzard in the memory of Nebraskans struck Lincoln one day about noon. The presses were grinding away at the *Star* and Sam battled his way through the wind and the driving sleet and snow to the paper. He was one of the few boys who showed up. Nobody paid much attention to him, so he gathered up his papers and prepared them for delivery. Then he set out on his rounds. It was almost impossible to see. The stinging particles of ice struck his face and almost blinded him. He found the street where his delivery started and began taking the papers up on the porches so they would not be soaked or blow away. Soon his hands were almost too numb to handle the papers, but he kept on.

In about two hours he had completed his route and went back to the paper. He found that two of his friends had been unable to make their way through the storm to deliver their route, so Sam started out again to deliver these papers too. Just as he was staggering back from delivering the second additional route, his face blue and his body shaking with cold, Sam encountered Mr. Jerner, the circulation manager. Jerner looked at him in astonishment.

"Where have you been?" he demanded. "This storm is too bad for anybody."

"I was just trying to help a couple of the fellows," chattered Sam.

"Well, get in here by the stove and warm up. This is once when the Pony Express isn't going to go through any more!"

After that incident, Sam was entrusted gradually with more and more responsibility until by the time he was thirteen, he was handling the *Star's* newsstand sales and the complaints about non-delivery to homes. His life was busy but happy. He would study his lessons until late at night, go to school, rush to the *Star*, do his work, go home and start studying again. If he had a few moments on Saturday night while the thunderous big presses were running the Sunday issue and shaking the *Star* building he would lie down on the rolls of newsprint and sleep.

"I learned then that the absence of noise can wake you just as quickly as noise itself," Sam remembers. "When the presses stopped I woke up at once—it was time to deliver the *Star*."

44

Sam appeared headed for a career in the newspaper business. Then a tinseled road to fame suddenly beckoned him, and he took his first entranced steps toward the glittering goal. . . .

* * *

Sam must have been born with music in his heart. It was as much a part of him as breathing. His lusty lungs as a baby gave promise of great vocal prowess, and this talent was supplemented by a natural instinct for instrumental playing. Almost from infancy he was attracted to musical instruments. He avidly tried out the piano, the violin and the banjo as he grew big enough to master them. The banjo became his favorite.

Somehow while he worked as a paper boy he found opportunity at odd moments to strum the banjo. By the time he was in his early teens he was an outstanding banjo performer. At first he played only for his own enjoyment or to entertain other paper boys or his school chums. Then after he had attained a neighborhood fame for his proficiency he attracted the attention of the local radio station, KFAB. He was invited to play on the air. His renditions were so enthusiastically received by listeners that he decided upon a daring step.

He organized "Sam Yorty's Melodors," a small dance orchestra. Sam was maestro and banjoist. The Melodors caught on quickly and soon were in demand for high school dances and even University of Nebraska affairs; an almost overwhelming accolade from the sophisticated "college set." Supreme recognition came with a professional engagement at a roadhouse known as the Chicken Little Inn. To the strains of "If You Knew Susie," "Linger a While," and other sure-fire favorites of the early 1920s the Melodors rocketed to one triumph after another. Success was so intoxicating that Sam gave up his job at the *Star* to devote all his spare time to music making.

Shortly after this the Melodors received an offer from the Loup County Fair, about two hundred miles from Lincoln, to play during the entire fair. This proof that the fame of the Melodors was spreading far led Sam into a grand gesture.

Up to this time when the Melodors received a contract to play at an out of town dance Sam had been renting a car for the occasion. Now, though, he decided on his daring move. He thought it would be cheaper to own a car than to keep renting one if the

Melodors were going to be traveling long distances. So he began looking around for a proper vehicle.

The fire chief in Lincoln owned a big Paige car. Sam and the Melodors had admired the chief riding around in this gorgeous car and when Sam heard that it might be possible to purchase it, he set out to try to make a deal. Sure enough the fire chief was receptive to the idea and almost before he knew it Sam was in possession of the Paige. When it was time to start to the Loup County Fair the Melodors and all their instruments and their luggage were loaded into the Paige and the journey started over the rather uncertain roads of Nebraska. Everything was dirt and always rutted from the previous rains.

Sam figured he had allowed plenty of time for the trip to the fair, but after the first fifteen miles out of Lincoln he was undecided whether they ever would complete the journey. The tires on the Paige proved to have been in the last stage of collapse at the time Sam bought the car. Every few miles there would be a resounding puncture or blowout and the perspiring musicians would have to get out and double as mechanics before they could proceed. In a short time, too, the car began to cough and wheeze and then stopped completely dead. The boys poked in its innards and eventually got it going again, at least sufficiently to arrive in the next town. Here there was a delay of several hours while the local garage man worked on the Paige. Sam's slim supply of money was dwindling for tire repair kits and the necessary parts which had to be purchased.

Mutiny was threatening also as the other boys tired of fighting the creaky car. They were all older than Sam and had an unspoken resentment of their leader being so much younger, and they now began to assert their superiority by holding back when it became necessary to change the tires. Sam fought it through, but by the time the Loup County Fair came in sight he was almost too tired to play his banjo.

His spirits were somewhat revived by the success of the Melodors during this engagement but when the fair was over and it was time to go back home the mutiny broke into the open. The other members of the orchestra refused to ride in the Paige. They demanded adequate transportation of some other form. Sam had to dig down again and buy them all bus tickets back to Lincoln. His job then was to try to get the car home all alone. To the accompaniment of blowouts and periodic collapses of the car he did suc-

ceed in driving back home. He arrived in a state of physical and
financial exhaustion. All the money received from the engagement
at the fair was gone and, in addition, Sam still owed his musicians.
The matter preyed on his mind to such an extent that he went to
his father's friend, Judge Comstock, and asked whether the other
musicians might sue him. Judge Comstock tried to counsel him and
give him reassurance in this regard, but Sam was disconsolate over
the whole affair.

Reluctantly, Sam made a big decision. He went home and took
his precious banjo out of the case and gazed at it. It represented
much of his savings and also something a great deal more than
mere money. It was the symbol of his prospective career. His transient success had led him into rosy dreams of appearances in
Chicago, New Orleans, and New York, where he would be acclaimed as the rival and successor of Eddie Peabody. Now, due to
the expenses of the old Paige car in the county fair fiasco, he was
not only faced with ruin, but also termination of his musical career.
It seemed impossible that he could recruit any other musicians to
equal the Melodors, and they were holding aloof because of their
experience on the trip to the fair. With a final glance at the banjo,
Sam put it back in its case and took it downtown to the music store
to see what he could get for it.

He sold the banjo, paid the musicians with the proceeds and
hoped he could return to the newspaper business, his old love. His
musical career was over for the time being. Even then, young as he
was, he began to wonder about the way things happened. In his
home he had heard his mother speak many times of the Irish
proverb:

"If you keep your eyes open you can see God's hand closing a
door you shouldn't have been going through."

Sam wondered whether God had shut the door on music because
something else was in store for him. Even at this time he had
begun to have inklings in his own mind, although he barely permitted himself to think about it, of a political destiny. At the moment, though, his chief concern was to start making some money
again. He headed for the *Star* and his friend, Mr. Jerner.

* * *

It proved simple to get his old job back. His record at the *Star*
was so good there was no difficulty in returning: the more glamor-
ous interlude with the Melodors simply had lured him away for a

47

while from the life into which he fitted so comfortably. Being around a newspaper was almost second-nature after the eight years which had elapsed since he first began selling papers on the corner of Eleventh Street and N.

At this time things were bad at home. Sam's father had suffered another fall similar to the first disastrous one. This time his leg was crushed so badly that he was compelled to give up his work as a painting contractor. Sam's father and mother by this time had reached a point, following many previous incidents and a long separation, where it was impossible for them to be reconciled. Their rift in fact had existed for such a long period due to incompatibility and the stress of monetary worries that their marriage definitely was doomed. Sam, of course, had observed for a considerable time the dissensions driving the couple apart and he now began to understand fully the meaning of a broken home. Practical considerations, however, prevailed in regard to the making of a living. Sam's father at one time had started a restaurant in Lincoln and it had to be operated during the period he was laid up. This duty fell upon Sam's mother.

The profits from the restaurant were problematical and usually did not materialize by the time all the help was paid off and the grocery bills had been met. Sam and his mother and sisters, Kathleen and Enid, lived over the restaurant during that particular interlude.

Domestic turmoil and the succession of accidents in which his father was involved increasingly impressed themselves upon Sam. He saw his mother working far too hard, driven by the necessity of making a bare living, and unhappy at the absence of a normal home life. A ferment began to build in Sam's blood. He wanted to get away. Lincoln was all he knew, yet he realized that somewhere out in the world was a place which would afford him an opportunity to test his abilities on his own in a new atmosphere. He knew that before long he must get away. At this time he was working on the *Star*, running a pop stand on the side and trying to cram at high school so as to speed up his graduation. He was taking all the necessary courses for college preparatory credits in a little more than three years, and it seemed that there were never enough hours in the day.

His natural instincts led him into some competitive sports, but he found that there was never enough time for the necessary practice to make him a star. He reveled in playing basketball, baseball, and soccer and he particularly loved the competition of track events.

He had discovered while in grade school there was one competitive event for which he could practice without taking too much time away from his studies or his money-making projects. This was the 40-yard dash, a grade school specialty in which he excelled. He decided he would try to enter the finals.

He trained himself to a razor edge and successfully began the series of eliminations. He was quite confident about victory and was determined to go all out to have this credit on his grade school record. Finally the great day came. When the gun sounded, Sam shot from the mark, raced straight and true and at the finish thought he had won, but he was placed second for having ducked under the tape instead of breaking it, as he had never trained with one. The declared winner due to this circumstance was Warren Pershing, son of General John J. Pershing hero of the Mexican border War against Pancho Villa and in World War I.

This was Sam's first bitter personal defeat. He learned that day that defeat sometimes is inevitable no matter how much you practice, particularly if you don't know all the rules. He did a lot of thinking about that reverse. It began to teach him a lesson. He did not like being second best but he also realized that to be first and remain first required a concentration of effort and the application of enough time for preparation to get the job done.

* * *

As Sam neared the end of his high school days he felt life was pushing him toward some definite move to put himself on his own. One factor that made him feel perhaps he could leave Lincoln with a clear conscience was the small success his mother now was achieving in making a living. She was such a tireless worker that even out of meager resources she was managing to bring forth a respectable living. Sam's father still was in bed with his injury; in fact he never recovered completely from this second fall. Sam's mother, as a little money began to come in, leased an apartment building and rented some of the quarters while she and Sam lived in one of the small apartments. Sam's "room" was a screenporch, where he spent the brief periods of sleep which were left to him from his numerous activities. His pay at the *Star* was sufficient to buy everything he really needed and to provide him with a feeling of independence.

Just at this time a fad in shoes gave Sam an opportunity to better himself financially. During the period of the Melodors he had begun to observe carefully the dress of the young men who

49

attended the dances. He noticed that shoe styles went in cycles. So now he went to work for a men's furnishing store in Lincoln called Leon's and immediately proved to be a top salesman in men's shoes. At this time the fad among the college men at the University of Nebraska was a certain type of thin-toed shoes called Dixie Ties. The spirit of conformity in regard to dress prevalent among young people in nearly all generations was in effect at this time, too. The Dixie Ties therefore were a "status symbol" and as such were bought by nearly all the college men who could afford them.

From the manager of the store, E. Burton Campbell, known as "Humpy," Sam learned the fine points of selling. The little techniques of watching for indications of buyer softening, the little tricks of the trade in encouraging interest in a particular item, and the necessity of knowing the product were all drilled into Sam.

"Look at me," Humpy would say. "Here I am, almost with an engineering degree, but not quite, and what am I doing—selling shoes! Now I've got three kids and I don't suppose I ever will get back to college to finish up on my engineering. You're young, Sam, and you should go on to college and stick it out and get your degree in whatever you want to do."

Sam listened and learned. From Humpy's advice Sam began to evaluate the life of a salesman and decided that he wanted something better. The urge to go somewhere, almost anywhere, was becoming overpowering. It was true that Lincoln was all he knew but he felt that there must be wonderful places to see and visit and perhaps live in if he could only get enough money together to go explore them in person. He was torn between two places for his first venture. One was Chicago and the other was Los Angeles. He had no real idea of the geography of California but he had heard of Stanford University, although never of Palo Alto where it was located. He had no idea, either, how far Stanford might be from Los Angeles or San Francisco.

Sam's mother was doing relatively well financially with her apartment managing work. His father once again was able to take small contracts but no large jobs. The tensions of continual financial crisis tended each day to widen the breach between Sam's parents, who remained separated. It was obvious there was no chance of any reconciliation.

At this time the man who was to be of great assistance to Sam in the future came upon the scene. He was Richard Barrett, later destined to be Sam's stepfather. Sam liked Barrett from the start and confided in him his hopes for getting away from Lincoln to some large city. Barrett encouraged him in the idea.

One day a friend of his own age came in to see Sam and yelled, "Hey, I'm going to California by way of Salt Lake City. Why don't you come along?"

"Where are you going from there?" asked Sam.

"Oh, Los Angeles, I guess."

The idea appealed to Sam and at noon he left Leon's Haberdashery Shop and went home to talk to his mother.

He found her sympathetic. With her intuitive Irish nature she had been aware for a long time of the boy's yearning to get away somewhere. She was acutely conscious of the hardship the domestic difficulties had brought to Sam. She assured Sam she could get along very well with her care of the apartment house, and consented that he make the trip.

Sam counted his savings and started for the station of the Denver and Rio Grande Western Railroad. On the way, he ran into Richard Barrett on the street.

"I'm going to get a chair car ticket to Salt Lake City on the way to Los Angeles," he said. "Why don't you come along?"

"Maybe I will," responded Barrett.

He too got a ticket and Sam, Barrett and Sam's friend started on their journey. As the train puffed out of Lincoln Sam looked excitedly out of the window because, although he had been to Denver, this was the beginning of his first long trip. Each mile clicked off by the wheels of the train seemed to open a more wonderful imaginative vista.

In Salt Lake City the wide streets, the evergreen trees in the parkways and surrounding the homes, the Mormon Temple and the Tabernacle fascinated him. Sam's money was so low he decided not to attempt to get a ticket to Los Angeles on the train, but to try to find some cheaper transportation. He and his friends heard that individual automobiles were running "jitney buses" to Southern California. They made an agreement with one of the drivers and started the long, dusty, bumpy trip across Utah and Nevada to the golden goal, Los Angeles.

It was April 1927.

CHAPTER VI

I would rather give a speech than eat.

SAM YORTY

All during the late 1920s Sam persisted in his law studies, and made the discovery that he was growing more skilled in debate. He enjoyed the distinction of being chosen on the Southwestern University's debate team while he was still a freshman. To Coach William Barber, Sam gives great credit for having taught him much about public speaking. Even in the midst of these activities, however, Sam was unable to resist the blandishments of the musical Muse.

For about a year he succumbed to the temptation of trying to resume his musical career; not this time as a banjo player but as an opera singer. He took lessons and was told that his large vocal chords were phenomenal but that a damaged cartilage in his nose, possibly incurred while playing football as a boy, was a handicap. Eventually he concluded that God was slamming another door in his face, and therefore gave up a possible opera career in favor, as it turned out, of his political activities.

For a time, though, he was too immersed in his law studies and his earning of a living to give full attention to political affairs, although his interest in this realm was growing all the time. As a matter of fact, he found that even in his own day-to-day activities he was coming in collision with "politics" in a sense which to him seemed quite sinister. This early impression has remained with him to this day.

Every time Sam sees the Spring Street steps of the City Hall, directly across from the old Hall of Records where a bronze George Washington stands as if admonishing all men to tell the truth, he thinks of the first time he ever went up them. He never was in the old red sandstone City Hall at Second and Broadway and he might not have entered the new one either if he had not been filled with rage and a grim determination to seek justice somehow, somewhere. He had been studying to become a motion picture projectionist so that he might increase his income.

He worked hard at learning every detail of the projection machines, the threading of the film, what to do when the film broke, and all the details necessary to qualify him for the necessary examination and the joining of the union. Then when he was ready he took the examination and felt he had passed with flying colors. To his dismay he received a notice in a few days that he had failed.

He was positive it was not due to any lack of preparation on his part because the questions had seemed simple and he had answered them all. His suspicions were aroused. He began a quiet investigation on his own and then, after making certain discoveries, he stormed down to the City Hall, ran up the Spring Street steps, and immediately began his first confrontation with "the City Hall gang."

What he had found out was that the examination was rigged so that ability had little to do with passage or failure.

His evidence was so carefully gathered and well documented that he forced a showdown and a Grand Jury investigation. From this there came the dismissal of a recreant examiner and a cleaning up of the projectionist examination situation. Sam Yorty had begun to make his mark at the City Hall while he was still only twenty years old.

For a time then, in fact, he worked as a projectionist while continuing his law courses.

He was becoming acquainted in Los Angeles, of course, but he retained a deep sentimental attachment for his home town.

He kept up his friendships in Lincoln whenever possible and, in particular, remembered the people who had advised and helped him in his high school days and in his jobs. Thinking of his friend "Humpy"—E. Burton Campbell—and "Humpy's" ambition to better himself, Sam sent word inquiring whether he might like to come to Los Angeles. When "Humpy" said he would, Sam was able to arrange for a job for him at Alexander & Oviatt's, where Campbell remained the rest of his working life.

* * *

Beyond his own sphere now Sam began to be aware of wider horizons. His budding political interests and ambitions coincided with a period of great activity in seeking philosophical and religious knowledge. His mind naturally was of such an inquiring nature that his quest for something fundamental and basic in life led him to take part in all sorts of study groups and clubs. He attended sessions of the "Parliament of Man," a particularly active forum which met in a building now a union headquarters on Loma Drive near Belmont High School. Here Sam entered a stimulating new field of thought in discussions of Plato, Aristotle, Sir Francis Bacon, and many others. He met Will Durant, then at his zenith, and was boyishly overwhelmed at the opportunity. From Durant he received the stimulus to go into Spinoza's dissertations and then on to Aurobindo and many realms of Eastern philosophy and religion.

He found that sometimes philosophy, religion, and history were closely entwined. This was particularly true in relation to the rise and development of the phenomenon known as a "city." Added stimulation for this subject was provided by his exciting surroundings in Los Angeles, so totally different from the small town atmosphere of Lincoln, which in his formative years had formed virtually his entire world. Los Angeles as the product of two civilizations—the Spanish and the Anglo-Saxon—formed an example of the spontaneous and rampant upsurge of urbanization, as if mushroom cells comprised of people were spreading over hill and valley in some wild and unrelated fashion. This was in distinct contrast to the classic pattern of cities which emerged from a blending of religion and practical necessity.

It struck Sam as strange when he read Durant's "Story of Civilization" and similar works that he could be meditating about the academic subject of ancient cities in the midst of the turmoil and bustle of more than a million human beings scuttling about the Los Angeles landscape. From Athens, as was dwelt upon in the philosophical groups he attended, had come ideas and concepts still powerful in the modern world two thousand years later. Yet Athens in the period of its greatest prominence could boast no more than 150,000 free men and 100,000 slaves, a total of about one-fourth that of Los Angeles at the time of Sam's arrival.

"What do we call a city?" he found himself inquiring along with Durant.

Florence in the flowering of its greatest artistic triumphs which were destined to influence men of all races for centuries was a "city" of a mere 74,000 persons. Milan, with its artists, artisans, and writers was less than 100,000. Pisa, with its tower leaning not quite so much then, was a trifling 30,000. The little English towns from which London and other cities evolved could boast—for all their influence upon the history of freedom due to Magna Carta and the Common Law—populations of only 6000 to 10,000 souls.

In his contact with eagerly inquiring minds of all ages Sam found challenging facets of the philosophy of cities arising at every turn in his reading and discussion. The groups dissected the Bible to detect the origins of Nineveh and Babylon and Jerusalem. They explored, almost as if it were contemporaneously, Homer's world of Athens and Sparta and Troy and Alexandria and Carthage. They examined the concept which had prompted man before the days of Christ to congregate together so that a city, or urban gathering place, was the common habitation of gods and men. They traced this on into the Middle Ages where it persisted in the form of each city having a patron saint. They found inexhaustible mental fodder in the exploration of the fact that the Dark Ages in Europe up until the tenth or eleventh centuries were due in reality to the absence of established communities. Men lived in small groups in virtual savagery for centuries, with the only flickering light of intellect coming from an occasional monk illuminating a manuscript.

Then came the beginning of the towns in the years from 900 to 1100, as the historians recited, and their splendid flourishing during the next two centuries presaging the birth of the Renaissance. The people, groping from the abyss for a better life, were finding almost instinctively that cities provided a place of mutual protection, a chance for religion, a more beneficial political system for the common man, military safety behind walls, convenient marketing facilities, and a companionship which stimulated latent artistic talents. When the Renaissance did come it was directly attributable to this mutual stimulation in the Italian cities, with the leaven spreading across the Continent to animate and expand the lives of people in Paris, London, Amsterdam, Lisbon, and Seville.

Sam began almost imperceptibly to translate the theoretical into the practical. Around him in Los Angeles he began to detect and analyze the effects of divergent ancient cultures. The Roman cities

55

laid out on the Etruscan pattern of Asia Minor with the carefully planned city center and the radiating streets merged and blended with the casual winding ways derived from Old England.

To Sam's mind came the thought, derived from his reading: Each leader of a city has the legacy and heritage of presiding over an institution dating back to the days when Zeus and Jupiter were partners in the enterprise.

* * *

CHAPTER VII

What do we want with this vast, worthless area, this region of savages and wild beasts, of shifting sands and whirlpools of dust, of cactus and prairie dogs? Of what use could we ever hope to put these great deserts or these great mountain ranges, impenetrable and covered to their base with eternal snow? Mr. President, I will never vote one cent from the public treasury to place the Pacific Coast one inch nearer Boston than it now is.

DANIEL WEBSTER

Sam chafed to reach twenty-one for just one reason—so he could vote. Already, at nineteen and twenty in California, he was immersed in political activities and campaigns, but he felt a bitter sense of being thwarted because he could not translate his sentiments into a ballot. At last, on October 1, 1930, he reached the long-awaited day of his majority at a peculiarly significant moment in history which was predominantly Californian in one aspect, but world-wide in its effects. He became legally qualified to vote under the age sanctions imposed by the United States government at exactly the halfway point in the administration of Herbert Clark Hoover, citizen of California and President of the United States. This was at a time when California was "safely Republican" in such an overwhelming fashion—the registration of voters was roughly 3 to 1 Republican over Democratic—that the GOP conducted affairs on the happy assumption that one-party rule was "here to stay."

Few observers yet could anticipate that the Great Depression which had begun just about a year before Sam's twenty-first birthday anniversary with the Stock Market crash of 1929 would lead in another twenty-five months from October 1, 1930, to the election of Democrat Franklin Delano Roosevelt to the White House.

Indeed, in California, the Republican grip was so strong in the 1930 election for governor that James Rolph, Jr., San Francisco Mayor, the Republican candidate, easily was victorious over Democrat Milton K. Young, apparently with public acceptance of the Hoover assertions that there were really no "bad times," just a "business adjustment" with a few Wall Street suicides.

Sam wasted his precious first vote. It went for Democrat Young. Both vanished down the drain.

* * *

Sam's questioning mind, stimulated by the kaleidoscope of the multifaceted Roosevelt "Program of Change" was ready to evaluate all manner of new approaches to the overwhelming problems of the early 1930s when the horrors of the Depression manifest themselves. Nearly all men were frightened. Almost everyone had a panacea. Desperation and poverty were breeding a thousand "remedies" a day in man's attempt to relieve the evils brought upon himself in the robot industrial age which had made him captive to chaos and hunger.

In the midst of these gropings for any sort of a "plan," a few achieved some public following under one name or another.

Among these was "Technocracy."

Nobody ever seemed able to explain exactly what it was except that it was to seek to be a scientific harnessing of the great forces which man had set in motion with his inventions for the benefit of everyone. Its nebulous character was an asset in a way because it meant so many different things to so many different people. To Sam Yorty, who became Secretary of the Technocracy organization, it was part of the challenging realm of knowledge which had not been fully explored—a sort of cross between idealism and The Machine to provide jobs and ward off the breadline. Although he was still in his early 20s, his political knowledge and experience were so far beyond that of most young men that he was accepted as an equal among political figures two or three times his age. The fact that he was willing to examine all sorts of approaches to the nation's ills was no handicap in this association. Experimentation and the effort to penetrate new realms of economic thought were so prevalent that the exceptions were the people who sat quietly in despair and refused to believe there could be any surcease to their miseries.

Two letters to his father written at this time disclose his remarkable tenacity of purpose and political aptitude:

April 7, 1931

Dear Dad:

. . . I have been fighting desperately to keep from getting in a rut like so many young men with ambition do. Adverse circumstances made it seem inevitable at times but by denying myself in many ways I believe I have won. It seems as tho I was just leaving one of the danger periods where many fall by the wayside because of immature marriages and desires for good times. It seems as tho aiming at success is more or less of a game in which you dodge certain obstacles that present themselves to every one at some time or other. Most of my former friends are now married and trying to make a living for their families. This forces them into a rut because they can no longer go to a school or take a chance in a line of business that does not guarantee an income sufficient to their needs. It gives me a feeling of joy to know that I have passed these things and that I realize the value of freedom. My grades are the best at the (motion-picture projectionist) operators training school, which gains me many privileges not enjoyed by most students and they have assured me of a good job when I finish in two months or less. Then at last I can study with peace of mind and no rush. I have been criticized for not taking some job just for the money in it but to me it meant more than that because I was afraid that once I began making a decent salary I would be unable to quit and thus I would go the way of the many. I would not write this to any one else but I know that you will understand my feelings. . . .

Lovingly,
Sam

May 3, 1933

Dear Dad:

The past few weeks have been very eventful for me but I hardly know where to begin to relate the occurrences. However the real high spot was related in that newpsaper clipping about my speech before the Municipal Light and Power Defense League. It was a beautiful affair attended by all of the political leaders in California that were in Los Angeles at the time. The only speakers were to be the three candidates for mayor indorsed by the League namely Frank Shaw, Chairman of the Board of Supervisors for Los Angeles County; Former Mayor George E. Cryer; and Assemblyman Chas. W. Dempster. Mr. Dempster had to be in Sacramento so I was selected to represent him. I don't know yet how it could be. It still seems like a fairytale dream. The room was all in orange and beautifully decorated. At one side the speakers' table was raised up quite a bit higher than the rest so that we looked down on the crowd. Mr. Cryer sat on my right and next to him was John B. Elliot, Chairman of the California State Democratic Committee. On my left was President Randall of the Los Angeles Council and other councilmen. Randall, Cryer and I had not conversed five minutes until we learned that we were all three from Nebraska. Shaw spoke first, Cryer next and then me. I was thrilled all right but I don't think I was as nervous as Cryer. It seemed strange to be sitting there and speaking on the same programme with the man who was mayor when I first came here. I knew that if I made a poor speech I was done for and I also knew that if it was good it would do me much good, so I guess it was a good one because I have heard about it ever since. Several people whom I did not know gave me their cards and said they would like to know me better. Others came over to shake my hand and compliment me. Mr. Elliot said it was fine and Cryer wrote my name down on a slip of paper altho I had to take a few shots at him in the talk but of course that's just politics. Since that day it seems like I know many important people. As yet I haven't tried to cash in. Altho my candidate was eliminated I have some offers to continue speaking in other campaigns until June when they will be over. I'm going to be careful who I speak for because I am going to be running before many years and I don't want to make any mistakes. Say Dad just between you and me, you know I wear a 15½ size collar and my throat and vocal chords are abnormally large so that I never have trouble being heard in the largest places. It is a wonderful asset for which nature is to be thanked. I would rather give a speech than eat and so I have been quite happy this year because I am always speaking somewhere. Now all I have to do is make money and I'll be pleased. I don't seem to be as good at money-making as I am at speaking. Perhaps it is because I cannot bring myself to the worship of gold. I am confident I shall get my share but it will be second to success and not the end or success itself. . . .

Your loving son,
Sam

In his political venturings Sam was ready to try *almost* anything. This included Technocracy.

Yet he possessed an inborn quality, nurtured and instilled by his father, to distinguish between proper experimentation in the American spirit and that other murky realm of vicious undermining of the American system by a foreign foe or domestic intolerance and bigotry. For this reason he was instinctively affronted by the two most dangerous and subversive movements of the 1930s, the Communist Party and the Ku Klux Klan. He had a kind of intuition which more and more permitted him to evaluate on the one hand the legitimate and enthusiastic exploration of a new approach to utilization of governmental and political power and, on the other hand, the stealthy effort of subversives to destroy the fundamental principles of U.S. life. This intuitive sense was not fullblown or entirely developed at the outset, of course. It was a matter of accumulated facts, observation and a definite Irish faculty of "feeling" in an almost extrasensory way.

In regard to the Ku Klux Klan he already had undergone enough personal experience in Nebraska as a boy to shape his undying opposition to it. He had actually spied on one outdoor Klan meeting at night and had been terrified by the experience. As for Communism, he was so unaware of its existence and aims during the first years of his residence in Los Angeles that considerable time elapsed before he began to suspect it as a cancerous and deadly foreign growth. Only when he saw many of his friends and companions in the political machinery of the Democratic party succumbing to its blight did he begin to be aware of it consciously. This was an attitude presaging a climactic moment in his political life a few years in the future.

Even in Technocracy which intrigued him for the possible good it might do among the hungry and miserable people around him Sam, as young as he was, was determined not to be drawn into any orbit which he considered contrary to the fundamental American pattern. This to him included Socialism which, despite its more or less academic nature and its repeated failures to gain any large-scale support in this country, was one of the recognized factors on the American political scene. Upton Sinclair, the author, at this time was a leading Socialist exponent and, in fact, he was the Socialist candidate for Governor of California in 1930; as a prelude to changing his registration and becoming the Democratic candidate in the celebrated campaign of 1934, in which his EPIC

(End Poverty in California) program stirred one of the bitterest fights in the state's history.

When Sam plunged into the study of Technocracy, he became so expert on the subject although he was only about twenty-four that he became a contributor to the Los Angeles *Citizen*, a periodical dealing with Labor and its problems. He wrote an article entitled "Technocracy or ?" He was proud enough of the effort to send the original manuscript after its publication to his father in Nebraska with the handwritten inscription at the top:

> Dedicated to my dear old Dad hoping that he will find in my humble efforts, a reflection of his own philosophy. . . .
>
> Your loving son,
> Sam

As if to protect himself from any supposition that he had abandoned his own concepts of the Democratic party and the American system, he included a definite assertion that: "those who stamp a label of Socialism on Technocracy are merely dodging and befogging the real issue." He wanted it known that he was not embracing any "isms" contrary to the Republic's basic characteristics.

In the article, though, he went all out to lambast the selfish accumulation of wealth to an undue degree.

"It seems clear," he wrote, "that our deluxe citizens are facing the dilemma of returning some of their wealth through charity and taxes, on the one hand; or of accepting a more judicious distribution of wealth on the other.

"Let us keep in mind that wealth is not a criterion of true worth and ability. The urge for acquisition is, according to Veblens and Spencer, an outgrowth of the honor attached to the savage collections of skulls and ancient trophies. . . .

"We cannot expect Technocracy to be a panacea. If it only stimulates our thoughts, so that we may guide ourselves more sanely in the light of the facts, it will have served an immeasurable purpose."

❂   ❂   ❂

About this time, because of his widening interests, Sam became convinced he ought to know more about California politics. He was making the strange discovery—a rather remarkable one for a person so young—that to understand the subject at all it was necessary to know everything about it from the start. He sensed that tradition, old feuds, trends of thought, voting peculiarities, party allegiances and defections and the inception of State Constitutional principles combined to form, as it were, a flowing river of political continuity. Eddies, whirlpools, and bayous might complicate the pattern, but down deep there was a basic current which could be followed by those with the proper political sounding tools.

He determined to acquire a set of those. Immediately, in conjunction with his law studies, his philosophical delvings and his general reading he began to delve in the murky waters of California's political past; determined to make his knowledge of it serve his future purposes and ambitions. This was a study destined to last the rest of his life, continually rewarding him over the years with new facets of political facts. First of all it became apparent to him that California's anomalies and paradoxes went right back to its beginnings in its "American phase" in 1846.

California was a maverick from the very moment of its beginning under the control of the United States. It never conformed; it never did anything according to the rules. When Commodore John Drake Sloat formally took possession of the nebulous region known as California by raising the American flag over Monterey on July 7, 1846, he set in motion a series of events which not only perplexed and confounded the Mexicans but also the rest of the United States. His seizure of California was one of the early moves in the conflict which became known as the Mexican War. In California itself there were a number of military engagements and shifting of control in various cities, notably in Los Angeles itself. But the net result when the California phase of the war came to an end under the Treaty of Cahuenga, signed near Los Angeles in January 1847, was the creation of an American appendage which really had no political status. California was of necessity under a kind of military rule because it did not fit into the standards previously established for potential states. In other parts of the country the territorial status or intermediate phase of preparation for statehood was the recognized procedure. But California, persisting in its already well-established position of being "different," was not of a mind to be a territory.

It was flamboyantly independent in its thinking and was so far away from the nominal seat of government in Washington, D.C., that it did pretty much as it pleased. In fact, inhabited as it was by strong-minded people who had come from all over the nation and indeed from the far corners of the earth, it declined to conform in any respect to what might have been expected of it. The citizens

63

decided that they would take matters into their own hands and set forth the conditions under which they would be willing to enter the Union. As a result, the people decided to have a Constitutional Convention to arrange for their entry into the Union as a full-fledged state. They scorned the idea that they even needed the intermediate stage of being a territory. It fascinated Sam to discover that, consequently, in September and October of 1849 a remarkable group of young men gathered as delegates to the California Constitutional Convention in Monterey. There, amid premonitory symptoms and stresses of the prospective Civil War they hammered out a State Constitution, allied with the "free" forces in the rest of the country rather than with the slavery element. The Constitution rather resembled that of Iowa in its major provisions and indeed was extremely forward-looking in its entire character.

Thereupon, California went boldly to Washington through its elected representatives and requested formal admission into the Union. This brash and upstart procedure shocked the sedate Senate and House of Representatives because the Congress had never had to contend with such a situation before. Complicating matters, as Sam found, was the fact that California was to become the 31st State—if the Congress decided to admit it at all—and therefore had assumed the crucial role of breaking the balance between the "free" and "slave" states in the United States Senate. These stood in precarious balance at fifteen states each at the moment California knocked on the door for statehood. It required about a year of negotiations and maneuvering before statehood finally was achieved on a "free" basis on September 9, 1850. During that time such political giants as Daniel Webster, Henry Clay, and John C. Calhoun made some of their climactic and most impassioned speeches over the California issue and the whole related aspect of slavery. In a very large sense the entrance of California, breaking the balance in favor of the "free" forces, set in motion the culminating animosities which led directly to the outbreak of the Civil War a decade later.

A paradox in the whole situation was that these momentous forces were instigated by men in California who were not really Californians at all. They were still impregnated with the spirit of the regions of the United States from which they had come. They had been "Californians" only for a year or two or three and their loyalties and allegiances and thinking still grew out of the more basic philosophies in which they had been reared in their respective states in the East or in the South.

Robert Semple, president of the Constitutional Convention in Monterey was a long, lanky Kentucky dentist. The first senators from California were John C. Frémont, the explorer, from Savannah, Georgia, who was despite his birthplace everlastingly a "free Stater," and William Gwin, who came from Tennessee. The first governor was Peter Burnett, who had come down from Oregon and yet was so new in Oregon that his real purposes and convictions dated like Gwin's to his native state of Tennessee.

All during the early days of California's tempestuous beginning when the Civil War was brewing here as elsewhere, there was a constantly mounting internal stress over the issue of slavery. Duels were fought repeatedly either over the issue of slavery—with the "Chivalry" as Southern supporters were known, arrayed against the Unionists—or over the very issue of lawlessness itself. San Francisco, which in a real sense meant California because of the concentration of population and politics there, fell under the domination of such blatant crooks that it required the formation of the Vigilantes and the appliance of lynch law to bring some sort of order out of the chaos. From all of this emerged an essential ingredient of California politics then and in the future—its utter unpredictableness.

Los Angeles during all this period, Sam learned, remained more or less the little village that it had been when the 1848 gold strike was made. But it too shared in the fierceness of political feeling engendered by the freedom vs. slavery issue. The community was overwhelmingly Democratic and pro-Southern. It was the home of Mrs. Albert Sidney Johnston, whose husband was destined to be second-in-command to Robert E. Lee and one of the great Confederate heroes until his death on the battlefield at Shiloh. General Johnston's brother-in-law, Dr. John S. Griffin, voiced such fiery Southern sentiments that he helped influence many others in the community. Nearby was one of the genuine "hot spots" of the Confederacy in the West known as "The Monte" or El Monte. This settlement had been created by Texans and others of Southern origin who maintained a little Confederacy of their own in the area of the San Gabriel River and the Rio Hondo. It was known that in the event of any clashes all the Los Angeles Confederates needed to do was to call on "the boys from The Monte" and they would respond en masse with their rifles to join in any insurrection that might be brewing.

"The Knights of the Golden Circle," a secret organization dedicated to the winning of the West for the Confederate cause, came so close at one time to bringing about the seizure of California that the repercussions were heard all the way to Washington, D.C., and resulted in military expeditions to crush unofficial Confederate outposts all through the western region. Many "Knights of the Golden Circle" and other Confederate sympathizers felt with some reason that if California and Cuba could be seized for the Confederate cause the whole trend of the war might be changed. The gold from the mines of California did, in fact, prove to be one of the decisive factors in the victory of the North because it was California gold which permitted the Federal government in Washington to maintain its credit with England and France and other countries from which it was obtaining the overwhelming munitions of war which finally crushed the Confederate defenses. If Cuba had been seized for a military and shipping base the sea routes of the Confederacy could have been protected for vitally needed munitions from abroad.

In a sense, then, the "Knights of the Golden Circle," Dr. Griffin and his allies, and others in the Los Angeles area became enormous factors in the Civil War. The fact that they lost caused not only immediate relief in Washington, D.C., but also influenced the entire course of human history.

California—and Los Angeles in particular in one instance—also directly decided two elections for President of the United States in an incontrovertible fashion.

The first was seemingly almost of contemporary interest because it involved the Los Angeles *Times* which, as Sam observed, was showing its increasing influence every day, even though the presidential election occurrence itself dated back to 1888. Democrat Grover Cleveland was seeking re-election in that year but was being challenged by Republican Benjamin Harrison. Among the chief issues was the assertedly undue friendship of President Cleveland for the British, who at the time were engaged in a bitter fight with American fishermen over fishing rights. The Democrats in their campaign were trying to avoid any appearance of friendliness toward the British, because they knew the temper of public opinion on the matter.

At this juncture the British Minister in Washington, D.C., L. S. Sackville-West, received a seemingly innocent request for information in a letter signed "Charles F. Murchison" from the little

66

town of Pomona, California. The letter asked that the Minister indicate to the writer, of English parentage, which presidential candidate would be favored by England. In a carefully worded but nevertheless plain reply, the unsuspecting Minister spoke forth in favor of Cleveland.

Then the trap was sprung. "Charles F. Murchison" turned out, in reality, to be George Osgoodby of Pomona, born of English parents in Monroe County, New York, and a staunch Republican. The ill-advised letter of Minister Sackville-West was published with a flourish in the rabidly Republican Los Angeles *Times* of Colonel (later General) Harrison Gray Otis on October 21, 1888. It created a national sensation by showing that a "foreign" envoy was daring to meddle in American politics.

So disastrous were the consequences that the Democrats suffered enormous losses of voters due to the close connections, thus revealed, of the Cleveland administration with the British. President Cleveland did in fact lose the election to Mr. Harrison, and nearly all observers credited the "Murchison" letter with having brought about the Democratic defeat.

The other instance—of unusual significance to Sam because it was linked with his own boyhood and the beginning of his devotion to Woodrow Wilson—was in the election of 1916, which was decided in Wilson's favor because of a slight to California's Governor, volcanic Hiram W. Johnson, by U. S. Supreme Court Justice Charles Evans Hughes, the Republican candidate. Johnson had been the running mate of Teddy Roosevelt in the Bull Moose campaign of 1912 and as such was detested by many Old Guard Republicans. William H. Crocker was one of the Old Guard in the Republican National Committee. It was charged he managed things so that Hughes failed to confer with Johnson although they were in the Virginia Hotel at the same time in Long Beach, California, in August 1916 during the presidential campaign. This was considered a gratuitous snub because it would have been natural for Hughes to see Johnson who was a candidate for U. S. Senator in California.

The snub—generally regarded as not having been Hughes fault—was nevertheless disastrous. When the votes were being counted on election night Hughes went to bed confident he had been elected President. The next morning he found that California, considered a sure thing in the GOP column, had actually gone for Wilson by 3773 votes, a defection attributed to Justice Hughes' snub of Governor Johnson, and thus had tipped the national election in Wilson's favor. To add gall for Hughes, Johnson was swept into the Senatorship with a 300,000-vote majority.

As Sam Yorty delved deeper and deeper into Los Angeles and California history then and later in his own career he became convinced that each political event held a lesson for him. Always he tried to relate the past to the present, and to profit by its example for himself.

CHAPTER VIII

. . . As rivers of water in a dry place. . . .

At the westernmost fringe of the cluster of buildings marking the Los Angeles Civic Center and Mall—several blocks from Sam's domain in the City Hall at the east end—great fountains gush perpetually around the modernistic headquarters of the Water & Power Department, which glows at night with innumerable electric lights. Nearby, over a cliff on the face of Fort Moore Hill directly west of the Plaza, a waterfall crashes continually beside a bas-relief memorial to the American military forces which helped take over California from Mexico in 1847. This too is lighted at night. Both are symbolic of the city's dependence upon water and power brought incredible distances across mountains and deserts to permit its teeming millions of citizens to survive.

Whenever Sam looks at the fountains and the waterfall and the lights he feels a glow of personal participation in what they represent. His own career has been tied in so closely with the water and power which form the twin bases of Los Angeles' existence that he could never underestimate their importance. Just as water is a predominant part of the human body, so is water a predominant factor in Sam Yorty's thinking. It is a part of his personal and political self. Naturally enough, Sam like almost all other new settlers coming to Los Angeles had no real idea of water scarcity as it prevails in the Far West. On the contrary, he was like so many Midwesterners who have been accustomed to living in the land of the big rivers where the flow never ceases. In his own home, in fact, the only real discussions he had ever heard of a "water problem" was the oft-repeated family story of the flood near Lincoln, before he was born, when his mother and father were almost swept away from the rooftop after his father had been injured on the plow blade.

Even when Sam arrived in Los Angeles there was no occasion for him to inquire too seriously into the water situation because a domestic supply came conveniently out of the tap and he gave little thought to its origin. Of course, even then in the late 1920s action was starting in informed circles in Los Angeles to augment the supply brought 250 miles from the Owens Valley by the aqueduct completed in 1913, under the skilled direction of William Mulholland, the imaginative engineer in whom Los Angeles had placed its trust to solve the city's water needs. Many sources were being evaluated by the engineers while decisions were pondered on a specific program. Even if there had been a program it might not have made much impression on Sam at that particular time. He was too immersed in the day-to-day problem of trying to complete law school and to earn a living. His time was too occupied between his jobs in the clothing store and his law studies at Southwestern University to permit much delving into other subjects. For more than two years in the lush late '20s he managed to make enough money to continue his reading of the law uninterruptedly.

Then came the Great Depression. Around him the devastating effects became apparent almost immediately in Los Angeles and Southern California. Some of the old-timers who had lived through the boom-and-bust days of 1885–87 said the current hard times were far worse because of Los Angeles' interim "progress." In the late '80s there was so little currency in circulation, anyway, that a reduction in supply merely resulted in more trade-and-barter. Most of the people even in the "downtown" area lived simply on the products of home gardens and neighboring fields; they kept cows and chickens and pigs. Actual starvation was hardly considered.

But in the early 1930s Sam saw around him thousands of persons roaming an asphalt desert in the midst of the great city, with the spectres of hunger and starvation goading them to madness and plunder. East Fifth Street in Los Angeles, immemorially the haunt of professional bums, now became a seething mass of hopeless men and women from all walks of life. They sat on the curbs, they slept in the gutters. Their common bond was that they were all broke. Sam saw Main Street turned into a gauntlet of beggars, so that a well-dressed person daring to try to go to the Pacific Electric Railway Station at Sixth and Main was besieged by an almost solid mass

70

of outstretched palms. The cry of "Brother, can you spare a dime!" ceased to be a joke as originally intended and became a dirge.

Long lines of hopeless men stood day and night at the Midnight Mission conducted by "Brother Tom" Liddecoat, who made a valiant effort to see that no one who applied to him went hungry. The Salvation Army worked overtime, hardly finding a moment for revival meetings due to the necessity of catering to the physical needs of so many starving people; souls had to give way for the time being to the stomach. Aimee Semple McPherson, the evangelist, recruited workers and gathered baskets of provisions which were sent indiscriminately to anyone who applied. Anonymous businessmen downtown contributed generously to "Brother Tom" and the Salvation Army and in many instances—such as that of Harry Chandler, the then-publisher of the Los Angeles *Times*— were hardly recognized for the sacrifices they made to alleviate the general misery.

Sam at first shared as best he could with the hungry people who held out their hands to him, but finally there was nothing left in his own pockets to give. He had given up his clothing store job long before to concentrate on his still-continuing law studies. His successful fight to gain a place in the projectionist union had finally been abortive after all.

The Olympic Theater had signed a contract with IATSE Local 150. It was a closed shop contract and the union had a closed charter so Sam lost his projectionist job although Sherrill Corwin, the theater owner, asked the union to permit Sam to continue working for him. Many senior union members were out of work. The union later made Sam an honorary life member but he never again worked as a projectionist after this experience.

Under the circumstances, if Sam was going to be able to continue at Southwestern he had to find work. He made the rounds day after day trying to find something to do. Fortunately, the City of Los Angeles itself, almost as if it were a human being, was making valiant efforts to combat the effects of the Depression. This spirit of persisting in the face of all sorts of adversities had been a characteristic of the community for a long time, dating back even as far as the great droughts of the 1860s. Its first aqueduct from the Owens Valley during a period when the amount of money to be spent was colossal in proportion to the then population of the community was an example of this spirit.

Now, amid the Depression, Los Angeles was embarking on a vast new undertaking to assure its future—a future which at this time seemed highly uncertain of ever materializing. The gray clouds of despair were blotting out the sunshine of optimism which the Chamber of Commerce and the All Year Club sought to keep alive in those citizens who had a moment to lift their eyes toward the economic sky. Specifically, the Los Angeles Water & Power Department was preparing to do its share to reap the benefits of the vast Boulder Dam Project. Boulder Dam—later rechristened Hoover Dam—was being constructed at Black Canyon on the Colorado River to tame the devastating river, provide a stable supply of irrigation water for the Imperial Valley and the Yuma, Arizona, region, and also to assure a domestic supply for Southern California.

As a part of this program the Los Angeles Water & Power Department was preparing to bring electric power on giant transmission lines hundreds of miles across the desert from Lake Mead behind Boulder Dam. This undertaking in the midst of a Depression was perhaps even more colossal in its over-all proportions than the Owens River Aqueduct job had been a generation before. The Water & Power Department was providing the essentials of life in Los Angeles from its current sources, but the Boulder Dam supply of power loomed as a potential benefit in relieving the effects of the unparalleled hard times. The many jobs to be created were certain to remove some hungry people from the streets.

Sam at least was not actually mowing lawns or raking leaves— yet. His early training in the debating society of Lincoln High School and now at Southwestern University was beginning to bear practical fruit. He found that he had a knack for making political speeches. He had become acquainted with some friends of John Baumgartner, a candidate for the Los Angeles City Council. Sam prevailed upon the leaders of the campaign to permit him to make speeches for Baumgartner.

During the successful Baumgartner campaign Sam attained a little local fame as a young man who could speak directly to the point and impress an audience.

At this time, too, Sam's stepfather, Richard Barrett, became a precinct worker for Baumgartner, and showed great aptitude in the work. During the campaign Sam met Joe Gallagher who was running the speakers' bureau. Joe was slightly older than Sam and was married and had several children. The two became good friends from the start.

Barrett's efforts were so effective that Baumgartner later helped him get a job with the Los Angeles Water & Power Department. In the campaign for mayor in 1933, Frank Shaw was a candidate. Sam applied to the Shaw leaders and was granted permission to "try out" with some speeches. Shaw was favored by the friends of the Department of Water & Power which was still controversial at the time. Sam went around expounding the virtues of Mr. Shaw and berating the opposition but when he got through, although Shaw won, all he had to show for his efforts was a raspy throat. One day Sam heard about the possibility of some work in the field for the Water & Power Department on the prospective transmission lines from Boulder Dam. He rushed immediately to get in an application for a job at the Department's building at Second and Broadway.

At last Sam arrived at the interviewing desk and indicated his desire to get outside the city—anywhere—on any kind of job. Apparently the interviewer had been encountering apathy among the ill-fed group which had preceded him, so he showed some interest if Sam would actually go out of town. Sam eagerly agreed.

Joe Gallagher already had been given a job with the Water & Power Department and was receiving the munificent sum of $300 a month, which he badly needed for his large family. Sam hoped his own salary might be as much as $150 a month. When the interviewer put down $200 a month he almost fainted with joy. The next thing for Sam was to find out what he was supposed to do. His title technically was that of a "field agent." This meant that he was to go literally along the line of the prospective right-of-way as laid out by the engineers for the big towers to carry the power lines, and negotiate with each owner of property for its acquisition.

It was a matter of walking. After his period of training had been completed he set forth on his mission with the knowledge that he was going to have to depend on his own two feet for getting from one place to another. He bought a pair of heavy-soled boots and some good socks and began to get in trim for the task. It was necessary for him to move to San Bernardino to be closer to his base of operation because his territory was to be the rough foothill country along the base of the mountains from San Bernardino to Los Angeles. Finally, he set forth with his maps and his plots and his survey sheets.

Before he was through, Sam the Walker could boast:

"I have walked the line!"

It was literally true that he had gone on foot from San Bernardino all the way into Los Angeles along the route of the giant power line. As the work had progressed and he had become acutely aware of the implications for all of Southern California in the electric current to be transmitted to it, the power line became almost a living thing to him. He could visualize the pulsations from the great masses of falling water at Boulder Dam being transformed into energy to help drive away the Depression and eventually to light big office buildings, drive productive machinery, illuminate homes, clear the darkness from lonely streets, perform household tasks in washing machines and dishwashers and clothes dryers and on down the line to the most humble uses of electricity. He felt that he was having a direct part in bringing this all about, that he was a portion of a worth-while team. He was filled with satisfaction in carrying on his assignment. From it came a sense of partnership with nature in transforming hitherto useless flood waters into the vital force of modern life.

One phase of the work was the study of water courses. Many of the stream beds were dry at certain periods of the year or indeed for several years at a time. But their potential flow and the riparian rights which attached to them were of enormous importance in evaluating the property. Sam's interest mounted daily in regard to this particular phase of his work. The importance of water in an arid land became daily more apparent to him, not theoretically or from the pages of a book, but in actuality in the midst of God's own handiwork.

❈ ❈ ❈

A distinct pattern was beginning to become apparent in Sam's life at this juncture although he himself, being the intimate participant in the events, was not really aware of it yet. Whole series of events, seemingly unrelated, yet forming definite connecting links were leading him to the right person at the right time to guide him along some still-unrecognized path.

It was now during one of these seemingly providential processes that Sam became acquainted with Dr. John R. Haynes, who at the opening of the Water & Power job sequence was not even a name in his thoughts. Sam was working directly with men who were shaping the day-to-day operations of a metropolis. His own job was humble, out there tramping the foothills and scrambling through rocky passes. Yet on those rare occasions when he was "in town," he was excited to be in the same building with the leaders of the whole far-flung operations of the Water & Power Department. In the halls he saw "the big bosses," William Mulholland and E. F. Scattergood, and sometimes Dr. Haynes, president of the Water & Power Commission and legendary political dynamo who already had left his imprint so deep upon the consciousness of Los Angeles and California.

This remarkable doctor, who had come to Los Angeles from Philadelphia and whose activities had been so eminently successful both in the medical and political fields, was a part of almost every civic movement. In addition to his work on the Water & Power Commission he belonged to numerous other leading groups. He was credited with being the father of the "Initiative, Referendum and Recall" reform in California which was approved by the voters on December 1, 1902.

Dr. Haynes soon became aware of the enthusiastic young man who was doing such an outstanding job in the field. Sam had the opportunity to meet him and gradually their acquaintance ripened into a friendship resembling that of patron and protégé. Dr. Haynes detected in Sam some of the qualities which had activated his own youthful life; he himself had become a medical doctor while he was still only twenty. This recognition of Sam's similar maturity at an early age resulted in Dr. Haynes engaging in long discussions concerning basic political philosophy. He explained his part in the initiative, referendum and recall movement and in other reforms for California as a state and Los Angeles as a city.

From these conversations Sam came to look upon Dr. Haynes as a political mentor and friend and sought to absorb all the wisdom he could from him. In this fashion he began to shape his own political aspirations, which were assuming definite form.

CHAPTER IX

The dimmycratic party ain't on speakin' terms with itsilf.

"Mr. Dooley"
(FINLEY PETER DUNNE)

Every time Sam drives from downtown toward his hilltop home in San Fernando Valley, he passes an area which appears rather nondescript to other observers but to him is of lasting sentimental significance. It is the scene of his first political campaign. Some of the houses and buildings are just the same as they were in that hectic spring of 1936, thirty years ago, when his young sister Enid got sore feet campaigning in his behalf, and Sam got elected to the California Assembly.

It was strictly a home-canned family affair—no campaign contributions, no fancy posters, no debates, no visible backers.

How it ever succeeded still remains a mystery in the minds of the defeated survivors, some of whom at the time described it as "The Third Battle of Bull Run," because there were so many scared participants all running in opposite directions. Only Sam and Enid apparently knew what they were doing, and they weren't entirely sure themselves.

Sam had been itching for some time to get elected to something, but he wasn't quite sure what, or how. The Depression was at its worst. Sam's family, by contrast with many other people, was getting along well. His mother had purchased a run-down four-family flat from an insurance company which had foreclosed on it. Sam, his stepfather Barrett, and Enid helped fix it up. Sam's mother rented out three flats and retained one. Enid and her husband were having no serious financial problems and Barrett was in a steady job with the Water & Power Department. Still, if Sam contemplated a political campaign he knew his own slender resources would be insufficient for a proper race, and he did not wish to impose on other members of the family. Yet he was obsessed with the desire to get into public service by way of the ballot box.

As early as the forepart of 1933 when he was twenty-three he had begun to be specific in regard to his ambition to engage in a campaign. On June 20 of that year he had written to his father in Lincoln:

Dear Dad,

. . . I am thinking rather seriously of running for the Legislature next year. Of course that is what I am endeavoring to build myself up to. It means I will have to save quite a bit to make the run. It is not my own idea as there are some people who want to back me. I have been offered funds from the big theatre interests because they want to control the Legislature but I refuse to take it because if I cannot go in free handed, I don't want to go at all. My chief worry is my age, but anyhow it is just a thot and I have a year to prepare. . . .

Your loving son,
Sam

This would have meant that he would have attempted the Assembly race in 1934. The fact that he did not run was due to three main factors: 1) his own realism which told him that the time was not right; 2) the lack of money; 3) the unprecedentedly scrambled nature of the governor's race which overshadowed everything else with its totally unbelievable character. This was the year that Upton Sinclair changed his registration from Socialist to Democrat and waged the "production for use" campaign which, until the last minute, threatened to defeat his Republican opponent Frank Merriam.

"I always considered Sinclair a Socialist and it left me nowhere to go that year," Sam says in retrospect.

In 1933, Sam had spoken only of running for the Legislature but by 1935 he was speaking of Congress. In a letter to his father he said:

Dear Dad,

. . . Things are going along well. Of course I am in a hot spot all the time because of jealousy. Then too the Councilman and Congressman from this district are worried about me so that they do everything they can to try and stop me but so far they have only hurt themselves. I certainly wish I was financially independent so I could really cut loose on some of these petty political figureheads. If I could get in Congress, I would join the Norris and Johnson groups because my sympathies are naturally with them. . . .

. . . I would just barely be old enough to run for Congress next fall. . . .

Lovingly,
Sam

He was living at the time at 465½ South Lake Street in the Westlake Park region. This was in the 64th Assembly District. Sam decided he would try to get the Democratic nomination after John McCarthy, the Democrat incumbent, decided not to run again.

Hopefully, Sam went to McCarthy and asked for his endorsement. McCarthy cannily declined, saying that with so many candidates in the field he had to remain neutral. This left Sam on his own. But so were his assorted opponents.

Eleven other candidates filed on the Democratic ticket. This made an even dozen Democratic aspirants, four Republicans, four Prohibitionists, two Socialists, three Progressives, a Communist category and a Commonwealth ticket although nobody got a vote in this latter listing.

From the start it was a mixed up mess under California's "cross filing" system then prevailing. Harry Lyons, Republican, was playing the field by running on the Republican, Democratic, Prohibition, and Socialist tickets. Walter E. Winebrenner finally outdid him by receiving votes in the Democratic, Prohibition, Socialist, Progressive, and Communist columns.

Sam figured correctly that after all the motley registrations had been completed his chief opposition on the Democratic ticket—and that was the only one for which as a loyal party man he had registered—would be from Winebrenner whose liberal leanings were well known and whose son was on the Los Angeles *Daily News*, the only Democratic newspaper in Los Angeles; and from Allen T. Richardson, a teacher and a Beau Brummell in his fastidious garb.

Sam felt pretty shabby by comparison. He always tried to be neat but he simply could not pay for fine suits.

It was a pinch penny deal from the word go as far as Sam was concerned. He couldn't afford a cheap campaign; it had to be practically a free one. Strategy had to take the place of money. It had to be doorbells instead of billboards. Sam had been studying his district for a long time and he knew it by heart. It extended roughly from Temple Street to Sunset Boulevard and from Bunker Hill Avenue to Hoover Street. It included mostly modest homes and small businesses and a large number of apartment houses. To add spice it included Angeles Temple, the church of Aimee Semple McPherson who was still expounding her Foursquare Gospel despite the sensation almost a decade before surrounding her disappearance in the ocean and reappearance in the desert.

Sam from the start adopted a daring policy which he and his sister kept as a secret to themselves. Uppermost in his mind was a piece of advice he had absorbed during his previous political activities in Los Angeles:

"Forget the apartment houses—they don't vote!"

In adopting this principle he was anticipating a sociological factor which was to become more and more apparent to analysts a quarter of a century hence; thus once again demonstrating his own prescience in anticipating political and sociological trends far ahead of their general acceptance.

On this theory of not wasting time on apartment dwellers, the campaign got under way on a carefully conceived line of approach. This involved principally his sister Enid, a five-foot-four beauty with dark red hair inherited from her Irish mother, and Enid's friend Joy, a blond out-of-work beauty operator, also a petite five feet four. Joy had been out of work like almost everybody else and was glad to try politics for a pittance. Each day Enid and she set forth carrying armfuls of specially prepared campaign material. This consisted of glowing write-ups from a supermarket paper which were paid for and written by Sam himself. Accompanying these write-ups were glossy-print glamour pictures of Sam with his mustache looking as mature as possible. Along with these Enid and Joy carried mimeographed petitions containing a pledge that the signers would vote for Sam.

The procedure was simple. Each girl would go to a modest home, ring the doorbell and then say to whoever answered:

"We're working for a mighty nice fellow who's running for the Assembly. His name is Sam Yorty and we'd like to have you vote for him."

At this point they would display Sam's picture and add whatever encomiums seemed appropriate for the person to whom they were talking. Nearly everybody was intrigued by Sam's picture and the girls' simple "pitch" for him. Ordinarily, as Sam well knew an unusual name like "Yorty" is bad in a political campaign. "Johnson," "Smith," and "Jones" are better. But the girls managed to capitalize even on a seeming handicap and to turn the name "Yorty" into an asset. They seized the chance whenever the opportunity arose to tell about Peter Jorty the American pioneer and how he was unable to pronounce the "J" and the "T" and his name thus became "Yordy" in the time of William Penn's heirs and then later "Yorty." This bit of enhanced genealogy practically put Sam in the Mayflower class.

As a climax the girls would say:

"Would you please sign our little petition that you will vote for Sam so we can show him that we're doing some good?"

Despite the reluctance of most people to sign petitions, this ingenious approach worked so well that every night the girls were able to bring home with their sore feet a batch of signed petitions. Then Sam had to get to work. He sat down each evening after coming home from work and wrote a personal thank you letter to every person who had signed the petition, voicing his deep appreciation for the pledge of support and promising when—not if —elected to remember the kindness of this particular individual. The pledges came in such gratifying numbers that at a point well along in the campaign Sam decided it was time for a "meet the candidate" gathering. He thought it would be nice to start making speeches to audiences to get in practice for the Assembly. The big problem was to find a free meeting place. He combed the district without success but finally discovered that he could get the Micheltorena School which was just outside the boundaries of the 64th District. He managed to scrape up enough money for a few posters which he put around in conspicuous places advertising the meeting. He ran notices in the supermarket paper. A friendly Indian, Joe Longfellow, who was publisher of the Westlake *Post* ran some notices gratis about the mass meeting.

On the appointed evening Sam was worried because he was delayed and he and Enid and Joy were fifteen minutes late in reaching the school. He and the girls felt terrible about leaving the audience waiting. He ran in the door of the school with the first words of his speech on his lips and then stopped cold. The only "audience" was a bored janitor wearily leaning against a blackboard. Sam was almost too crushed to be civil but he did remember his manners enough to tip the janitor a quarter. Then he went home to write thank you letters and to forget all about "mass meetings."

From then on the feet of Enid and Joy got sorer and sorer. They redoubled their efforts, carefully avoiding all the apartment houses and continuing to concentrate on the small homes. They found that some of the people on whom they called were members of Aimee's church and in each case they pictured Sam as a deeply religious young man who deserved the support of everybody in the Foursquare Church. The message got around and Sam found himself being smiled at on the streets by church members who had been persuaded that he was practically ready to take up evangelism himself.

At last in a flurry of final doorbell ringing and "thank you" letter writing the campaign came to its final day and election night arrived. Sam, Enid, and Joy were exhausted. Sam was appalled too at the cost of the campaign which out of absolute necessity for a few printing bills, the pictures, the petitions, and the publicity in the supermarket news had run up despite all efforts of economy to almost $1000. All of this had come from within the family, including Sam's mother, Enid and her husband, and Sam himself. No outside contribution had been received.

On the ballot Sam was listed rather grandiloquently as "manufacturer." This was essentially true because he was in a small business of manufacturing cosmetics under the trade-name of Laline with Enid and his brother-in-law, in addition to his clothing store job and his continuing law studies.

When the moment came for the polls to close Sam was at the office of the Registrar of Voters waiting for the ballot tabulation. He was tired but hopeful.

This initial optimism changed to consternation and bewilderment when the bulk of the votes had been counted. The returns showed Allen Richardson far ahead with Winebrenner second and Sam trailing far down in the pack.

This was far more shattering for Sam in regard to the apparent breaking of faith by the people who had signed the petitions to vote for him than to his self-esteem as such. He felt as if personal friends had deserted him for no reason. He had genuinely believed that the small home owners at whom he had directed his campaign were sincere in their reactions to the presentations of Enid and

Joy. Now it seemed that it all had been a mockery to shame and disillusion him. He knew from careful counting that almost two thousand voters had committed themselves on the petitions and yet this was not apparent in the vote returns.

Sam, disconsolate and disheveled, was plunged into even deeper gloom when the immaculate Richardson clad in a fresh white suit appeared and calmly took his commanding lead as a matter of course. At 1 A.M. Sam went home dejected and hurt. He undressed and went to bed but was unable to sleep.

"How could they do that to me?" he kept asking himself in bewilderment, totally unable to comprehend what might have motivated the voters in such a hyprocritical gesture. At 4:30 A.M., an hour when things seemed the darkest, he could stand it no longer. He had to know his ultimate degradation. He telephoned the Registrar of Voters and asked how he stood.

"You're ahead by 177 votes," said the voice over the wire. "That was a mistake earlier in the evening in the tally and it has just now been caught and corrected. But this is still unofficial."
apartment, Sam leaped up and threw on his clothes and grabbed
With a yell for his stepfather who was sleeping in the next
a flashlight.

"We've got to check the polling places," he cried to the astonished Barrett. "I'm ahead downtown but let's get the figures off the tally sheets."

They plunged into the darkness where there was as yet no hint of dawn, except in Sam's excited mind. Down alleys, up to little houses, back to garages they went to check all of the polling places. With the flashlight they illuminated the figures of the leaders on the tally sheets and then dashed on to the next place. They were working from south to north and thus were in the area of the apartment houses when they started jotting down the figures. Sam was getting practically no votes here and the returns looked worse and worse. As the sun came up they were still making their frenzied canvass and hope was rising. They had reached the region of the small homes where Sam's pledges had been obtained. Now his faith which had been so brutally shaken was reasserting itself in the essential decency of human nature. The people who had promised had not let him down after all.

Finally he and his stepfather came to the last of the polling places and checked the figures once again. Sam truly had won by

177 votes, shabby as he was, over play-the-field Winebrenner and by 327 votes over white-suit Richardson.

Harry Lyons had easily won the Republican nomination.

Sam's confidence was restored. He felt he knew the secret now. He was ready for Lyons in the November general election.

* * *

In the interim between the primary and the general election, Sam took time for a vacation at Avalon on Santa Catalina Island. From there he wrote his father:

Dear Dad:

I am taking a little rest before starting in to manage Roosevelt's campaign in my district and my own campaign for the State Legislature.

I really went through a dog fight in the primaries because I had eleven opponents and the power-trust and chain stores tried very hard to defeat me. All they accomplished was to make me more determined than ever to continue to expose them at every opportunity.

Give my love to Grandma.

As ever,
Sam

At the top of the letter, now in Sam's personal papers, is the handwritten parental notation, *"The beginning of Sam's wonderful political career."*

Franklin D. Roosevelt was running that year for a second term against the jolly hayseed Governor Alf Landon of Kansas.

The popularity of FDR was at its zenith.

Once, when Sam got a little worried about his Assembly race against Lyons, he was reassured by the Los Angeles County State Senator, Culbert Olson elected in the melee of 1934, who said: "Forget it! You can't lose. You're on the ticket with FDR!"

So it was.

When the ballots were counted in November, Sam the Democrat had overwhelmed Harry Lyons the Republican 17,791 to 9564.

Next stop: Sacramento.

CHAPTER X

You don't hold your own in the world by standing on guard, but by attacking, and getting well hammered yourself.

GEORGE BERNARD SHAW

An elderly man came up to Sam at a public meeting following the mayor's re-election in 1965 and shook him warmly by the hand.

"I've always wanted to meet you," he said. "I used to vote for your father way back when he was in the Legislature in the 1930s."

"Thank you, but that wasn't my father," replied Sam. "That was me."

He was naturally pleased that anyone remembered his efforts prior to U.S. participation in World War II in Stop Hitler movements, and to foil Japanese spies masquerading as "fishermen" off the coast of California, but it dramatically accented the long stretch of his political service. Sam Yorty's precociousness in fact has had a strange sequel in this fourth phase of his office-holding career. He has outlasted nearly all his original contemporaries with whom he served in his first job as California Assemblyman thirty years ago. In 1936 he was acclaimed as the youngest candidate elected to a state office in the entire United States. Most of the other Assemblymen were ten to thirty years older than he. As a result, when he looks about him now when he himself is fifty-six he finds few familiar faces left in public positions. Age has taken its toll of his one-time companions. He is, in a sense, on a lonely plateau. It gives him a rather nostalgic perspective on the American political scene of the last generation.

As he went to Sacramento for that original term when he was barely twenty-seven he was filled with youthful excitement and zeal.

The beautiful California capitol set in the midst of its redwoods, deodars, and vast lawns close to the mighty Sacramento River represented all the majesty of government to Sam Yorty. As he entered the door for the first time and gazed at the gilt-framed portraits of governors and of Captain John Sutter, the Swiss founder of the capital city and member of the 1849 Constitutional Convention, he realized he was entering in reality the realm of legislative procedure about which he had dreamed since boyhood.

Out there in the city itself, with its tall almost funereal trees lining the streets, were the gingerbread governor's mansion and the old fort of Captain Sutter, emblematic of the pioneer spirit of California's golden-tinted past. Sam's ambition was whetted by his physical surroundings. From his reading of California history he knew the stirring scenes which had taken place on the streets of Sacramento and in the capitol itself. Duels had flared over the question of slavery. The Legislature had figured in dramas revolving around the issue of Secession. Wild rumors of a Southern Confederacy "take over" of California had swept the corridors. The Legislature had gone so far in 1859 as to vote for splitting of California into two states, one south of the Tehachapi Range to be known as "Lexington," although Congress failed to follow through and make it a reality. The wordy battles over revision of the State Constitution in 1879 had raged in the Assembly and Senate.

Evidences of the history being made were apparent even in the year 1936 when he was arriving. Indigents and bums from all over the United States, harried by the Depression and snow and sleet in the East, had swarmed "on the rods" of the railroads to the comparative warmth of Sacramento, a favorite harboring place. They existed as a dirty, begging, uncouth fringe in the waterfront dives and old buildings within a few blocks of the capitol. They touched Sam's heart and the hearts of many others. Some of his legislation in behalf of the poor and needy was accented by this horde of pitiful rejects from the ranks of society.

Sam, still a bachelor, took a room at the Sacramento Hotel. In the official roster of the Legislature, though, he gave his address as "Assembly Chamber" as if he were so devoted to his new job he was going to stay in the capitol all the time, day and night. Some people unkindly hinted maybe he did. They said he could not possibly think up so much legislation to introduce unless he did spend twenty-four hours a day at it.

Indeed, Sam did seem to be using a shotgun to introduce bills

85

during his terms in the Legislature. The range and variety of subjects was so great that his opponents accused him of writing bills just to get his name in the paper. These offerings included a Labor Relations Bill labeled "The Little Wagner Act," a measure to make incompatibility a grounds for divorce in California, a bill reducing the "waiting period" on interlocutory divorce decrees from one year to six months, a proposal to set up state-operated pari-mutuel horse race betting machines to help eliminate "bookies," bills to set up a unicameral or one-house State Legislature, to create county youth authorities, to force chattel mortgage reform, to disclose the names of the principal stockholders of private utility corporations, to create a "Little Hatch Bill" to take politics out of relief, a measure to sanction producer and consumer co-operatives, a bill to put the state in the public utilities business, permitting state drilling for oil in the tidelands, forbidding Nazi Bund assemblies in uniform, for regulation of farm wages and hours. He introduced bills to ban "refill" bootleg operations, for a mortgage moratorium for small home owners, for anti-usury restrictions, limiting service charges and interest rates, and many others.

All during these years in the Legislature, as he traveled back and forth from Sacramento to Los Angeles he was learning legislative procedures, making friends, making enemies too, and attempting to chart a consistent course in his over-all approaches to measures for the betterment of California. His political studies and philosophical ponderings ever since he was a boy were being drawn together now in a cohesive pattern in behalf of the ordinary citizen. It was during this time that he was subjected to criticism from many quarters for the apparent ultra-liberalism of his views. The Republican press in particular attacked him with scarcely disguised insinuations of close affiliation with Communism itself. Some of the people closest to Sam were unworried by these accusations but they were puzzled by another of his qualities which rather frightened them. This was his seemingly uncanny ability to anticipate social change and political trends long before they had become apparent to men twice his age and with many times his experience. They began to ask:

"Did it all come from the Little People of the Ould Sod? Is there a fey quality of the incipient seer in Sam Yorty derived from the genes of his mother's blood lines in the land of the shamrocks?"

Nobody could say for sure, but Sam did in truth astound and confound both his friends and his adversaries with the prophetic nature of many of his utterances and predictions in the tempestuous years from 1936 to 1940. He was "ahead of his times" by three to fifteen years on many subjects. Often he was derided for his ideas. Time alone was able to vindicate him. The very fact of his youthfulness added to the derision with which his pleas were greeted.

"That crazy kid is popping off again," said the Sacramento crowd in the capitol.

It actually was a far cry a generation ago from Sacramento to the problems of the Negroes in the Southern states. Still, the objective of social justice was one of those raised by Sam Yorty at a time when the Negro rights movement was hardly taking form. It was so much a part of his basic belief that he did not need to attach it to any formal movement or campaign. His aims were spontaneous and part of a pattern which continued unabated in his political career. Indicative of this feeling was a statement he made in Sacramento early in 1939, dissecting not only the Negro problem but its relation to the Democratic party:

"Raising Negro workers in the South from their present oppressed status is the key to a thorough victory for all labor progressive forces in the United States. In my opinion, the backwardness of the Southern states coupled with their strength in the Democratic party makes a real fundamental program of social welfare impossible of accomplishment by the party as it is now constituted. The Southern states fail to realize that the economic problems can be solved only by raising the living standards and purchasing power of all the people. In their desire to maintain their supremacy and to keep the Negro workers in a state of peonage, they are blocking all fundamental reform measures and retarding the progress of the entire nation. If they persist in their course, they will eventually carry democracy to the brink of destruction in the United States.

"Some of the Southern states were intent on preventing Negro workers from being protected by the Fair Labor Standards Act (wages and hours) when employed to do work other than agricultural labor, which the Act exempts. They contend that once the Negro workers receive the 25 cents an hour minimum provided by the Fair Labor Standards Act, it would be difficult to keep them out at work from dawn until dusk in the cotton fields at the 75 cents a day wage now paid in the South.

"It must be apparent to every thinking person that the problem of increasing the educational opportunities and the working and living standards of the Southern Negroes is one which all people in the United States must join together to solve. They must do this not merely for the benefit of the Negro workers themselves, but also for the benefit of all workers who cannot advance very far ahead of those in the lowest brackets without causing economic dislocations."

Sam Yorty became one of the first supporters and advocates of Dr. Francis E. Townsend, who, in the midst of the Depression conceived the idea of "The Townsend Plan" to pay every citizen over sixty a government pension of $200 per month for life. Dr. Townsend, a physician in South Dakota's Black Hills had retired to California but had seen his own savings swept away in the Depression. This experience and his observation of the suffering of other poor old people led him to evolve his plan for the pension to be paid from a transactions tax.

The idea gained national attention almost immediately. Yet within two years Dr. Townsend was involved, in 1936, in a Congressional investigation regarding the raising of funds for "promotion."

To Sam Yorty, himself engrossed with the problems of the poor and the elderly, the Townsend Plan appeared to be a useful device to focus attention on a problem too long neglected. He still gives it credit for having led the nation toward the humanitarian goal which eventuated in Social Security under Federal auspices. But, he says sadly, Dr. Townsend was "misled and used" under unfortunate circumstances, following the initial presentation of the pension proposal.

On another front, Assemblyman Yorty showed singular insight into a grave threat to the security of the United States. This was when, in 1939, more than two years prior to Pearl Harbor, he began to demand the curtailment of alien Japanese "fishermen" along the California coast. Sam said that some were not fishermen at all; that they were military spies plotting an attack on the United States. He told the Legislature he could prove it. This was at a time when Japanese "good will" missions were at their height, and when the "Moral Rearmament" Buchmanites of the "Oxford Movement" seemingly were assuring everybody that everybody in the world loved everybody else, or should.

Sam Yorty was impeded by national security considerations from disclosing the sources of his information about the danger to California from alien Japanese "fishermen." He was receiving information from the United States Navy that the supposed "fishermen" off the California coast were in reality Japanese Naval officers and other espionage agents, but he was unable to obtain permission to disclose to his fellow legislators where he was getting the facts. As early as December 30, 1938, almost three years before Pearl Harbor, Sam Yorty announced his intention in Sacramento to seek legislation to bar "enemy spies," and did introduce it January 10, 1939. He cited instances of Japanese observers following the United States Navy far to sea and watching maneuvers.

"An idea of how effective these spying activities can be may be determined by referring to history," Yorty said. "During the Russo-Japanese War several members of the Japanese fishing fleet were decorated for destroying the Russian Naval fleet. They worked the same old trick they are working now and we have been . . . sound asleep . . . I propose to put a stop to it. We make it too easy for enemy spies—and there are plenty of them, as so recently indicated by arrests both in New York and Los Angeles—to study our coast defense and our Navy. We must awaken to the threat."

At the same time he expressed the hope of obtaining a closed sesssion of the Legislative Committee entrusted with the matter to hear an investigator disclose factual material. All during the first part of 1939 Yorty battled vainly to have the legislation withdrawn from the Fish and Game Committee. Sam was ridiculed by some of the legislators, and one of them, Assemblyman Augustus F. Hawkins of Los Angeles County, was quoted as declaring the spy stories were "a bugaboo." This outright ridicule was given tacit support by the indifference of most of the people of California. They were being lulled at this time by all sorts of Japanese propaganda and "peace" moves and there was little general understanding of any overt menace from the Japanese military forces.

Sam's Irish "sixth sense," however, was telling him all this time that he was correct in his suspicions about Japanese spies disguised as fishermen. Finally during 1939 when his efforts to arouse his fellow legislators had failed and he was still under secrecy restrictions from the Navy as to the source of his information, he decided he must make a supreme effort to put over his point. He sent an all-out appeal to the District Commandant of the Navy at San Diego to send an authorized spokesman to a closed meeting of the Legislative Committee at which the facts could be disclosed in secrecy so as to protect national security. His request was so fervent that it was granted. A remarkable officer was sent to Sacramento to make the disclosures for the Navy.

He was Captain Ellis Mark Zacharias. His role later in World War II as Rear-Admiral Zacharias was so important in its impact upon the United States war effort against Japan that it was credited with being one of the decisive factors leading up to the Japanese surrender. Captain Zacharias, a native of Jacksonville, Florida, had served several times as Naval Attaché to the American Embassy in Tokyo prior to his assignment to San Diego. He had made a life-long study of espionage, and was convinced that spies often set the stage for conquest before open warfare began. He had written in this regard: "When Genghis Khan's nomad horsemen galloped over Asia and Eastern Europe in the thirteenth century, trained spies always were sent ahead to search out each city's defense secrets and to spread confusion and fear among its citizens."

During the last few months of the war with Japan Admiral Zacharias from a little cubicle in Washington, D.C., broadcast appeals in Japanese which were acclaimed as superior to those of the famous propagandists Lord Haw-Haw, Tokyo Rose and Axis Sally.

In 1939, however, when he went to Sacramento to talk to the California Legislators, the United States was still nominally at peace and he was in a most delicate position regarding comments about the Japanese. The things he told the Legislators were so shocking and so carefully documented that they could no longer possibly doubt the validity of the charges of wholesale Japanese spying along the California coast. Captain Zacharias completely vindicated the accuracy of Sam Yorty's assertions, with the permission of Rear Admiral Sinclair Gannon, the Commandant of the Eleventh Naval District at San Diego.

Even so, the Legislature unaccountably failed to take action to curb the alien Japanese spying activities. Sam Yorty's pleas were unavailing. The Japanese espionage, later known as "the prelude to Pearl Harbor" continued in California's coastal waters.

CHAPTER XI

Love, from whom the world began, hath the secret of the sun.

ROBERT BRIDGES

When Sam on a November afternoon at the age of twenty-nine years and thirty-eight days went into the Palm Springs Post Office to mail a letter he was totally unaware he was going to emerge with a "Canceled" mark on his single life. He saw a blond girl putting stamps on envelopes at the counter and he felt an immediate impulse to assist her in such exhausting work.

"Can I help you?" he blurted impulsively.

The blonde looked up, startled, and then seeing a personable young man obviously strong enough to lick stamps, she accepted aid gracefully. Sam took the opportunity to introduce his friend, Frank Egger, and this naturally paved the way for him to introduce himself. Then as he continued to lick stamps, he waited for reciprocation.

Laughing at his forwardness, the girl said:

"My name is Betty Hensel."

Sam licked his stamps as slowly as possible and wondered impolitely to whom all the letters were going. Between stamps he managed enough conversation to discover that Betty Hensel had come to California from La Grange, Illinois, for the Notre Dame-USC football game. She and her mother and her brother Norman who had attended Notre Dame were guests on a special train of Notre Dame fans in charge of State Senator George Maypole of Chicago who conducted an annual excursion.

"Oh, I used to see Knute Rockne when he came to my home town in Lincoln for Notre Dame to play Nebraska," exclaimed Sam, as if this constituted a close bond between the girl as a Notre

Dame fan, and himself. "I even sold him some socks once in the men's store where I worked."

The girl's eyes twinkled.

She was fully aware that Sam by slow stamp licking had managed to elicit a certain amount of biographical material from her but that he now saw he was fighting a losing battle because the envelopes were running out. Desperately he sought some device by which he could prolong the conversation or arrange another one. By this time he had managed to impart the information that he was a newly re-elected Assemblyman of the State of California in the just-concluded 1938 elections and a confidant of the new governor, Culbert Olson, who was actually in Palm Springs too at the home of Joe Schenck, the movie magnate. Betty appeared impressed and seeing his obvious hesitation at the impasse they had reached due to the end of the stamp licking, hopefully inquired, "Would you like to meet my mother and brother?"

Sam seized this opportunity and obtained the address of the cottage rented by the Hensel family. He parted unwillingly from the girl as if he feared he might never see her again and then made his way in a trance-like state to the old Del Tahquitz Hotel where he was staying with his friends Frank Egger and David Gill. All Palm Springs had assumed a new aspect. He felt as if he were seeing it for the first time. Across Palm Canyon Drive from the Post Office was the Desert Inn of Mrs. Nellie (Mother) Coffman with its spacious lawns and small private bungalows stretching out from the low graceful main building amid its date palm trees. Overhead towered the sun-kissed peaks of San Jacinto and Tahquitz where the dreadful Cahuilla Indian god who had given his name to the latter mountain was reputed to hold lovely maidens captive in icy palaces. A little way up the street was the El Mirador Hotel, the new and ostentatious rival of the Desert Inn. Off to the north the sharply etched hills reflected the last rays of the sun setting over Mount San Jacinto. Close by were the celebrated Indian springs which had given Palm Springs its name and now attracted visitors from all over the world to this health spot emerging as an international spa.

Ocotillos, ironwood trees, palos verdes, mesquites, and giant saguaro cactus bespoke the desert atmosphere even though orange and lemon and grapefruit trees with ripening fruit at this November season lent a tropical touch to the landscape. To Sam at that moment in his exhilarated state each growing thing was a glorious manifestation of the bounty of nature.

Sam confesses the next three days and evenings were at the same time the most glorious and the most terrifying in his memory. He could not bear the thought of losing this girl and he was determined to defy the hordes of eastern admirers she appeared to have if her letter writing was any indication. He suffered pangs of jealousy for hated rivals he had never seen. He met Betty's mother, Mrs. Elizabeth Hensel, and her brother Norman. Each evening he was permitted to go out with Betty on multiple dates with a group of young friends. Each hour Sam became more convinced he could not let the enchantment end.

On the third evening he managed to get Betty alone and somehow to speak out his plea—this boy orator who had been deserted by all the words he once knew—in the one phrase:

"Don't go back to Chicago!"

Betty accepted.

She knew a proposal when it came from the one person she wanted to make it even though there wasn't a single "love" or "dove" or "June" or "moon" in the whole thing.

Sam dashed in late that night and woke up David Gill at the Tahquitz and began excitedly to announce that he was engaged. David turned over with a snort and went back to sleep but even this attempted throwing of cold water on Sam's excitement was ineffectual.

Almost from the moment he met her, Sam coined a pet name for Betty Hansel. He began calling her "Betts," and still does.

The next day before they told Mrs. Hensel about their plans, Sam took Betts aside and said to her:

"I've got to tell you one thing. I come from a broken home and I know what that means. I just want one wife and you'll have to get used to me from now on."

She nodded, and they went to find the family. It was a surprising disclosure but the impetuosity and sincerity of Sam and Betty overcame any hesitancy. The wedding date was set for December 1 in Los Angeles, the early date being chosen because Governor Olson had asked Sam to proceed to Sacramento early to assist in the development of the legislative program under the new Democratic regime. Sam even was being talked of as a possible candidate for Speaker of the Assembly, and it was important to him to be on the scene before the Legislature actually convened.

Sam, although religiously and philosophically inclined, was not at the time a formal member of any church but he had a good friend in Los Angeles, Monsignor O'Halloran of the Sacred Blood parish. Sam with Betty's acquiescence asked Monsignor O'Halloran to perform the ceremony at a side altar, as was permitted under Catholic procedure, in the church at Sixth Street and Occidental Boulevard.

"He looked wonderful in his robes," Sam recalls sentimentally even today.

Sam's political friends had rallied around. Phil Gibson who later was to become Chief Justice of the California Supreme Court was there. Jack Tenney of the Assembly took movies. John R. Kelley of the Los Angeles Water & Power Department, with whom Sam had worked during the Depression, was best man.

Mrs. Hensel, Norman, and the attendant friends joined in a wedding breakfast at the Mayfair Hotel. The only sadness in the Hensel family was at the absence of Betty's father to share in his daughter's radiant happiness. He was an inventor and salesman who had died when he was just past forty.

Sam took his bride first to the Ansonia Apartments at Sixth and Lake streets in Los Angeles and then they prepared to go north for the prospective session of the Legislature. Sam even in the first flush of love for his bride was conscious of a serious fact. In the stormy days he saw ahead for himself in the world of politics he knew he would need a loyal and devoted partner to sustain him. He was supremely confident he had found her.

*　*　*

Now that he had acquired a wife, Sam decided he must make every effort to complete his law studies along with his work in the Legislature so he could round out his nearly 12 years of effort to become a lawyer. The year following his marriage he did in fact take the State Bar Examination, passed, and was admitted to the practice of law in California, subsequently adding to his education by taking post-graduate work at the University of Southern California and at the Extension Division of the University of California.

CHAPTER XII

God grants liberty only to those who love it, and are always ready to guard and defend it.

DANIEL WEBSTER

Sam was swept into a realization of the meaning of Communism and into violent collision with its leaders almost before his mind could absorb the enormity of the evil force he was combatting. His grappling with the subject actually overlapped his efforts in regard to the Japanese spies. Like so many dedicated Democrats of the early part of the Franklin Delano Roosevelt administration Sam entered zealously and sincerely into many of the governmental remedies and experiments which sought to wipe out the Depression and insure that the United States would not again be subjected to such a dreadful scourge. He considered these to be legitimate efforts to explore new realms of cooperation between people themselves and between the government and the people. In his relative inexperience he was not prepared for infiltration of foreign agents bent upon wrecking the American government into the party he idolized. "Communism" was, in reality, merely a word to him; he had not encountered it in practical politics.

As the end of his first term in the Assembly neared and the elections of 1938 approached, Sam had been labeled a "left winger" and a "liberal" and had aligned himself almost exclusively with other California members of the Legislature who were described in the same terms. This in itself did not worry him. He had, indeed, introduced some measures which verged on the extreme. He had earned the name of being "wild-eyed." Still, in his own mind he was a forward-looking Democrat, supporting FDR, aiding progressive legislation, espousing unions, seeking to reduce poverty, trying to help the underdog. This, in his opinion, did not warrant the

95

ferociousness of abuse heaped on him from some quarters, notably the Republican press and Republican party leaders.

The plain inference of many of these accusations was that Sam Yorty was a Communist. The imputation was repeated so many times that many California citizens actually believed it. Sam himself did not bother to deny it because in his own mind it was too far-fetched to deserve notice. But the time arrived—much sooner than he might have expected—when it became necessary for him to announce himself not only as a non-Communist but an enemy of Communism and all it stood for.

"Just before the election in 1938," relates Yorty, "I was shocked by a Los Angeles *Times* front page headline reflecting a charge that the Democratic party's leading candidates were Communists —Culbert L. Olson, candidate for Governor; Ellis Patterson for Lieutenant Governor; Ben Rosenthal, John Gee Clark, Jack B. Tenney, and Sam Yorty, candidates for re-election to the Legislature. The story was purportedly based upon testimony before the House Un-American Activities Committee—the Dies Committee—which made it privileged and gave the newspapers legal protection from a libel suit.

"I felt sick, disgusted, and angry. This was sordid politics—the kind that discourages many people from seeking political offices and does a disservice to our people and our nation. The voters of California were not fooled—we all won! Since, in my own heart, I knew the charge was a vicious lie, and since the voters proved they also knew it was a lie, I dismissed the matter from my mind, and went on with my work. At some later date Tenney became curious about the so-called 'testimony before the Dies Committee' and traced the source. He discovered that a certain Arthur James Kent, known as the 'Red Burglar,' had made an affidavit while in the Los Angeles County Jail calling the Democratic leaders Communists. This affidavit was flown to Dies. No doubt by pre-arrangement, he released it without notice or hearing so the Republican press could use it with impunity—which it did. Kent told Tenney he did not know any of us.

"While the fraud on the public did not work, Kent was paid off for his effort. On his last day in office, the defeated Republican governor commuted Kent's sentence to 'time served' and released him from jail because of his 'cooperation with the Dies Committee.' When Tenney looked Kent up he was again serving a jail term.

"When I was chairman of the State Committee on Un-American

Activities, I always remembered the abuse of power by Dies and never permitted the State Committee to be used in such a manner. We confronted the suspected Communists with their accusers at open hearings. The Kent affidavit made it possible for all manner of demagogues to repeat the lie with complete immunity from libel or slander actions. When I served in Congress with Martin Dies, he once boasted in the Democratic cloakroom: 'I am a demagogue and I admit it'—and so he was. His tactics discredited his committee and helped the Communists by disgusting and confusing many sincere citizens. So many loose and unfounded charges were made by the headline-seeking Dies that people were unable to distinguish fact from falsity and did not believe his charges even when true."

The "testimony" of Kent the "Red Burglar" had been released in Washington, D.C., by Dies and of course was available to newspapers and radio stations all over the United States and abroad. The Communists subsequently made a concerted and sustained effort to destroy Sam Yorty; an effort which has continued to the present day. It manifested itself in 1939 when he was a candidate for City Council in Los Angeles, in 1940 when he was heading the California Legislature's Committee on Un-American Activities, in 1960 when he supported Richard Nixon—long-time hated enemy of the Communists—in the presidential race, and at various times in between; and in 1961 and 1965 during his races for mayor of Los Angeles.

A pattern of consistency has run through Yorty's attempts for more than twenty-five years to awaken the American people to the danger of Communism, and the Communists' unremitting assaults upon him. His description of this perpetual warfare dates back to his days in the Legislature and his council race in 1939:

"My awareness of the Communists in the Democratic Party in California and their disciplined conspiratorial activity developed rather rapidly in 1938 and 1939 after I once learned how to observe them in action, especially in their 'fronts' like the 'League for Peace and Freedom'; 'Hollywood Anti-Nazi League' and many others. I saw them disrupting labor unions in their efforts to infiltrate and control them. They had virtual control of the Young Democrats. They were determined to control the State Relief Administration and they were undermining Governor Culbert Olson in doing so. My growing awareness of the activities of the party at that time made it possible for me to understand some past actions and I began to put the pieces together.

"Many things that had happened fell into place: The obvious shock shown by a bright young Democrat when I told him I thought he had a promising future but to avoid getting mixed up with the Communists. He later turned out to be one. Then there was the strange sudden shift from me to another candidate in the 1939 City Council race and the attempt to keep me from even speaking about my suspicions at one of my own Council campaign meetings, after which some campaign workers deserted me. They grabbed my scarce literature and dumped it into gutters. At last, I decided the Reds had to be exposed. I told the editor of a 'progressive' weekly newspaper of my decision. His paper supported many Democrats and by a co-operative arrangement which involved changing one page for each Assembly district, we were able to get special editions for our district at little cost.

"The California press was practically all Republican in those days and so was the business community. Democratic campaigns had to be run on a shoe string. So the 'progressive' paper and the inexpensive special editions were a great help. The editor and publisher took great exception to my determination to expose the Communists. He argued heatedly that I was wrong in my suspicions, that the Communists were really just 'good liberals,' that some of the members might be doing what I said but, if so, their actions were contrary to the wishes of their leaders. He said I would ruin myself and the Democratic party and that he was sure the members causing the trouble and disruption could be stopped if I were willing to make my complaint directly to the responsible leaders. He asked me if I would give them a chance to rectify matters before requesting a legislative inquiry. At his urging I agreed to make my charges to them personally but I told him I would not talk to them alone; that they could come to my apartment in Sacramento, but that I wanted a witness present—Jack B. Tenney, an Assemblyman and a labor leader. The editor arranged the meeting.

"I later learned the two men to whom I made my complaint were top echelon Communists. They listened politely and disclaimed any knowledge of the efforts of which I complained. They said they would look into the charges and if true, they would correct the situation and urge their members to desist. They were not in good faith. The disruptive tactics continued and a systematic campaign to discredit me was launched. All manner of lies were concocted and spewed out at Democratic party meetings which were systematically covered by 'Party Liners.' People who had been friendly suddenly quit speaking. I could practically identify the Communists and their cohorts by the change in attitudes. The campaign against me was virulent and vicious. It was calculated to destroy me and drive me out of the Democratic Party.

"It has now been carried on with intermittent intensity and in various forms for more than twenty-five years. The same sort of campaign drove Jack B. Tenney out of the Democratic party and ultimately caused him to embrace extreme causes—a far cry from his more natural and becoming tolerant attitude. He went so far that at one point I found it painfully necessary to oppose some of his more extreme legislative proposals.

"Once when I was an Assemblyman, I was called on the telephone by a person who represented what he described as a new daily newspaper to present labor's point of view. He asked me for a comment. I said labor's point of view was not always adequately presented in the press and I congratulated them. The newspaper turned out to be the 'People's World,' and I have been repeatedly accused of 'endorsing' a Communist newspaper."

It was late in 1939 about a year after his marriage while Sam was serving his second term that he became convinced the State Relief Administration under Governor Olson was dominated by Communists. The governor refused to believe it, or to take action. During these days of stress Betty Yorty the bride was becoming acquainted with the wild and tempestuous nature of California politics. She stood resolutely by Sam but she actually feared for his personal safety many times during this period of his violent conflict with the Communists and their allies. Fortunately some Democrats who had come to the same conclusion as Sam began to aid him in obtaining specific evidence of Communist activities within the Olson administration. He was not alone in his efforts.

The bulk of the evidence centered around the Los Angeles County offices of the State Relief Administration headed by Director Sam Houston Allan.

It became more and more apparent that Governor Olson would not admit the presence of Communists in the Relief Administration. Yorty by this time, despite his previous identification as a leader of the Olson administration was so certain of his evidence that he decided to seek a full-fledged investigation into the matter in the Assembly. The fight by now had raged to a point where there was no apparent possibility of any reconciliation between Olson, intent upon protecting his administrative record and those who felt that

99

California was in mortal peril from a Communist plot to disrupt the state through the virtual conscripting of relief recipients by Communists in state positions. In the midst of the controversy Democratic party leaders put great pressure on Yorty because they said he was about to destroy the effectiveness of the party in California by his charges. Yorty immediately replied that under the circumstances the only thing for the Democrats to do was to try to clean their own house before the Republicans brought up the issue.

The climactic day came on February 1, 1940. In a dramatic debate in the Assembly Yorty's resolution for committee investigation of Communist activities in the State Relief Administration in Los Angeles County was passed by a vote of 51 ayes to 21 noes.

A factor in the overwhelming vote was the coincident passage of a resolution of sympathy for Finland which had just been overrun by Soviet Russia. The resolution branded Russia as the world's "most brutal and degraded tyranny."

From then on for months the "Little Dies Committee," as the investigating group became known, engaged in a series of sensational hearings up and down California, from Stockton and San Francisco to Los Angeles. The committee appointed by Speaker Gordon Garland of the Assembly included Yorty as Chairman, Jack Tenney and Seth Millington, all Democrats; and Lee T. Bashore and Harrison Call, Republicans, with some others added later. The investigation was aimed principally at officials of the Communist Party, the Workers Alliance and Labor's Non-Partisan League, all of whom were accused of participating in or aiding the State Relief Administration infiltration.

In his summing up of the committee's objectives Yorty said:

"The Communist Party is simply awaiting a crisis.

"Through its efforts in the SRA, it is endeavoring to aggravate the present crisis brought about by unemployment in the State and nation.

"It is attempting to do this by maliciously endeavoring to increase relief costs to such an extent that taxpayers will be unable to carry the burden, and all relief will thereby be jeopardized. This program is calculated eventually to deny relief to the destitute and cause unbearable suffering . . . useful to them in their revolutionary agitation."

Then he added:

"One of the 'startling disclosures' was the fact that a large percentage of the Communists working in the SRA were graduates of the State-supported University of California."

Within a few days of the passage of the resolution by the Assembly the hearings were launched in the midst of fist shaking and shouts. On February 5, in Los Angeles, Yorty himself became involved in a violent exchange. Don Healey, secretary of Labor's Non-Partisan League, when asked whether he sought Relief Administration jobs for members of his group said:

"You ought to know, Sam, because I saw you at the SRA office headquarters when you were trying to get positions for your own workers."

"That is a lie!" shouted Yorty.

The original targets of the investigation, the officers of the SRA in Los Angeles County, suddenly had been removed from the arena by Governor Olson. Four days before the Assembly investigation was ordered the governor in a surprise move fired the SRA director and a hundred members of his administrative staff effective as of March 1. In the meantime Yorty was under violent attack by the *People's World,* which headlined:

YORTY ASKS
WITCH HUNT
IN SRA

The committee widened its hearings following disclosures of alleged Communist activities in many spheres. Yorty who had been such a staunch champion of labor unions now declared that in justice to legitimate workers he was compelled to expose unions which had come under the domination of Communists.

A few days later in Stockton the investigation created a new sensation when twelve SRA workers were arrested for refusing to answer questions of the Yorty Committee. Police backed a patrol wagon up to the front door of the SRA offices and carried them off to the police station.

During his open break with the governor, Yorty made an outright charge that Olson was aiming at "a veritable dictatorship" in California.

In Sacramento Yorty said:

"The last time I spoke to the governor he told me 'I believe in a dictatorship of democracy'; I replied, 'Governor, I don't believe in any kind of dictatorship.'

101

"I feel the governor is playing a dangerous game in failing to rid his administration of Communists.

"As an American and as a Democrat I cannot support his policy of inaction. The governor is not the Democratic party. His dictatorial demands that his orders be carried out do not make those orders either right or consistent with the platform of the Democratic party.

"Today only a fearless Legislature which refuses to be browbeaten is protecting California against the establishment of a veritable dictatorship. I won't be driven out of my party by Communists or by a leader with a dictator complex."

The inquiry went on unabated into May 1940. The final report was filed with the Assembly May 24. The report itself was accompanied by an organization chart of the Communist Party in California.

"The chart alone is conclusive evidence of the stark reality of the Fifth Column (traitors and spies) in California," Yorty declared.

"Americans already have delayed too long in facing the problem which these Fifth Columns have created. We must not continue to make the mistake of being apathetic and tolerant toward their treasonable activities. If we do, our inexcusable apathy and misguided tolerance eventually will be discovered among the tools used to destroy our government, our Constitution, and our freedom."

The committee report itself written by Yorty and signed by the members exposed the whole Communist procedure:

". . . It is evident that a relatively small organized force can render a whole nation helpless by coordinating its activities with forces driving from the outside.

"The great masses of the people are always completely unarmed and unorganized. When confronted with an organized and disciplined group, they find themselves helpless. The Communist, or Bolshevik Party, has already demonstrated the ability of a small organized group to overthrow a government when that government is in a state of crisis resulting from either internal conditions, or the necessity of defending itself against outside forces . . . The Communist Party is bent upon overthrowing the American Government in order to substitute a dictatorship for our democracy. These traitors probably do not have the power to accomplish this objective today without outside assistance. But they are preparing to strike whenever we face a crisis of sufficient gravity to weaken our resistance. As part of our national defense we must stop them before they are able to attain sufficient strength to accomplish their objectives . . .

". . . Communist discipline, when understood, explains the success of the Communist Party in organizing demonstrations such as that fostered by Labor's Non-Partisan League and the Workers Alliance in Sacramento on February 25, 1940.

"There is no doubt that the so-called Workers Alliance march on the State Capitol was, in reality, a Communist political demonstration, of the type used by the Communists, as part of the revolutionary training of the masses. Evidence adduced before the committee establishes the fact that letters directing Workers Alliance members to march on the Capitol were sent out from the state office and signed by the State President of the Workers Alliance, Mr. Alex Noral, who not only admitted his membership in the Communist Party, but also exhibited his official membership book. This is only one concrete example of the disciplined activity of many similar Communist-organized and directed demonstrations, which have been prevalent in California in recent years. It is worthy of note here that similar demonstrations were employed to protest lay-offs of unnecessary SRA personnel, by the Communist-controlled union to which many members of the relief staff belong.

"The Communist Party is today endeavoring to deceive the American people into believing that the party is not international in character, foreign directed, or planning to overthrow the American government by force and violence . . .

". . . Many people have been fooled by this Communist scheme because of their failure to realize that the party is a disciplined army of termites.

"The whole history of the Communists proves that they would never hesitate to lie in stating their immediate or ultimate objectives . . .

". . . Communists in the State Relief Administration have used as a smoke screen for their activities a CIO union called the State, County and Municipal Workers of America.

"Your committee knows that the leadership of this SRA group is Communistic . . ."

". . . The *People's World* has recently devoted much space to attacks on the American preparedness program and the work of J. Edgar Hoover. To find such a subversive newspaper openly and widely supported by members of the State Relief Administration staff affiliated with the SCMWA is shocking and disgusting . . .

"An administration not willing to face the facts, and to make a thorough check on the activities of these subversive groups, cannot hope to cope with the problem which they create . . . American liberties and freedom were won at the sacrifice of the lives of many of our forefathers. Subversive elements working in the United States today would destroy the liberties and freedom guaranteed by our Constitution. They would place us under the iron heel of dictatorship along with the other millions of human beings now suffering from oppression. To fight against this is the present duty of every American . . ."

As the culmination of its report, the committee recommended an immediate further investigation of subversive activities throughout California, new laws by the United States and California to control "Fifth Column" propagandists, a study of the state educational system to strengthen appreciation of American democracy, and constant vigilance against subversives.

The report was signed by

> *"Samuel William Yorty,* CHAIRMAN
> *Jack B. Tenney*
> *Lee Bashore*
> *Chester Gannon*
> *James Phillips"*

The report aroused California. From then on, the war against Communism was intensified in the state. Later in the decade of the 1940s the national struggle against Communist infiltration into government positions was intensified under such leaders as Representative Richard M. Nixon who had been elected to Congress from the 12th California District. The Yorty report had helped materially in alerting the American people to the danger confronting them.

* * *

Perennially the old accusations of Sam having been a Communist or a Communist dupe crops up again. As recently as the campaign for Senator in 1954 it was raked up once more on the basis of the accusation by Kent, the "Red Burglar." *Time* magazine made a statement to this effect and Sam Yorty wrote a letter about it. *Time* recanted and wrote in an ensuing issue:

"*Time* erred. *Time* is glad to set the record straight."

In his letter Sam had shown another example of his prescience in regard to coming events because this was at a time before the term Birch Society was well known throughout the country, and he said:

"The extreme right-wingers and extreme left-wingers are closer together than is generally recognized. The rest of us are in between extremes, fighting to preserve our democracy against both."

A strange sequel developed recently in Los Angeles to the "Red Burglar" story. Kent was discovered by a member of Mayor Yorty's staff, Ray Parker, to be occupying an executive position in a manufacturing plant. The company with which Kent, the burglary expert, was associated was making tempered steel tools.

CHAPTER XIII

In peace, as a wise man, he should make suitable preparation for war.

HORACE

In the two or three years preceding the entrance of the United States into World War II, Sam Yorty like other young Americans was fired with patriotic zeal. The uncertainty of the international military situation posed a quandary for Sam. He was immersed in his work in the Legislature and trying also to chart his course for the future.

The success of his efforts in the fight against Communism and his great interest in the state-wide affairs of California led him to a bold step. He entered the Democratic primary for the United States Senate in 1940, seeking to challenge U. S. Senator Hiram Johnson—the same man who had figured 24 years before in the Wilson-Hughes political drama—in the general election. Under California's cross-filing system in existence at the time, Johnson defeated Sam in the primary.

❄   ❄   ❄

The alien Japanese "fishermen" about whom Sam had been derided in 1939 became on December 7, 1941, the aggressors of Pearl Harbor. Sam at the time was thirty-two years of age. Under normal circumstances the dawning of a new year on January 1, 1942, would have signaled excitement over an election year in California. But in the apprehension and preparation of the war, the fact was obscured.

Everything was in a state of uncertainty. Japanese in California had been sent to concentration camps, constant vigilance was being exercised against expected air attacks, enemy submarines were known to be off the coast. Air raid wardens were being trained, civilians were being warned of prospective shortages, politics seemed to have declared a moratorium.

Sam talked things over with Betts. He was uncertain what he should do. He was pulled by patriotic feelings toward enlistment. Yet he knew that a strong wartime government in California was a necessity. His ambition had been whetted due to his successes in the Legislature. He wanted to continue to serve—but should it be on the home front or in the armed services? As 1942 progressed he was impelled toward a gesture which never really materialized. He felt that young as he was he could give the State of California a good administration as governor. He actually went so far early in 1942 as tentatively to announce his possible candidacy for the position. Then Earl Warren whose political star at that time was beginning to move toward its ascendancy announced on the Republican ticket for governor. Warren had been Attorney General and his success in that position had given ample notification to all observers that he was of the caliber from which governors are made. As soon as Warren announced, Sam Yorty withdrew from the contest.

Immediately thereafter he made preparations to enlist in the Air Force. Pending the acceptance of his enlistment, Sam remained nominally in the contest for his former Assembly seat. Soon, though, his enlistment was accepted and he was notified that he was to go to the U. S. Air Force Officers' Training School in Miami Beach, Florida. This changed all plans for the re-election campaign. He disclosed the fact that he had entered the armed services and therefore could not personally campaign for the Assembly.

It was not long after he had gone to training school in Florida when Sam's associates in Sacramento were shocked at being approached by FBI agents and military intelligence men inquiring about Sam Yorty. They harked back immediately to the accusations against Sam by the "Red Burglar" in connection with Communism and wondered what on earth had happened in Miami Beach. The answer was simple. Sam was being considered for code and cipher school in the encoding and decoding section of the Army Airways Communication Service. The FBI and military intelligence were checking up on his records to make sure he was qualified as to loyalty and in every other respect to be entrusted with this delicate undertaking.

Sam plunged into military affairs with the same zeal he had shown for politics.

"Cipher school is the most sensitive assignment in the military," Sam Yorty declares. "When you get in that room you are performing a function which requires all your faculties."

Sam persisted in his studies and graduated from Officers' Training School with the highest honors in the class. He was valedictorian and delivered an address on the purposes of America in the war. Then he found that being a lieutenant in the Air Force did not necessarily mean "military service" in the sense he had intended. He was first assigned to the code and cipher school at Boland Field, Virginia. This was so far from the war zone that he began to chafe under the monotony of the work and finally was transferred to Honolulu. This also seemed too far away from the war. He finally requested and obtained a transfer to the Southwest Pacific in Brisbane, Australia. Still, though, he was continuing to contend with codes in the cipher room. It seemed that he would never get to the war itself. He decided upon a radical step. In Brisbane was the Intelligence Officer (G-2) on General MacArthur's staff. Sam heard that he needed trained men badly, particularly those from the legal profession, to handle intelligence problems in the war zone itself. Strictly against "channels" protocol, Sam went to this officer and requested transfer to the fighting zone. Despite the fact that he had not gone through channels, his qualifications were studied and he received the coveted assignment. He was sent to New Guinea in the thick of the conflict, when Japanese bombing raids were almost incessant.

Later, while he was in the Philippines area he was keeping up a steady correspondence with political leaders in Los Angeles. By this time his close friends included many leading figures in the city. He corresponded with George Killion, a long-time confidant and now president of the President Lines; Harry J. Bauer, president of the Edison Company; Will H. Fischer, vice-president of the Edison Company; John B. Elliott, Democratic leader; and Manchester Boddy, publisher of the Los Angeles *Daily News,* the only Democratic newspaper in the city.

During the final portion of the Pacific struggle he served on the Civil Affairs Staff of General MacArthur and as a Civil Affairs officer with the Sixth Army on Leyte Island.

While on New Guinea Island in 1943 at Port Moresby and Tsilli Tsilli he engaged in a typical Yorty activity. He formed discussion group—"spit and argue clubs"—among GIs. His aim was to keep the young men in the service from getting bored and mentally sterile. He felt they needed the challenge so as to prepare them better for civilian life and the task of upbuilding the United States on their return home. News of the "spit and argue clubs" was spread all over the Pacific theater of war and reached as far as Washington, D.C.

Because of his long overseas service in New Guinea and the Philippines Captain Yorty was sent home from Leyte for a rest. He was assigned as Intelligence Officer at Florence, South Carolina, at the time the war ended. He then was sent to Fort MacArthur at San Pedro, California, for discharge.

By coincidence, he saw Ronald Reagan, the film actor, likewise destined to be a political figure in California, discharged on the same day.

As soon as he was out of the service, Sam Yorty again harkened to the siren call of politics.

* * *

Sam had come back to Los Angeles in 1945 after VJ Day with his captain's bars and discovered, although it took him awhile for the full realization, that Fate once again had guided him toward an association which was to shape and mold his entire future. Just as Mrs. Grubb, his teacher, and Dr. Haynes, his counselor on affairs political, had directed him along paths designed to make the best use of his innate talents, so now another mentor was waiting to assist him. This was John B. Elliott, the most respected of Southern California Democratic leaders, whose distinguished career was destined to stretch over a period in excess of fifty years. Ever since 1933 when Sam had written to his father enthusiastically about having met so many political leaders all in one day, Elliott had been one of his political idols. Elliott had been brought up in the political tradition, too. He could remember as a boy of fourteen marching in a torchlight parade with his father through the streets of Fort Stock, Kansas, on behalf of Grover Cleveland who was running to recover the presidency from the man who had defeated him in 1888, Benjamin Harrison. Elliott went into the newspaper business and became a political reporter and editorial writer. He moved to California and joined the staff of the Los Angeles *Times* under General Otis. General Otis was known as a martinet who demanded total service from his employees. When he found that

Elliott, after hours, was working for the Associated Press, he called him in and gave him a choice of working full time either for the *Times* or the AP.

Elliott, because of the higher wage involved, decided on the AP. He became an important Associated Press executive in Washington, D.C., and then came back to Los Angeles and became highly successful in business.

Politically, he was so apt that he gravitated to high positions in the Democratic party, figuring prominently in the campaigns of Woodrow Wilson. He became Collector of Customs in Los Angeles and Chairman of the Democratic State Central Committee.

Like Dr. Haynes, he recognized a special quality in Sam Yorty. All during the period of Sam's early campaigns in some of which he met defeat, Elliott was his friend and adviser. He went on Sam's note at the bank when Sam had to borrow for a campaign and Sam always got the money paid back. By the time Sam had returned from the war Elliott was convinced of his maturity and capability. He encouraged Sam, who was still only thirty-five, to run for mayor of Los Angeles.

Sam did run, and was defeated. This defeat was relatively unimportant. The genuinely important thing was that in the race he became acquainted with and gained the confidence of one of the most remarkable women in California politics. Eleanor Chambers who had resided in Los Angeles since she was eight years old had come into political prominence during the early years of the Franklin Delano Roosevelt administration, and in the intervening period until 1945 had played a progressively greater role in local, state, and national political affairs. Her unerring instinct for the right move at the right time had gained her the confidence of Democratic leaders and the grudging respect of Republican opponents.

In 1945, Elliott asked her to manage Sam Yorty's campaign for mayor. Mrs. Chambers was deeply committed to the President's War Relief Control program, after having served on a presidential committee for a census of congested production areas, and she hesitated. Elliott arranged for her to meet Sam and Betty Yorty. She "took" to them and they "took" to her. She agreed to manage the campaign. Out of this grew an enduring friendship for Sam and Betty, and an incalculable political asset for Sam's career.

Necessarily, however, a recess from politics was imperative for Sam after the unsuccessful mayoralty effort in 1945. He had to make a living like so many other servicemen coming back and trying to fit once again into civilian life. He resumed his practice of law but hoped that it might be only a stopgap until he could get into the political arena again.

During this homecoming time, in 1946, the Yortys' only child, their son Bill, was born. With an addition to the family, Sam and Betty were uncertain what life held for them politically but they were sure that their efforts toward each goal would have new meaning and importance because of Bill.

In his law practice, Sam suddenly found himself drifting almost without realizing it into a sphere he did not particularly relish. Due to two or three sensational cases in which he was successful as a criminal lawyer in obtaining acquittals for his clients, he began to be besieged by would-be clients seeking his aid in all kinds of criminal cases. This development came about because of Attorney Yorty's participation as defense counsel for a war hero, and a child prodigy.

The hero was accused of robberies. Attorney Yorty trying the case before Judge Walter Gates succeeded in obtaining the release of the hero on the ground that he had been suffering from insanity at the time of the robberies but was sane at the time of the trial. The prodigy who was accused of setting fire to a Catholic church in the Westwood area, also won an acquittal from a jury which accepted Attorney Yorty's explanation that the prodigy was "not conscious" of what he was doing at the time of the fire due to the effects of a disease, Japanese encephalitis.

Due to the publicity in these cases Attorney Yorty suddenly found himself with all sorts of potential criminal defenses. He decided to end this type of practice. He turned his attention to civil cases and became counsel for oil companies, and manufacturers, giving up the criminal end of the business.

The fleeting nature of human life was the factor which brought Sam Yorty back into elective circles. When he had gone to war in 1942 his seat in the Assembly from the 46th District was won by John C. Lyons. Now, in 1949, seven years later, Lyons died.

"I learned of his death from Eugene Blalock, Los Angeles attorney, who telephoned me and called me 'Assemblyman,'" Sam Yorty recalls. "I laughed at this. He said, 'Haven't you heard the news?'

"'What news?'" I asked.

"'John Lyons has died and some of us think you should go back to the Assembly,' Blalock replied.

"I scoffed at the idea. My law practice was growing rapidly. After a night's reflection, though, the idea began to intrigue me and I decided to run."

A special election was called.

Many of Sam's former constituents remembered him and new residents were able to evaluate him during the campaign. Mrs. Chambers had determined that she would like to make up for the set-back suffered in 1945 and she devoted all her efforts to helping Sam regain his place in the Legislature. The effort was successful. Sam won.

The next year an opportunity presented itself for him to run for Congress in the 14th California District.

"Go ahead and try," advised Betty Yorty and Eleanor Chambers.

Sam thought it was a good opportunity. He announced his candidacy and, in 1950, halfway through the administration of Harry S. Truman as President, was elected as Representative from the district in which he had lived for such a long time.

CHAPTER XIV

National injustice is the surest road to national down-
fall.

WILLIAM E. GLADSTONE

Sam's entry onto the national scene found him already well known to many members of Congress because of his active participation in one of the great issues of the day. This concerned the furious struggle between the Federal government and a number of the states over the rights to billions of dollars worth of "tidelands" oil. Sam Yorty out of personal conviction as well as for business purposes had become counsel even before his election to Congress for the "States' rights" side of the issue. In essence, the controversy revolved around the question whether, at the time of the formation of the Union, the respective states had retained the rights to their "tidelands," which in general meant three miles from shore (except in Texas and possibly Louisiana where, due to special circumstances, it was ten and one-half miles).

Sam before plunging into the big issues facing Congress found the House to be a friendly place. For the first three or four days after he was sworn in he wandered into a small lunchroom in the Capitol and was treated with every courtesy. About the fourth day, though, he observed that there were no other recognizable Democrats in sight.

He asked about it and was told:

"Why should there be? This is the Republican lunchroom."

The seemingly prosaic and academic tidelands question which in the 1700s revolved largely about fish, clams and oysters, suddenly took on major importance when gigantic petroleum deposits were located under the marginal seas and became more accessible due to improved drilling methods. Supposedly the states were fully protected in their claims to the "tidelands" which had been guaranteed to them in more than fifty Supreme Court decisions over a period of approximately 150 years. But in 1946 the United States Supreme Court reversed all its previous doctrine and caused consternation among the states by declaring the "tidelands" to be the property of the Federal government. By the time Sam went to Congress the entire "tidelands" issue had injected itself into partisan politics on a national scale. The Democrats for the most part were going along with the Federal position. The Republicans on the contrary were espousing States' rights.

Representative Yorty was put in the anomalous position of being a supporter of the state viewpoint although he had just been elected as a Democrat, and President Truman was for Federal ownership. As a matter of fact, other individual Democrats because of their belief in the basic principle also were supporting the tidelands' stand of the states. These included Speaker of the House Sam Rayburn and Francis E. Walter, an influential Democratic Representative from Pennsylvania.

The tendency of Representative Yorty in refusing to "go along" on all issues merely because of actual or supposed policy of the Democratic administration was an integral part of his political nature. It was on the eve of General Dwight D. Eisenhower's candidacy for the presidency on the Republican ticket that the extraordinary cleavage had developed between the parties on the immemorial States' rights issue which had existed since—and even before—the creation of the Republic at the Constitutional Convention of 1789. By now, though, a strange reversal of position had taken place. The Democrats who had existed as a political entity since Thomas Jefferson's first term at the start of the 1800s had been traditionally the defenders of States' rights. This was a geographical as well as a political position because of the concentration of Democrats and Democratic thinking in the South prior to, during and after the War between the States. The Republicans, inheritors of the Alexander Hamilton banner, the Whig legacy, and the Lincoln philosophy of preserving the Union had, on the other hand, been proverbially allied with the position of a strong central government (to give, as their political opponents said, a firmer grip of the moneyed class on the reins of government).

In the political upheavals of the Franklin Delano Roosevelt New Deal era and its successor, the Truman period, there had come, along with the amazing coup by which FDR captured the Negro vote from under the noses of the GOP, a radical shifting of emphasis. The Democrats by long tenure in office and from the deep satisfaction of abiding power had come to treasure the strong Federal position that they occupied. The distribution of Federal largesse was such a powerful weapon for gaining votes when it was carried out from Washington without regard to state lines, that the once-revered Democratic battle cry of "States' rights" became more and more muted, and almost disappeared altogether.

The Republicans, on the other hand, long out of power and hungry for some of the manna of the political Promised Land which had been denied them so long, began to capitalize on the States' rights matter from two approaches. One was that of genuine conviction that the pendulum had swung too far to the left in denying basic American principles to the component parts of the Union. The other was the less virtuous consideration of expediency. It was noted by many Republican leaders that there was genuine dissatisfaction in many states because of the slighting by the Federal government of long-existing state privileges and the sometimes ruthless trampling of state prerogatives.

During the Truman "second term" starting in 1948 after his upset defeat of Thomas E. Dewey, one dramatic issue after another specifically pinpointing this shifting of the poles by the parties on the home rule matter loomed on the political horizon. One of the most easily observable of these was the tidelands question.

The oil-rich tidelands of California, Texas, Louisiana, and some of the other states were precipitating the showdown struggle as Sam entered Congress.

The "tidelands" question became a vital factor in the 1952 presidential race when General Eisenhower forcefully advocated the States' rights position. This stand was credited with winning him great support and with his carrying Texas over Adlai Stevenson. Congress in 1953, accepting the verdict of the people in the 1952 election, did in fact override the Supreme Court's granting of the "tidelands" to the Federal government and ratified them to the states.

Even while this was transpiring Sam was becoming notably involved in another States' rights question which necessitated his pleading vainly with the President from his own party, Harry Truman, to disavow the actions of the U. S. Justice Department. This amazing episode was uncovered in California. It concerned an overt attempt by the United States Attorney General's office to seize private property rights, under the guise of military necessity and on an assertion of "paramount Federal rights" without regard for the Fifth Amendment's "due process of law" guarantee. The move ostensibly was in behalf of U. S. Marine Camp Joseph Pendleton at Oceanside, California, in a dispute with upstream water rights owners on a small stream known as the Santa Margarita River, a watercourse bearing the same name as the vast and famous 200,000 acre Santa Margarita Rancho on which Camp Pendleton had been created in the World War II era.

The circumstances, incredible as they were, might not have come to public attention nationally if the apparently surreptitious move of the Attorney General's office had been consummated by capitulation of the water rights owners. One small rancher, owner of twenty acres at the little upstream town of Fallbrook, however, was so affronted when Federal papers were served on him demanding that he surrender his water rights without compensation that he wrote "a letter to the Editor."

This letter aroused the interest of L. D. Hotchkiss, editor of the Los Angeles *Times*. He assigned the writer of this book, a former State Editor, City Editor, and Editorial Page Editor of the *Times*, who had specialized for many years in water controversies and water law, to investigate the letter from the small ranch owner in Fallbrook. From this grew the nationally celebrated "Fallbrook Case."

It developed that hundreds of water rights owners in and around this small avocado-growing community of Fallbrook were being sued under the "paramount rights" theory. These ranged from people of national reputation such as Frank Capra down to "Aunt Eadie" who lived in a shack near the river and drew her meager water supply from a well. The assertion in the complaint was that the water was needed for military purposes at Camp Pendleton and that therefore the Federal government had the privilege of taking it without compensation.

This view was so contrary to all accepted U.S. water law, both state and Federal, that an incredulous outcry arose against the proceedings. At first it was charged that the Los Angeles *Times* for reasons of its own, presumably because of large land holdings in the Fallbrook area, was presenting the matter for its own selfish purposes. This was refuted when it was disclosed that the *Times* did not have any such holdings. The articles, in fact, had grown entirely out of the inquiry following the letter of the small rancher with his twenty-acre holdings.

The first news story in the *Times* exposing the "paramount rights" scheme stirred Representative Sam Yorty to immediate action in Washington. He inserted the story in the Congressional Record, thus being primarily responsible for bringing it to national attention, and began an investigation of the circumstances surrounding the launching of the unprecedented legal action.

At first the Attorney General's office in Washington attempted to give the impression that the water suits had been instigated by the Marines at Camp Pendleton. It soon was shown, though, that the origin of the suits was within the Attorney General's office itself, apparently motivated by a desire to see whether the "paramount rights" theory could be "put over" quietly so as to establish a precedent. This precedent then presumably could have been used to permit the Federal government to take over property rights of any nature without due process of law on the assertion of "paramount rights" or "national necessity." The evidence of the nature of the original Fallbrook suits and the prospective subsequent consequences was so conclusive and so documented by the formal written words of the Attorney General's office itself that Congress, prodded by Sam Yorty, became curious about the whole matter. It was at this time that a remarkable triumvirate of California representatives went into action on a totally non-partisan basis in opposition to the water rights seizures. Harry Truman was President, but the outcry from sincere Democrats was as loud as that from Republicans. In addition to Sam, the others in the triumvirate were Clair Engle, Democrat, and Representative Norris Poulson, Republican. Engle later was to become U. S. Senator and die in middle age of a brain tumor, and Poulson was to become mayor of Los Angeles and then be beaten by Sam Yorty.

At that time, in 1951 and 1952, they all were working together intent upon preventing the Attorney General from seizing the water rights of the Fallbrook people. The first objective was to seek if possible to save the thousands of prospective defendants at Fallbrook from the gruelling and expensive ordeal of trying to defend suits aimed at them by the Attorney General. Sam Yorty and the others realized fully that if these suits were allowed to proceed it would be years before there could be any decisive ruling in the high courts. Congressional action to halt the Attorney General and decide the basic issue appeared to be the desirable course. Representative Yorty amended the Navy Department bill to bar use of funds for the suit in 1952. At this time in 1952 a delegation went from Fallbrook to Washington to plead its case direct with Congress. Bill Heald, president of the Fallbrook Public Utilities District; George Yackey, general manager; and Board Members Raymond (Jim) Wayman and Vic Westfield had decided to plead their case in person. Aided by Yorty, Engle, and Poulson they found Congress receptive.

A color motion picture *The Fallbrook Story* had been made gratuitously by a team consisting of a script writer, a director, and a cameraman in California, and this had aroused widespread sympathy for the people who were being sued. The House of Representatives was so impressed by the clear-cut nature of the case and the attempted injustice by the Attorney General that it unanimously passed a remedial bill in behalf of the Fallbrook people. Victory appeared in sight. But one Senator in a key committee position blocked the entire proceedings in the Senate. Senator Joseph O'Mahoney of Wyoming, chairman of the Interior and Insular Affairs Committee, refused to bring the measure before his committee. This obvious attempt to thwart the will of Congress on a far-fetched technicality aroused a wave of protest even in his own state. As it happened, Senator O'Mahoney was up for re-election. He was opposed by Governor Frank Barrett of Wyoming, a staunch supporter of the principles embodied in the Fallbrook Bill.

In Los Angeles, numerous copies of *The Fallbrook Story* film were made with a sequel attached at the end explaining how Senator O'Mahoney had, without good reason, blocked the legislation in Congress. These films were then shown in every city, town, and hamlet in Wyoming during the campaign. The effect was so devastating that Senator O'Mahoney, despite his long years of service in Congress, was overwhelmingly defeated. Even so, the Fallbrook cause had received such a severe setback and the Attorney General's suits had proceeded so far in the courts that the case floundered into an agonizingly slow series of legal proceedings.

In the original suits some of the defendants were convicted by United States District Judge Leon R. Yankwich in Los Angeles. These convictions later were set aside by the U. S. Appellate Court with strong admonitions to Judge Yankwich in regard to his faulty conclusions.

Subsequently the cases were tried again before United States District Judge James Carter in San Diego. During the long proceedings the Fallbrook people were represented by Phil Swing and Franz Sachse, Swing dying before the proceedings were completed. Eventually the Fallbrook people triumphed when the findings of Judge Carter in their favor were upheld by the U. S. Appellate Court. But, typical of American judicial proceedings, more than twelve years had elapsed before the Attorney General's unwarranted action, as exposed by the Los Angeles *Times* and denounced by Representatives Yorty, Engle, and Poulson, had been repudiated.

* * *

Sam Yorty was one of the best friends the Air Force had in Congress, because of his own experience in it and his continuing study of the subject of air power. He was determined that the United States must maintain its full strength in the air to counteract growing Russian might. Early in the Eisenhower administration, soon after Charles E. Wilson, president of General Motors, became Secretary of Defense, Sam was catapulted into national prominence because of a spectacular clash over Air Force matters. Wilson, with characteristic vigor, attacked all manner of problems in the Defense Department and launched a sweeping effort to save five billion dollars on the military budget. This aroused many Congressmen who were worried over the defense status of the nation.

Wilson was questioned on his viewpoints concerning the entire question of American air power. He denied changing his mind on the importance of airplanes or of losing confidence in the Strategic Air Command. However, he said, the former goal of 143 Wings by June 30, 1955, could not be reached anyway, so it had been reduced to 120, which he contended could be attained. Senator Burnett Maybank, Democrat of South Carolina, asked Wilson directly whether the 120 Wing Air Force would constitute an offensive or defensive force in the United States. Wilson wavered in his reply. This prompted Maine's Senator Margaret Chase Smith to ask "Is the new budget based on economy or security?"

Sam Yorty broke open the whole situation by a simple device. He telephoned the Air Force Liaison Office on Capitol Hill and asked straight out what the effect of the enormous cut in the budget would be. The reply was staggering. The Air Force candidly said that if the cuts were to be made contracts would have to be canceled and that "large segments of the aircraft industry would be cut so sharply that they could not adequately respond to later aircraft orders."

This meant, of course, that the national defense was being jeopardized through crippling of the industry's capacity. The Air Force spokesmen likewise said that the goal of 120 Wings could not be reached until June 30, 1956, a year after the date set by Wilson, and that even so it would have insufficient equipment and manpower under the pending budget.

The disclosure of these facts by Representative Yorty stirred up a national storm. *Time* magazine and others picked up the story from the newspapers so that nearly everyone in the United States was aware that former Captain Sam Yorty of the Air Force had come in direct confrontation with the Secretary of Defense. Yorty himself in fact asked that Wilson resign.

"We cannot afford to have the Defense Department headed by a defeatist Secretary whose vision is so circumscribed by dollars, profits and grossly exaggerated economic strain," said Yorty. "His unwise direction leaves us helpless targets of mounting Russian air strength." The attack was bolstered by a statement of Air Force Lieutenant General Roger W. Ramey that the United States lacked the air power to repel an all-out Communist attack in the Far East or at home.

Yorty wired President Eisenhower:

THIS CONFIRMS THE SOUNDNESS OF MY FEARS WHEN I OPPOSED YOUR AIR FORCE CUTS AND TRIED UNSUCCESSFULLY TO GET AN APPOINTMENT WITH YOU TO DISCUSS THEM. SECRETARY WILSON STANDS CONVICTED BY GENERAL RAMEY OF RETARDING OUR PROGRESS IN A RACE IN WHICH OUR SURVIVAL IS AT STAKE.

Yorty later added "a second-best Air Force is an open invitation to Communist aggression."

He continued the attacks by charging that Wilson's policies "have sharply reduced American military power in the face of Russia's continued rapid and menacing build up." He declared Wilson was "recklessly painting a rosy picture based upon sheer fantasy while worried military leaders are trying to give the people a glimpse of the truth."

To this day Yorty contends the effect of the Wilson policies has been felt with devastating impact upon the Air Force program. It is not so much, he points out, in fighter planes as in transport aircraft which in long-range war must assume a particularly vital role. Thus in Viet Nam the need for transport aircraft has been demonstrated time and again. It takes a period of many years from the drawing board to the completed plane, including all the steps of

Congressional approval, the letting of contracts, the design and manufacture of the planes themselves. So more than a decade after the Wilson action, Sam Yorty declares the Air Force suffers from that ill-calculated move.

His fight on the issue at the time, plus his courageous stand on the tidelands and Fallbrook questions, won him a coveted privilege. He was chosen as the Democratic nominee for United States Senator from California in 1954. It was a slam-bang campaign as far as the Senate was concerned but the race for governor was rather one-sided. In the balloting Republican Goodwin J. Knight swamped Democrat Richard Graves, and Sam Yorty lost to Senator Thomas H. Kuchel due in part, Sam believed, to the Knight sweep, because Sam had led the Democratic ticket.

Rather grimly, Sam went back to practicing law in Los Angeles.

CHAPTER XV

Sam Yorty is the most dissident Democrat.

JIBE FROM A
RIVAL POLITICAL CAMP

Total political effacement was impossible for Sam Yorty, even though he himself was absent from the active jousting lists as an actual candidate during that period of seven years from the time of his unsuccessful race for United States Senate in 1954 until the announcement of his candidacy for Mayor of Los Angeles early in 1961. It had been necessary, of course, for him to resign his seat in the House to make the 1954 Senatorial race. He and Betts resumed their life in Los Angeles, with Sam concentrating on his law cases and Betts finding time for art lessons and social activities and Bill's school life.

Sam emerged briefly, in 1956, while unsuccessfully seeking the endorsement of the California Democratic Council in Fresno for another try at the Senatorship to utter some pointed words about the opposition forces which thwarted him. The CDC was formed in 1953 as a state-wide organization of local grassroots clubs with about 500 units and 50,000 dues-paying members, as a sequel to the first campaign of Adlai Stevenson for President. It flourished for a time—although finally falling into debt and acrimonious internal difficulties in 1965—and its endorsement still was coveted in the 1956 pre-primary skirmishing for the Democratic nomination for U. S. Senator in 1956.

Sam had begun to distrust what he considered to be the leftist leanings of the CDC but he accepted its endorsement in 1954. By 1956, however, when he was skirmishing with Richard Richards, State Senator from Los Angeles County, for the U. S. Senate endorsement he was ready to blow off the lid.

Belligerently on the CDC convention floor, he accused the organization of being a boss-ridden, closed, illegal conspiracy against the unorganized Democratic voters of California. While being jeered and booed, he roared:

"I charge that this convention is wired, packed, rigged, and stacked." He withdrew his name and walked out.

Subsequently, he charged the CDC with having been taken over by the extreme Left, and did everything he could to destroy its effect on voters. This fight still was being carried on in his capacity as an individual Democrat when the 1960 presidential year arrived. In the campaign between John F. Kennedy and Vice-President Richard M. Nixon, Sam Yorty made one of his characteristic gestures; enraging many party "regulars" on the Democratic side of the fence, and mystifying the Republicans.

He came out for Nixon.

Sam's "defection," for which some Democratic leaders immediately attempted to pillory him, was based on two main reasons.

In the first place, he was among the ranks of those including Mrs. Franklin D. Roosevelt and Harry S. Truman who expressed the belief that John F. Kennedy was not "ready" to be President of the United States. Secondly, he was firmly of the opinion that the election of a Californian—Nixon—was more important in the light of the state's growing role in national affairs and vital need for economic impetus—meaning space and defense contracts—than was partisan politics.

His conclusion to take the possibly disastrous step of leaving the Democratic party and actively supporting Nixon was brought to a climactic point in a conversation at the Beverly Hills Hotel during the pre-convention maneuvering of the 1960 campaign.

All during the period prior to the Democratic Convention in Los Angeles Sam was a strong supporter of Lyndon Johnson for President. He wrote to all members of the California delegation to the convention asking their help for Johnson. Governor Brown headed the California delegation and left Yorty off it. In the conversation at the Beverly Hills Hotel the subject of the Kennedy tactics was uppermost.

"The Kennedys are using unlimited money to get control of state delegations, by means of retainers paid to lawyers who can influence individual delegates," Sam was told by highly placed Democrats he believed.

This coincided with Sam's own observations and conclusions.

This monetary aspect and his already-strong conviction that Kennedy was not ready for the task led him after the convention to support Nixon's candidacy.

"I think it is dangerous when any man can purchase the presidency," Sam Yorty declared.

Even the fact that Johnson accepted the second spot on the Kennedy ticket was unable to outweigh Sam's feelings concerning Kennedy himself. In regard to the monetary phase, Sam Yorty quoted Senator Humphrey during the primary campaign as saying:

"Kennedy is the spoiled candidate and he and that young emotional juvenile, Bobby, are spending with wild abandon."

These views and others on Sam's basic beliefs as expressed in 1960 became known to at least some California voters. Yorty explained his abandonment of the Democratic ticket and his support of Nixon by voicing his stand on many issues in a prepared document, *I Cannot Take Kennedy*.

In this, he expressed his own opinions on subjects ranging from unions to vigilance concerning Communism and from undue concentration of Federal power to water rights, the implications and indeed the avowed intent being to show that Nixon's views more closely were aligned with these expressions than were Kennedy's. Taken together, the Yorty statements formed a political credo arising consistently out of his beliefs voiced many times previously.

They were credited with being one factor in helping to carry California for Nixon by approximately 35,000 votes.

In *I Cannot Take Kennedy* Sam wrote:

"I have been a Democrat all my life, and served five terms in elective office as a Democrat. My roots are deep in the Democratic party, but I cannot convince myself that John F. Kennedy is ready to be President of the United States at this critical point in our history. Of course, I could remain silent and escape the partisan abuse which will be heaped upon me for expressing my opinions but I am not sure but what silence for personal reasons would be cowardly in view of the gravity of the decision which we must all make in November.

"First of all, it seems to me this is primarily a contest between two men and only secondarily a contest either between two political parties, or two political theories.

"In my opinion, the Kennedy clan destroyed the internal integrity of the Democratic party in their rush to catapult the young

Senator into control of the party by an abuse of the power of lavish amounts of money.

"It was the big city machines that cinched the nomination for Kennedy.

"Kennedy should certainly not be condemned by his father's immense wealth, but neither should we as Democrats be captured by use of it. If those of us who are Democrats feel compelled to vote for Kennedy irrespective of how he got the nomination, we are captives. I for one do not propose to be an accessory after the fact to what went on leading up to and in Los Angeles."

Sam Yorty then went on to explain his own feelings, starting out with union leaders.

"For my part, I have always enjoyed a cordial association with Labor during my terms in elective office," he wrote, "but I must confess that the attitude of their leaders is sometimes very puzzling. For instance, they spent years denouncing the Taft-Hartley Act as a 'Slave Labor' law and threatened all who voted for it with being purged from public office at the polls. Yet, I have seen them turn around and support candidates who voted for the Taft-Hartley Act while at the same time condemning others for doing so. . . .

"Organized Labor has a broad base and a large membership but professional Labor leaders are, as a rule, not very interested in the problems of unorganized workers except insofar as these problems affect Unions in one way or another. There are many workers not organized into Unions who have no professional special pleaders for their interests, and who must look directly to their elected representatives for whatever protection their rights or interests require, either relative to Unions or otherwise. Of course, most Labor leaders would like to force all workers to join Unions. They would like, if possible, to do this with the help of the coercive power of government. It is nice to have the government force your customers to buy your product instead of having to sell it to them."

He turned then to his foes in the California Democratic Council.

"The Communists in the so-called 'CDC' are too wise to openly endorse known Communists but they fight to prevent endorsement of candidates who do more than give lip service to the fight against them," he charged. "For over twenty years I have had to fight the Communists in the Democratic party in my State every time I have been a candidate. And I am sad to say, that during these years Republicans who knew better, or should have, customarily abetted the Communist 'smears' either directly or simply by refraining from disseminating the truth. The truth would have helped me defeat my Republican opponents and this fact put too much strain on their pretended impartiality.

"In California today, the position of a militant anti-Communist in the Democratic party is an uncomfortable one. Most of the leaders are anti-Communist but they are in many cases either naive or too cowardly to do anything more than merely talk about the evils of Communism while contending that the threat is greatly overrated—a theme the Communists foster and love to hear repeated. . . .

"They (the Communists) seek to use the Constitution as a protective umbrella for their subversion. Sometimes I think certain of our judges provide such an over-extended legal umbrella for Communists that their decisions ignore the facts of life in this twentieth century. . . ."

His next target was the bureaucracy in the national capital.

"For most of us Washington is a long way off and just the cost of going there and staying long enough to try to see important Federal officials can be prohibitive," he wrote. "It is better for us when our government is kept as close to home as possible. . . .

"The more power there is centered in Washington, the greater the temptation for selfish interests to try to control it for their own purposes, and the more difficult it becomes for the local citizens to restrain abuse of such power. As government gets farther away from the local level, it becomes less understanding, more impersonal, and the bureaucrats more brazen.

"Right now those of us who live in the West are witnessing a massive Federal attack upon the historic jurisdiction of our state laws over our water rights. Fantastic claims are being asserted for plenary Federal power. Oppressive law suits asserting Federal superiority have been filed against thousands of our citizens. One filed under Truman is being continued on under Eisenhower. It seems that no matter which party is in power the career Federal officials go on their way asserting their unbridled claims of Federal authority. The answer, the only answer, is for us to stop surrendering power to the Federal government, and to stop looking to Washington for the solution of all of our problems. The tendency to do so is destroying the fundamental structure of our Federal-State system. . . .

"I do not have a great deal of faith in the Washington planners who think they can master-mind the workings of our infinitely complex American economy . . . Believe me, the Washington bureaucrats are far from omniscient. Any businessman who has to deal with them is soon painfully aware of this fact.

"Each Federal control seems to breed a need for more controls to make the first one work. Because of this, each surrender of power to Washington tends to 'snowball' and transform our free economy into a controlled one. Ultimately this process can cause the channels of commerce to become choked with red tape. Then our free enterprise system fails to function efficiently. Los Angeles will not soon forget that rental units, which were in short supply under Federal rent control, miraculously became plentiful when the controls were belatedly removed. I say belatedly, advisedly. Once a bureaucracy of office holders is built up to administer a government control, they do not surrender their powers without a fight. As far as I am concerned, the less government we have in business, the better. . . .

"As a practicing attorney, I am repeatedly made aware of the awesome power which the Federal government can turn against a citizen, rightly or wrongly. It takes a very rich client to pay for the legal services required to counter the efforts of the multitude of full time Federal investigators, agents, attorney, and the staffs of tax supported employees at their disposal. So difficult is the position of the citizen when the arsenal of Federal power is arrayed against him, that many are forced to submit to injustice simply because of lack of adequate funds to fight for justice."

All these viewpoints from a political figure classified as a "maverick" naturally created animosity toward Sam Yorty in the Kennedy administration on the eve of the 1961 mayoralty race in Los Angeles.

CHAPTER XVI

I have endured a great deal of ridicule without much malice.

ABRAHAM LINCOLN

Betty Yorty confesses she was shaking with nervousness when she and Sam went to the City Hall in January 1961 for him to file as a candidate for mayor. It had been seven years since Sam had been in a political race. The relative quiet of that intervening period had been nice in a way, she felt. Still, if Sam wanted to run, she was game. Money was lacking for any kind of spectacular campaign, but that had been true before. The main thing was that Sam believed he could win, money or no money.

Until the actual day of his filing, there had been little public attention paid to the possibility of Sam Yorty running. The normal speculation about various political and business figures in the community had been indulged in but the assumption that Mayor Poulson would announce for a third term and be elected in routine fashion was firmly fixed in almost everyone's mind. Two Republicans, Pat McGee, a former Assemblyman, and Joe Holt, a Representative in Congress, were mentioned as possibilities, although political experts considered they would be wasting their time against Poulson.

Sam was fully aware of the hopelessness under normal circumstances of defeating an incumbent. It was part of his political creed which had been hammered into him the hard way. Yet several factors prompted him to believe that there might be a fighting chance to overcome the seeming impregnability of Poulson's position. Chief among these was the oft-expressed opinion which he heard from ordinary people that "Poulson had been in long enough." Another was the conviction that the Poulson "image" as a dynamic and successful mayor had been created by highly paid public relations people, and that it was not valid and could be punctured. Further, Sam was bored by the practice of law in comparison with the fascination of public service.

"I knew that it was now or never," he explains. "I had been out of office seven years and realized that the voters soon would forget me entirely. Of course it was a tremendous gamble. I knew that I normally couldn't beat the incumbent—but I felt in this case he would beat himself. Incumbency is such a factor in politics that almost anybody of reasonable capabilities can stay in if he gets there unless he is involved in situations where he destroys his own chances. I felt pretty confident, knowing Poulson as I did from our days in Congress together, that he would do many things to hurt himself and to help me. It was a great temptation to run but I continued to waver."

Encouragement given by a Negro friend finally tipped the scales for Sam. He met Everett Porter, an attorney and an influential leader in the Negro community, in the Courthouse one day in late 1960.

"I think you ought to run for mayor," Porter said. "I'll support you if you do."

Then Jimmy Bolger, one-time secretary of former Police Chief James Davis and later a member of the Board of Public Works called up to tell Sam that a number of people in the community wanted a candidate against Mayor Poulson and would Sam consider running.

"I'd like to see a poll," Sam replied, "to find out whether there is a real negative feeling about Poulson."

A professional group, Hal Avery's Opinion Research, conducted such a survey in the central part of the city. This poll showed 32 percent for Poulson, 25 percent for Yorty, with 17 percent and 12 percent for other candidates and a smattering of "undecideds."

"This showed such a negative factor for Poulson that my suppositions were borne out," Sam relates. "The high recognition factor of the name 'Yorty' after seven years since my last campaign was a pleasant surprise. I came to the conclusion that Poulson couldn't win in the primary and that I would get in the run-off with him. It was in the run-off that I counted on him defeating himself. So I decided to run."

As soon as Sam filed Betty quit shaking and pitched in to help in the old familiar way. Word was flashed to Cambria Pines and started things happening up there. Eleanor Chambers, perennial campaign manager for Sam, got the "message" at her hilltop home and started packing her car for a long stay in Los Angeles. She knew she just had to pitch in once more for Sam. It had gotten to be a habit. The other races had been challenge enough and some had been won and some had been lost, but this promised to be the biggest fight yet.

Like all of Sam's campaigns this one had to be done on a shoe-string, but it was just about the most frayed shoestring of all. By dint of persuasion about cheap rent Sam and Betty and Eleanor did manage to get the use of an old loft-building at Wilshire Boulevard and Catalina Street. They got hold of three old mimeograph machines and prepared to turn out their own campaign literature because they couldn't afford to have it printed. They partitioned off the loft so as to provide space for TV coverage if any developed, and arranged some makeshift offices in the rest of the space.

"As it turned out we could have used twice as much space," recounts Eleanor Chambers. "It almost made me cry to see what happened. People who remembered kindnesses that Sam had shown them way back in his days in the Legislature or in Congress came flocking in to help. Many of them were really poor people but they brought in tiny sums as campaign contributions—actually quarters, half-dollars and dollar bills. A lot of them volunteered to do office work, stuff envelopes and ring doorbells. It was the most heartening thing that could have happened for Sam, struggling along without any really adequate campaign funds, to see that his friends remembered him."

Sam was convinced the people were anxious "for something to happen" on the matters which touched their everyday lives, and were resentful that Mayor Poulson's administration had failed to bestir itself to solve the problems. He kept up a steady fire on these issues. His urging of new methods of trash collection was repeated again and again. Smog was choking the whole area. Traffic hazards and tie-ups were becoming worse daily due to lack of mass rapid transit. Property taxes were increasingly burdensome. The "spot zoning" of residential areas was becoming a threat to home-owners. The city needed a civic auditorium and convention center, a zoo, more cultural opportunities. The state was unsympathetic to Los Angeles because the control of the State Senate was in the north; reapportionment of the Legislature was necessary.

Almost nightly on TV Sam kept parading these civic needs and promising quietly to start practical efforts to meet them. He became convinced he was on the right track. His appearances on television programs aroused so much public interest that the TV stations became aware Sam was an asset in raising their viewer rating, and as a result he was able to obtain much free time on news and commentary spots. This was an essential because the Yorty campaign did not have the money to buy expensive TV and radio time.

He was not alone in his efforts on television. One of his strongest supporters from the start was George Putnam, then news commentator on KTTV, Channel 11, which paradoxically was owned by the Los Angeles *Times*. Viewers thus were treated to the spectacle of an outspoken commentator on a *Times*-owned subsidiary urging the election of Yorty while the *Times* itself was doing everything within its power to assure the re-election of Poulson.

"I don't think I could have won without George Putnam's help," Yorty comments. "He was under pressure from all sides to stop backing me. Poulson supporters sued him because of his exposé of a Los Angeles harbor oil lease deal of which I had made an issue."

Putnam persisted in his outspoken backing of Sam despite any of the alleged pressures and kept presenting Sam's side of the campaign issues right up to the last moment.

In an entirely different category one little thing bothered Sam as the campaign progressed. It was a physical liability. What should he do about his mustache?

"I grew the mustache when about nineteen or so, trying to look older," he recounted later. "It was sort of brown and with the advent of TV it became a nuisance. If I blackened it, I looked like a city slicker type and if I didn't blacken it for TV my lip looked dirty and the mustache didn't show up as such. One night when getting ready to go on with George Putnam during the campaign I said the mustache was a nuisance. One of George's secretaries said, 'The villain always wears the mustache. Why don't you take it off?'

"I did, and was pleased to be told I looked younger although most friends did not notice that the change was caused by eliminating the mustache."

Mustache or no mustache, Sam used a language, a directly colloquial speech infused with genuine feeling and personal recollections distinctly different from anything Norris Poulson was able to articulate. Sam spoke with sympathy and understanding, because of his own experiences, of the needs of injured people, of poor people, of people from broken homes, of people with dogs, of the aspirations of young politicians, of the religious oppressed, of racial minorities, of ambitious students with no money and of the job seekers out pounding the pavements for some kind of honorable work. These were the things everybody understood. Sam was not "putting on" or making "campaign speeches." He was discussing things of which he had intimate knowledge. Also, he was not ashamed to keep talking about the everyday things shunned by most politicians: The necessity of keeping Los Angeles supplied with water, the need to end the "tin can monopoly" by means of his oft-mentioned combined trash collection, the need for band concerts and more picnic places.

This was tame stuff to the ears of what Sam described as "the downtown crowd," and they were not content to let a campaign roll along on such a commonplace level.

Things began to get dirty and became dirtier as the date of the April 4 primary rolled around and the run-off election campaign got under way. Poulson topped the ballot in the primary with 179,273 votes, Yorty was second with 122,478 votes, and Pat McGee was third with 115,635. This bore out Sam's expectation based on the original Opinion Research poll taken several months before. But his strong showing merely served to intensify the attacks on him.

Mayor Poulson made the direct accusation at a press conference April 5, immediately after the primary that Yorty's campaign was "backed by the underworld." Five days later Yorty sued Poulson for $2,200,000, charging interference with his Constitutional right to seek public office in an election free from improper practices and slander. Yorty disclosed the filing of the suit after a press conference in the City Council chamber. Mayor Poulson had been invited to attend but declined to interrupt a Palm Springs vacation. He dictated a statement that he would not take part in "the cheap political matinee." Later in the campaign, just prior to election day, May 31, the taking of depositions in this suit resulted in tumultuous scenes and the breaking up of one session.

Before these wild outbursts took place, however, the opponents and their partisans had engaged in controversies involving everybody from Democratic State Senator Richard Richards to Republican McGee who came out for Poulson after his own unsuccessful effort in the primary.

The Los Angeles *Times* in an editorial April 27 said:

". . . (There) . . . were good enough reasons for urging Mr. Poulson's re-election. Meanwhile a more compelling reason has developed: the alternative to his re-election is municipal calamity. If his opponent, a partisan political adventurer named Samuel W. Yorty, were elected, the moral underpinning of good city government would be dangerously impaired."

The newspaper added that:

"Another example of Mr. Yorty's destructive method was his recent imputation against the expertly advised and deliberately enacted rubbish collection and disposal program. He called it phony.

"Why does Mr. Yorty want to walk into the mayorship over the municipal wreckage of which he would be saboteur-in-chief?"

It is true that Sam was hitting hard on the rubbish program. By this time his campaign tactics of direct approach to the people by way of TV programs had won him, apparently, such a following that he was afforded many opportunities to appear on non-paid programs and newscasts, which he used to the utmost to express his views on simple issues appealing to housewives. He urged over and over again a simplification of rubbish pick-up procedures and the use of one container for tin cans and combustible rubbish. This was a hot issue at the time because householders were compelled by the city to separate tin cans so they could be sold for reprocessing. Sam found early in the campaign that his stand on this matter was understood by everybody and seemingly was popular with a large proportion of the population.

The attacks on Sam covered a variety of subjects. One was the disclosure that he had participated as a part-owner—his interest being received as a legal fee for representing the other owners—in a small private rubbish dump near San Pedro along the Dominguez Channel adjacent to Broadway and Main Street. Another was that he had received a $12,500 fee for attempting to obtain a gambling license for a Las Vegas casino, the New Frontier Hotel. Sam said this was not true; that the applicants had been sued in California and he represented them in the law suit. Stockholders had reputedly lost more than $1,000,000 in the venture, leading to the litigation.

Yorty was making some charges too. About a month after the primary he declared that Mayor Poulson had land and cattle holdings worth $250,000 at Baker, Oregon, and demanded that the mayor explain "where he got the money when his public salary was $25,000 a year." Sam offered to open his own Federal income-tax records to the public if Poulson would do likewise.

"These are the biggest lies yet injected into the campaign by Sam Yorty," Mayor Poulson replied as he minimized the value of the Oregon property.

This particular subject was good for headlines for several days, with Mayor Poulson offering to sell his reputed prize bulls for a virtual pittance, and Sam continuing to ask how Poulson could afford all that land and the bulls anyway.

In the lulls the candidates traded charges about their respective backers. The mayor presented a list of more than one hundred citizens supporting him and challenged Sam to do the same. Sam immediately came back with a list of 517 which had to be printed in small type to squeeze into the newspapers. Sam said he would fire all the police commissioners if he were elected, and the police commissioners said he wouldn't get the chance because they would quit. Senator Richards attacked Yorty as "not a responsible Democrat." In response Sam snapped:

"I'm not surprised that Paul Ziffren's (former Democratic national committeeman) fair-haired boy, Richards, has been ordered to join the City Hall machine in making an attack on me . . . Richards is part of the Ziffren operation calculated either to rule or ruin the Democratic Party in California . . . I was in the Legislature of California fighting for the Democratic Party before Ziffren brought his Chicago tactics to our State."

All these things were the inevitable repartee of a conventional political campaign. Underlying these matters, however, was a constant repetitive pounding away by Sam at the inadequacies and complacencies of the current regime, an almost intangible element which he brought home forcefully to the ordinary citizen. He dwelt upon the lack of over-all planning in Los Angeles, the minimal concern for the ordinary citizen, the virtual contempt for the "little man" who sought to remedy unfairness in civic procedure and, always, the need to put those doggone cans in with the rest of the rubbish.

Day by day the three old mimeograph machines ground out their quota of Yorty material under the direction of Betty and Eleanor, and night after night Sam kept sitting there on one TV program after another ripping away at the Poulson weaknesses. He knew his messages were going over because of the enthusiastic letters and personal calls of volunteers who swamped his campaign headquarters. The volunteers by this time were canvassing the city on Sam's behalf, virtually using a trash can as his knightly symbol. It was something the women voters could understand, and they responded to it.

The formal campaign wound up in a flurry of screams and shouts of "lie" over the "underworld" accusation and its attendant suit and deposition taking. But the real leaven of the political showdown was working in the minds of the people who saw Sam on TV and detected something more than mere "campaign talk." They sensed a genuineness and a concern for individuals. They harked back to his support of Richard Nixon for President the previous year and the creed of personal rights he espoused at that time. They remembered his sustained and never-ending attacks on Communism. They heeded his pleas for a concerted effort on the part of Los Angeles' citizens to create the kind of community they did not yet have but which he described as a meaningful possibility. They pondered his pledges to utilize members of minority races in the civic administration. They listened attentively to his declaration as a suburb dweller himself in San Fernando Valley that suburbs must play a greater part in a new and better Los Angeles.

All the while Sam was convinced Poulson was beating himself through complacency and ineptitude. Sam, of course, did some things to help along this objective. Even Fate took a hand. Poulson contracted acute laryngitis and was virtually bereft of his voice during the latter part of the campaign. His appearance on television did much to hurt the "image" which Sam contended had been built up originally by press agents.

As Election Day came Betty Yorty quit shaking. She was too tired.

Sam's total vote mounted up to 273,701 with Mayor Poulson being able to gather only 257,073 votes.

As the unmistakable "trend" of the ballots had set in and Sam realized he was going to be mayor, a host of memories of previous election nights welled up within him amid the congratulations and tumult of his headquarters, packed with beaming well-wishers. This was his sixth and most meaningful election to public office, coming as it did in his mature years when he felt better qualified than ever before to undertake a heavy task ahead. He was buoyed by confidence, smiling, elated. Yet, in the midst of the rejoicing, he

135

recalled distinctly how it felt to lose, too. He had experienced that often enough in the past. He was sure the remembrance of defeats would give him a measure of humility now; it had a lasting therapeutic effect to be defeated sometimes. It made you want to win all the more the next time.

Betty, he noticed, didn't look tired any more. Her face was aglow with pleasure. The lines of fatigue were chased away. She was laughing and talking, greeting the ever-growing influx of celebrants. Sam knew her belief in him had provided the final necessary ingredient for victory, the inspiration he needed to become, in fact, the Mayor of El Pueblo de la Nuestra Señora la Reina de Los Angeles de Porciuncula.

Sam grinned and manfully held out his sore right arm for more handshakes.

CHAPTER XVII

The world is too much with us . . .

WILLIAM WORDSWORTH

Mankind's affairs everywhere were very much with Sam Yorty that day he first took his oath of office as mayor. He could not have escaped them if he had wished to do so.

Every pressure, every tension communicated itself almost instantaneously to Los Angeles as to all great American cities; no longer was it possible for "foreign affairs" to be concentrated solely in Washington, D.C. The net effect of wars, famines, uprisings, massacres, embargoes, moon shots, and atom tests were felt immediately.

Just forty-four days before Sam was elected, the "incredible blunder" of newly inaugurated President John F. Kennedy at the Bay of Pigs had shaken the American people. The abortive Cuban invasion by exile forces seeking to overthrow Fidel Castro came on April 17, 1961, and by May 31 when the Los Angeles mayoralty election occurred some of the ugly details of U.S. inaction and false assurances had leaked out.

These, by indirection, served to aid Yorty's candidacy because of his outspoken assertion that John F. Kennedy was not "ready" for the presidency. Now, though, as the day approached for Sam to take over the city government of Los Angeles as its chief executive, he was too overwhelmed in local detail to be giving much thought to any differences with the President. In the period between Election Day, May 31, and the date of his inaugural, June 30, Sam had managed to start some sort of healing process in the municipality after the bitter charges of the campaign. Still, many of the underlying difficulties remained. Retiring Mayor Poulson with whom Sam had been on such close terms in Congress during the great water battles of a few years before, had participated sportingly in preparations for the take-over of the executive reins by Sam despite the bitterness of the campaign. The ceremony was arranged for the traditional temporary stands always erected for special occasions on the steps of the Spring Street entrance of the City Hall.

George Jessel, the perennial one, was chosen to be Master of Ceremonies. When the time came for the actual taking of the oath by Samuel William Yorty as mayor he had been joined in the ceremony not only by Poulson but also by former Mayor Fletcher Bowron. The news photographers were able to take the proverbial picture of the new and former mayors clasping hands in token of civic unity.

Despite this symbolic evidence of amity Sam nevertheless knew he was on a lonely pinnacle where every move would be closely observed and probably criticized. As he intoned the words of the oath at 12:20 P.M. he could look out at a city which contained many hostile elements as well as those friendly ones which had contributed to his election. He could not help but be mindful, too, of the headlong sweep of world events continuing while he himself sought to bring some order into the local orbit over which he was to preside.

In the early editions of the press on inauguration day Mickey Cohen, the mobster, got bigger headlines for being convicted on eight counts of United States income tax evasion than Sam did for becoming mayor. Even the Bay of Pigs scandal still was manifesting its dismal aftermath in columns adjacent to the news stories of Sam's induction. The abortive "Tractors for Freedom Committee" headed by Mrs. Franklin D. Roosevelt, Dr. Milton Eisenhower, and the Auto Workers' Walter Reuther was disbanding with a curt refusal to give Fidel Castro "$28,000,000 or $28" in exchange for the 1197 prisoners still held from the unsuccessful invasion. Dick Nixon down in Long Beach at the 43rd annual convention of the California American Legion was demanding military and diplomatic firmness in dealing with Communism and urging against admission of Red China to the United Nations. President Kennedy, trying to retrieve his prestige after the Cuban fiasco, was signing the broadened Social Security Benefits Bill and the New Housing Bill which represented victories for his administration. Adolf Eichmann, on trial in Jerusalem for the murder of 6,000,000 Jews, was trying to save his own life by testifying that his role in the massacres consisted only of providing the cattle cars for conveyance of the victims to the extermination camps.

On a happier note, Willie Davis of the ex-Brooklyn-now-Los-Angeles-Dodgers was running wild with consecutive triples and an almost-steal of home, while the incredible Whitey Ford of the Yankees was chalking up his eighth win in a month.

All these things, the vital, the grisly and the trivial were equally unimportant to Sam at the moment. He was face to face on his own with the multiple and multiplying problems of Los Angeles, some of which were battering him almost before he could get off the inaugural stand. Defiance, criticism, and attacks continued to be the dominating factors in his immediate environment. Furthermore, Sam was supposed to be primed for any sort of questions on a "Meet Your Mayor" telecast set for Saturday evening, July 1, the day following the inaugural ceremony.

With these distractions as a background, Sam Yorty spoke his beliefs in his inaugural speech.

"This ceremony typifies one of the principal tenets of our democracy: the orderly transfer of executive responsibility carried out in accordance with the will of the people as expressed by them through the instrumentalities of the secret ballot," he stated. "I think it is fitting that this ceremony be brought out here into the open where all who so desire may witness it. This is in keeping with my firm resolve that your city government be conducted, like this ceremony, in the open. An informed citizenry being a cornerstone of good government and a strong bulwark against abuse of the great power entrusted to public servants by the people, I will make every effort to keep you as informed about the conduct of your government as it is within my power to do.

"We will share the facts together, and together we will experience the exciting challenge and opportunity of demonstrating that American local government can meet the responsibilities of changing times in a changing world where too many millions have lost, or have never had, the right to govern themselves—a right which we must protect, preserve, cherish, and perfect so that the truth of God's plan for man's freedom shall shine forth and enlighten an ever-widening circle of our globe within which free men may live and work together in peace, harmony and good will.

"Good government and the preservation of freedom begins with each individual citizen and is the responsibility of all of us and all levels of government. If we meet the great challenge of our day

139

at the local level, our national government with its grave responsibilities, can better meet that challenge at the national level.

"Each one of us is therefore a pillar in the house of democracy, and the strength of our house depends upon our willingness and ability to cast aside selfish considerations and share wholeheartedly in the task of forging a greater city as a strong unit of a greater nation, and a hopeful beacon for those who long to break the bonds of tyranny as did our forefathers when they established our nation.

"We have much for which to be thankful. In our busy day it is well that we pause regularly to count our many blessings. I shall be ever mindful that the governmental power which I shall exercise comes from you, the sovereign citizens of Los Angeles. I want to emphasize the word *sovereign* because in this election you have aroused the interest of the entire free world by proving that no one can speak for the people without their consent. The people can speak for themselves. You have made this abundantly clear and in doing so you have emboldened and enheartened those who might otherwise have felt it impossible successfully to challenge combinations of power—power in actual fact built more on illusion and delusion than upon any substantial basis. Truth is a force to be reckoned with. So long as we preserve our means of conveying truth, we need have no fear of overcoming entrenched interests and preserving our rights freely to choose those to whom we desire to entrust the responsibility of government."

After taking the oath Sam looked over at Betty, radiant in a summer costume for the ceremony, smiled at her, then took a deep breath.

He was mayor now.

All he had to do was start mayoring.

CHAPTER XVIII

*The Promised Land always lies on the other side of a
wilderness.*

HAVELOCK ELLIS

Thwarting experiences harass every conscientious public official
going into office with high aims and ambitions, but the most thwarting is the instant collision with multiplied trivia. Great goals sometimes are lost in the ensuing confusion. Little details smother initiative and progress. Stagnaton triumphs.

Fortunately for Los Angeles, Sam Yorty was ready for these
perils because of his previous experience during his cumulative five
terms to elective office as Assemblyman in the California Legislature and a Representative in the United States Congress. He knew
how to handle the multitudinous bothersome details of setting up
an office, selecting a staff, keeping major objectives in sight while
attending to smaller demands, delegating authority, originating
municipal programs, and keeping in touch with the public which
had elected him. No sooner had he stepped from the inauguration
stand than he began to hammer away at his tasks. Many were
prosaic, others plain bothersome. A great number involved political
considerations which necessarily would cause him to tread warily.

Most pressing were some of the "routine" items: Political replace-
ments and the announcement of assistants. One of the strongest
beliefs held by Sam Yorty was that the success of any top official
depends to a great degree upon the genuine loyalty of his chief
aides. He was convinced that no amount of reward in the way of
salary or political favor could equal genuine fealty.

It was in line with this belief that he named as his own Chief
Executive Assistant the remarkable woman who not only had been
his campaign manager in the race for mayor but also his manager

in other notable contests in the past. It surprised no one when he selected Mrs. Eleanor Chambers to be his principal assistant.

Sam and Betty Yorty were devoted to Eleanor Chambers, whose ebullience, loyalty, and common sense had made her a close personal friend as well as a political adviser. Mrs. Chambers, born in Elmira, New York, had come to California at the age of eight, and, as her associates said, had "entered politics soon thereafter." She became a powerful figure in state Democratic circles after having been appointed to the State Central Committee with the support of Senators William Gibbs McAdoo and Sheridan Downey. She served as head of the Division of Service Projects of the Works Progress Administration for President Franklin D. Roosevelt, and later served in numerous Federal positions in Washington.

For Sam, she agreed to take the job which was the equivalent of deputy mayor (before it was formally so designated), although the responsibility meant a drastic reduction in the time she could spend at her beloved home in Cambria Pines.

As the Associate Executive Assistant Sam chose Joseph M. Quinn, who had been president of City News Service and one of the few avowed Yorty supporters in the metropolitan press during the mayoralty campaign.

Quinn had gone to Washington and New York for a series of newspaper and wire service meetings immediately after the mayoralty election in which he had been of such great assistance to Sam. Sam Yorty called him in New York and asked that he return. Quinn came back to Los Angeles and was offered the other deputy mayor job. He asked time to think it over. Then he accepted, although it meant a radical departure from his previous work with the United Press, as a war correspondent in Korea, and as head of City News Service and publisher of *Business News Wire, Los Angeles Enterprise,* and *Los Angeles Newsletter.*

He, like Mrs. Chambers, was a native of New York State, his home city being Buffalo.

During the campaign, great assistance had been given to the Yorty cause by a specially gifted Pennsylvania woman, Mrs. Dorothy Moore, a graduate of the University of Pittsburgh. She had been associated in business with her husband in Texas and in Canada. She had been a Congressional secretary in Washington, D.C., for Representative James B. VanZandt of Pennsylvania and for Representative O. Clark Fisher of Texas and Senators Warren G. Magnuson of Washington State and Hubert H. Humphrey of

Minnesota. Her poise and competence led Mayor Yorty to ask her to become his personal secretary.

Filling positions as administrative assistants to be "on the firing line" in daily affairs of his office, the mayor chose Frank O'Sullivan, an experienced executive from the Chief Administrative Officer's staff; Bob Goe, newspaperman; Ronald Ellensohn, insurance broker; and Jack Brown, former assistant political editor of the Los Angeles *Examiner*, for liaison with the Legislature and Sacramento affairs. Ray Parker, newspaperman, was selected for press relations and for liaison with the police department, and Bill Morrison, a veteran of the Chief Administrative Officer's staff, was given the job of legislative analyst dealing with City Council affairs.

One more immediate necessity faced by the mayor was to fill the job which in most cities would be known as that of "City Manager," but in Los Angeles was designated by charter amendment as "City Administrative Officer." Because of the relative newness of the position and unusual circumstances surrounding it, the prospective selection by Yorty was of major political significance. It represented a test of his judgment and selective capacity. He was being watched closely by both friends and critics.

A furor had been stirred up over the resignation of Samuel Leask, Jr., City Administrative Officer because when Sam was elected Leask was the only person who had served in the position since its creation ten years before. The job, long discussed in municipal circles had failed to materialize until the Los Angeles city elections in the spring of 1951. At that time the voters approved a charter amendment—one of the hundred adopted at various times to try to make the 1925 Charter work better—setting up the office so as to give some administrative relief to the mayor.

It was pointed out by the Los Angeles *Times* when the office was created that it was an appointive selection of the mayor so it would not "detract from the authority of the mayor."

In its appraisal of the job's purpose the *Times* said:

"The City Administrative Officer will direct, co-ordinate and expedite the business management of the city. He will plan ahead for future contingencies, keep the Mayor and Council advised of the condition, finances and future needs of the city, making recommendations for improvements.

"He will assist in preparing the budget, in researching in the realm of improvements, in putting into effect procedures and forms, programs and standards which will return the taxpayer more for his dollar. His authority—but under the control of the Mayor—will extend over the several city departments in the matter of transferring funds and transferring personnel so as to make the city's working staff and financial resources more flexible than at present.

"Essentially it is the city manager form of government with modifications specifically to conform to conditions in Los Angeles. In that it is nothing new and it has been under consideration here for several years."

Leask was appointed by Mayor Fletcher Bowron as the culmination of a successful business career. At first an official of the May Company Department Stores, Leask had performed public service during World War II and then had become an officer of J. W. Robinson Company Department Stores and had attained the presidency of the California Retailers' Association. Commendation was won by Leask for the most part in his pioneering of the new position.

Leask served until Sam Yorty's swearing in. When he resigned in line with customary procedure when a new administration takes over, Mayor Yorty named George A. Terhune, a long-time municipal official on an interim basis. Terhune served only for six months.

Mayor Yorty took his time and eventually appointed C. Erwin Piper, president of the Los Angeles Board of Public Works as Chief Administrative Officer. Piper had won distinction throughout the United States as an agent of the FBI. This experience in a job requiring the utmost attention to detail in addition to other strong qualities fitted him, in Mayor Yorty's opinion, for the exacting requirements of the CAO's position.

At the time Leask resigned, the Los Angeles *Times* printed the editorial deploring the loss of a man of Leask's stature and propounding the question whether Police Chief Parker would be able to stay in office, due to Yorty's supposedly critical attitude toward him. The latter point assumed national significance during the Watts riots in August 1965 when Parker not only still was in office under the Yorty regime but won all-out support from the mayor when Parker came under scathing fire from some civil rights leaders including Martin Luther King.

During those first few days of his term in July 1961 Sam Yorty was contending with two sets of immediate problems which had no visible connection at the time with the future. One was the setting up of his own administrative staff and outlining his executive and legislative aims. The other was getting rid of persistent holdovers from the Poulson administration who did not wish to be shelved. Chief among these was Lloyd Wright who flatly refused to quit as a member of the Department of Water & Power Commission. Others were Harry C. Dow and Don Belding of the Airport Commission who likewise declined to submit their resignations.

Yorty immediately emphasized his belief that commissioners "serve at the pleasure of the mayor," thus presaging a wholesale sweep of such office holders which came as something of a shock at the start of his own second term four years later. For the moment, though, after succeeding in disposing of Wright and Dow, the mayor turned to what he considered to be more constructive matters in the city for which he had such great ambitions.

In this connection he summed up, almost as a creed, his approach to municipal affairs:

"I felt that city government had too narrow a base," he said in retrospect. "Too few people were involved in elections and in the government process for such a large city. This was illustrated in the election for mayor.

"A few persons had become accustomed to picking a candidate and electing him, always from the central area. This overemphasized the downtown section and disregarded to a large extent the feeling of people in the outlying sections—such as those in the San Fernando Valley and in the harbor area which were physically a considerable distance from the City Hall and the Civic Center but still were a vital and integral part of the community.

"I thought this conflict between 'downtown' and the 'suburbs' was wrong. When I was elected I believed that I had a unique opportunity to correct this situation and bring the suburbs more into municipal affairs, on account of the fact that I was the first mayor elected from a suburb, which in my case happened to be the San Fernando Valley.

"My philosophy is that a city is like a wheel—the center, or downtown, is important but so are the spokes and the rim, the suburbs. My aim all along has been to draw together the hub, the spokes and the rim into a working unit so that each plays its proper role and the wheel rolls properly along for efficient government.

"I think we have done that.

"We have a growing awareness now of the proper structure of the city and of the necessary coordination of the departments within the city to carry out the wishes of the electorate in all sections.

"A good example of this tendency is the city's birthday celebration on September 4. Until I came into office as Mayor there had been, to all intents and purposes, just one observance and this was at the Plaza. This last year (1965) we succeeded in changing all that in line with the idea of spreading out into the suburbs instead of concentrating just on downtown. We had the Plaza dinner which was attended by around 1500 people but we also had a lot of other things which gained attention. In Hollywood Bowl we had a special birthday program and we jammed it with a crowd of 17,000. Many of these people had never even been in the Bowl before. We brought them in buses from all over the city and the whole thing was a big success.

"Then we had a Cabrillo play at San Pedro and a ceremony at San Fernando Mission. The whole city government, social leaders, and people of all types got to join in these programs which would not have been possible if the birthday ceremony had been confined just to the Plaza.

"Some people have talked about the friction I've had in office. Of course you have to have some friction if you're going to change things for the better or get improvements made.

"When I came into office I found out why Mayor Poulson had gotten along with little friction. He let the Council take control and of course if the Mayor didn't stand up for his objectives there wouldn't be much friction. Just about the only difficulties you heard anything about were when a couple of Councilmen like Carl Runberg and John Holland sounded off in the fight over the bringing of the Dodgers to Chavez Ravine. The apparent harmony was all due to the Mayor letting things slide and letting the Council have its way on nearly everything.

"The city was run by the civil service general managers of the departments who never met together in any coordinated fashion or checked with the mayor. They spent bond funds and did everything else pretty much on their own. As a result there was no unity of approach and things were going off in every direction.

"I decided that if the city was going to get anywhere in the way we wanted it to, there had to be central direction and coordination. When this word got around and I began putting it into effect we did begin to have great friction. Secret meetings were held by the general managers of the departments who were afraid they were going to lose the dominant roles they had been playing, because of my new approach. I started having meetings with them and appointed some of my staff members for liaison. I also arranged for the department heads to begin having general meetings so there would be some knowledge among them of what was going on in all the other phases of city government.

"An illustration of the way I had to fight this thing through came in connection with the proposal for a new fire department building at Second and Hill Streets. The way they had it planned it was going to be a six-story affair just for the fire people on a site they owned away from the Civic Center. When I found out about it I felt the building was too small and that all of the factors hadn't been given due weight. Considering the land value it was, uneconomic—an underdevelopment.

"'It's got to be bigger,' I told them.

"I insisted on a check with other departments to find out their future needs for additional quarters because, of course, for a long time the City Hall itself has been inadequate. When the investigation was done we found that it was more economical and efficient to house the fire department in the City Hall Annex back of the City Hall in the Civic Center utilizing other city-owned property and making it possible to sell the valuable fire department-owned property.

"I ordered all the department heads to check with the Mayor on things like this so we wouldn't be falling into such mistakes."

Amid a flood of such issues, Sam Yorty began stroking his way toward solutions. In the process he encountered challenging problems in the metropolis and fierce political opposition and obstruction. Through it all he began to display the quality of stubborn determination and guttiness which apparently won him wide-spread support from citizens. He was not always successful in his initial efforts for the objectives toward which he was striving but he was making it plain that regardless of consequences he was going to keep up the basic fight.

CHAPTER XIX

*The very essence of a free government consists in
considering offices as public trusts, and not for the
benefit of an individual or a party.*

JOHN C. CALHOUN

When Sam set up shop in the City Hall, one of the first things
he did was to put "Pinky" Snyder in a place of honor at the
entrance to the mayor's suite of offices.

This was nice for "Pinky" because he had been neglected for a
long time.

In fact—in the form of an oil painting—Mayor "Pinky" was lost
on a dusty shelf somewhere in a City Hall closet until Sam dug
him out, along with the portraits of other former mayors which
likewise were dusted off and hung in the corridors of the mayor's
office.

"Pinky's" distinction was that he was the last Democratic mayor
of Los Angeles until Sam came along. He served way back in the
term from 1919 until 1921, although he had been mayor previously
in 1896 to 1898 and 1900 to 1904. Of course, the fact that the
Honorable Meredith P. ("Pinky"—on Account of his Whiskers)
Snyder was a Democrat was supposed to be of no importance
because the job of mayor in Los Angeles is officially "non-
partisan." Still, it was a fact that every mayor for forty years since
1921—even though nominally "non-partisan"—had been a registered
Republican. This coincided with the almost-uninterrupted Republican control of major offices in California during virtually the entire
period of the twentieth century.

In the City Hall, the sight of a Democrat—except humbly craving
some boon as a mere citizen—was a rarity for decades. Sam, though,
was the kind of Democrat who put genuine meaning into the

148

supposed "non-partisanship" of the mayor's office. He appointed some Republicans to his staff and to commissions. Even the atmosphere of the City Hall began to change. Sam regarded this edifice in its historic connotation, remembering the area as it was when he arrived in Los Angeles and its background in the evolution of the downtown area.

The City Hall in its massive bulk sits athwart what used to be three historic streets in Los Angeles before they were obliterated by its construction. One was New High Street, which ran roughly north and south at an angle between Main and Spring streets. Two other small thoroughfares bore three names between them—Jail, Court, and Franklin streets. The City Hall covers all of the space between the present First and Temple streets and Main and Spring streets. Its most pretentious entrance is that on Spring Street facing toward the future Mall which will be completed when the present old Hall of Records is removed. It is on the Spring Street steps that the platforms traditionally are erected for the more important ceremonies, the greeting of distinguished guests, the observation of Mexican Independence Day, September 16, always a great occasion in Los Angeles because of the large Mexican-American population; and an occasional impromptu political conference between councilmen or hangers-on. On the First Street side where the steps are not quite so imposing, events such as band concerts and ceremonies involving flag raising honoring foreign nations take place, quite often.

Inside, the "main" floor bears the Spring Street designation. On one side of the long north-south corridor in the south wing, the City Council chamber is on the west side and the mayor's offices on the east side. The mayor's office is entered through an imposing doorway near the east side of the building. A back door, used only by the mayor's staff and newspapermen, leads off the big corridor.

Sam's formal office, with beautifully decorated ceiling and a huge desk in front of the American, California and Los Angeles flags at the west end, looks out through huge windows to the trees and flowers on the south lawn. Sam actually utilizes a small anteroom for his work desk.

The offices of his assistants are arranged along two corridors which meet at right angles outside his own office door, close to "Pinky" Snyder's portrait. His personal secretary, Dorothy Moore, has a large office near the mayor's work room. Outside Mrs.

Moore's office door sits a charming young woman, guardian of the portals, Miss Helen Romero, selected as one of the city employees' "Princesses" who in turn screens and channels telephone calls and those visitors who have penetrated beyond the receptionist. She is beset on the telephone with crackpots, "old friends of Sam" who, it turns out, in many instances never knew him at all, or thought they had in Georgia, Florida, or Texas when he was never there; and the people who are genuinely supposed to get through to Mrs. Moore, or, eventually, to the mayor.

Always during the day, there is a cheerful bustle, people coming and going, looking at the oil paintings of the former mayors on the walls, studying cartoon jibes at Sam from the talented pen of the late Bruce Russell of the *Times*, reading Sam's framed first inaugural address, or having a cup of coffee. Such a cheerful and purposeful atmosphere prevails that it seems more like an efficient modern business office than the traditional hang-out of political loiterers.

"Before we came in here it used to be like a funeral parlor," said Deputy Mayor Joe Quinn. "Sam has livened everything up."

Down the north-south inner hall in a big cheerful room Deputy Mayor Eleanor Chambers, Sam's campaign manager, carries on the demanding job of running the offices, helping select commissioners, advising, smoothing out, watching political trends, and greeting distinguished visitors. Deputy Mayor Quinn, laboring over policy trends, meeting dignitaries at airports, making speeches in lieu of the mayor, is close to Sam's office down the east-west hall.

When Sam arrives around 10 A.M. the office is galvanized, not at all by assistants trying to "impress the boss," but as if a dynamo had been turned on. Things happen when Sam is around. In the midst of serious conferences and exacting day-to-day obligations, there is always the intriguing question:

"What's going to happen next?"

* * *

California's political peculiarities always have been a mystery in the East—and ofttimes in California itself—and Los Angeles in its municipal elections has shared in creating situations which defied any rational explanation. The pattern of local government which Sam Yorty inherited from his predecessors in 1961 was a literal crazy-quilt of tradition, "reforms," contradictions, improvisations, stop-gap ordinances and charter revisions. The much-amended

City Charter under which the swollen municipality was attempting to operate was thirty-six years old.

This charter, in fact, was one of those instruments designed in the 1920s to "divide" responsibility between the mayor as chief executive and the City Council as the legislative body, and keep both "weak," with the aim of preventing the dishonesty which could occur when one branch—if in the hands of unscrupulous officials—became dominant enough to "sell" municipal favors without restraint. The practical result was to hamstring both branches of government. As Los Angeles grew, the inevitable impasses between mayor and council, each jealous of presumed prerogatives, became increasingly dangerous from an administrative standpoint. Successive mayors and councils chafed under their restraints and the consequent and obvious lack of coordinated government. Still, despite many reports and investigations, no major effort was put under way to replace the outmoded charter.

Many amendments—the number is more than 500—have been made to the charter since its adoption in 1925. Yet these in many instances, according to those most intimately connected with trying to run the day-to-day business of Los Angeles, have failed woefully to effect any material betterment.

Public understanding of the situation has been lacking for decades because of a simple circumstance. The more people who crowded into Los Angeles, the fewer who understood the basic problems of the city's government. Settlers from New York, Chicago, Albany, Keokuk, Omaha, Fort Worth, Cincinnati, St. Louis, Peoria, and a thousand other cities and hamlets were totally unaware of Los Angeles' civic affairs; they were intent only upon climate, their businesses, surfing, the movies, weekends in the mountains and deserts, TV studios and baseball. Appeals for them to understand and participate in their city government fell, for the most part, upon unheeding ears.

When elections came around they voted for party "regulars" as they had done at home or stayed away from the polls entirely out of disinterest.

Los Angeles municipal executives—many of them dedicated public servants who had been at their posts for years despite the comings or goings of elected officials—were as thwarted as the successive mayors and city councilmen. Lack of coordination between departments became more and more apparent because of the deficiency of the charter in providing any real executive authority in the mayor's office.

When the 1925 Charter was adopted it was at a moment in the city's development when ambition and idealism were blended. The population was at that magic figure between 500,000 and 1,000,000 at which cities are still small enough to be intimately aware of their own affairs, and yet big enough to embark upon magnificent projects designed for the future. The new City Hall towering against the blue skies—it was still the era before smog—was an example of the spirit of the times. To go with their City Hall the people adopted the charter which they considered a worthy corollary. They could not foresee its deficiencies in the days to come.

Sam's inheritance of this much-mangled instrument led him to strong efforts to correct its evils in one sweeping move.

Sam held definite views on the procedure by which the charter could be completely overhauled, even if it involved a freeholders' election. First of all he wanted a thorough study made of the need by professional analysts. For this purpose he proposed to the City Council that, as a preliminary to major changes an appropriation of $50,000 be provided for this initial study. The proposal, coming during the period of major conflicts between the mayor and some members of the City Council, was unsuccessful.

In summing up his own views on this fundamental aspect of city government Mayor Yorty said:

"I am not the first mayor to recognize the shortcomings of the 1925 Los Angeles Charter as the basic law for the government of Los Angeles in 1965. The inadequacies of the charter have also been experienced by former mayors; pointed out by students of government; the subject of numerous articles and commentaries; and deplored by many citizens committees. Yet, during this entire generation in which Los Angeles has witnessed one of the most amazing population and construction growths in history, this basic legal document has not once been thoroughly overhauled.

"What are the conclusions reached by practically all informed observers with respect to the charter. The objections can be summarized like this:

a. The charter is far too lengthy and cumbersome;

b. It has been altered more than 500 times since 1925 and is now an accumulated patchwork which has been constructed over a period of four decades;

c. It contains matters of administrative detail which should more logically be contained in an adminstrative code;

d. Minor matters are expanded unnecessarily and major matters are constricted;

e. It provides for dual authority in city operation which is inconsistent with accepted principles of direct lines of control and authority commensurate with responsibility.

"Disagreements between the mayor and the city council have been widely publicized, leading some citizens to inquire 'I wonder why they can't seem to get along?' The answer to that question is basically simple.

"The charter by its very terms contains built-in conflict. Section 40 of the charter designates the mayor as the executive officer of the city and, among other things, he is given the responsibility for exercising a careful supervision over all its affairs, enforcing the ordinances of the city and securing co-operation between the various departments. But Section 22 of the City Charter invests the council with authority to create positions, fix salaries and provide quarters, equipment and supplies.

"The chief executive of this city up to this time has no authority to appoint or remove the managers of the various city departments, except in a few minor instances, and except for one personal secretary he cannot appoint or remove anybody without the approval of the City Council! Yet many citizens logically look to the mayor for leadership and direction since he is the only policy-making officer elected by all the citizens of Los Angeles. The city attorney and the controller perform specialized functions.

"It is fundamental that any executive entrusted with the responsibility for co-ordinating and administering the affairs of a structure as varied and complex as the government of the City of Los Angeles must have a degree of control which can only be exercised by the right to direct key personnel. This fact was strongly emphasized in the 1962 report of the Municipal Manpower Commission in its publication 'Government Manpower for Tomorrow's Cities,' which states in part:

"'Government, like business, has moved beyond the stage where it can afford the uncertain performance of weak management.

"'The executives of growing, changing, urban governments must have authority over the personnel on whom they depend to get their work done. Mayors, city managers, department heads and others of like rank in urban counties must have greater authority to hire, to promote, to discipline and to fire. It is particularly important to place control of APT (administrative, professional, technical) personnel in the executive.

"'Where patronage and spoils still prevail, or threaten, means should and can be devised to safeguard personnel from arbitrary or discriminatory treatment, but without depriving the chief executive of essential authority to hire, promote, discipline, and dismiss personnel.'

"In public administration terms Los Angeles has what is called a 'weak' mayor type of government because of the restriction placed upon the authority of the chief executive in such governments. This has been pointed out and correction has been urged many times all the way from special charter study committees appointed from the University of California and the University of Southern California in 1934 to the charter study prepared at the request of Town Hall in 1963.

"The deficiencies inherent in the current charter were commented on in no uncertain terms by former Mayors Poulson and Bowron. I hope it would not be an exaggeration to state that our determined efforts have resulted in increased public awareness of the need for charter reform."

One possibility which was discussed was the borough system—under which local areas in a city have administrative powers themselves. Some advocates proposed boroughs as a governmental simplification and advance to help take care of the mounting needs of the metropolis. Others denounced this as a move in the direction of corrupt regimes, including ward bosses, such as those in some eastern cities.

Los Angeles under the California Constitution actually possesses the power to create boroughs. In fact, the checkered history of politics in the city and in the state regarding the creation of boroughs dates back to the "Progressive" movement in the first decade of this century when growing cities were attempting to meet their new problems.

It was an era of reform. The "muckrakers" like Lincoln Steffens and Upton Sinclair were exposing sickening details of municipal corruption and bribery at a time when citizens of the United States, in a relatively peaceful era under jovial and easygoing President William Howard Taft, had time to turn their attention to municipal sins.

In California the militant "Progressive" wing of the dominant

Republican party with the fiery Governor Hiram Johnson in the vanguard was embarking upon all sorts of efforts to clean up messes and bring more decency into local government. These attempts included not only cities but counties. The Constitutional Amendment moves in the years around 1910 sought to give greater flexibility in both municipal and county realms so as to assist in the general objective of "home rule."

Los Angeles by this time was recognizing the hand of destiny and glorying in its own tremendous strides in population. In the decade between 1900 and 1910 the city more than tripled its population, jumping from 102,479 to 319,198. In its enthusiasm it looked around for methods by which it could increase its size and importance.

A problem in Los Angeles, in fact, led to exploration of the borough idea. This was the unprecedented attempt of the city to obtain a harbor although the sea was more than twenty miles away. To attain this goal it was necessary for the city of Los Angeles to consolidate with Wilmington and San Pedro. It was thought that a localized borough government for the harbor area might provide the answer. This was because the harbor, if annexed, was to be made a part of the city by means of a narrow "shoestring strip" running down through other territory to the prospective annexation, far distant from the central city.

The citizens of Los Angeles dutifully amended the then-existing City Charter so areas within the city could organize boroughs. A Constitutional Amendment was sought at the same time to give validity to the procedure. When a Constitutional Amendment giving greater powers to cities was adopted in 1911 the part about boroughs was amended so that the entire city had to be divided into boroughs instead of just one part of it. This killed the borough idea for Wilmington and San Pedro at the time. About forty years later, however, in 1952, a State Constitutional Amendment was adopted permitting chartered cities in California to create a single borough if it desired rather than dividing the entire city. The way thus is clear legally for boroughs but no decision has been reached whether it is desirable to create them.

The discussions for civic betterment ranged through such a variety of suggestions in addition to boroughs that they stirred up full-scale debates of their own. Some people wanted to embark upon further major annexations. Others advocated a program of decentralization. The mayor studied all the proposals but kept pushing for charter revision as the necessary first step. He realized more keenly by now the handicaps under which his predecessors had labored.

* * *

Sam confounds his more serious contemporaries with some of his unexpected little adventures in going off on tangents. This was manifest when he became irked at the smug air of superiority he encountered when he talked to residents of Boston and Philadelphia, as summed up in inimitable fashion by the late Mr. Justice Oliver Wendell Holmes of the United States Supreme Court who, in his salty fashion, had remarked about a Bostonian moving to Los Angeles:

"How could anyone give up 300 years of culture for 30 degrees of temperature!"

Sam decided that what Los Angeles needed was a longer pedigree. He wanted to outdo Boston. To this end, he encouraged the Los Angeles Cultural Heritage Commission to seek legitimate historical proof that Los Angeles as an inhabited spot had existed for more than the mere 180-year span covered by the records when Sam was elected mayor.

"What was here before the Spaniards came?" he asked.

"Yang-na," responded the Cultural Heritage Commission.

"Fine!" said Sam. "What was Yang-na?"

"An Indian community right where the modern city stands."

"How long was it here?"

"Oh, maybe a thousand years."

"Okeh," said Sam, "let's advertise we're older than Boston, maybe a thousand years older. And we've still got Indians here to prove it."

Dr. Carl S. Dentzel, director of the Southwest Museum and at the time president of the Cultural Heritage Commission, who himself possessed a sense of humor, joined heartily in helping to give to Yang-na—which was really only a cluster of a few brush huts—all the splendid proportions of a Western Athens. Los Angeles, thus duly provided with a noble pedigree for the benefit of Boston, was able to turn back with a chuckle to its own concerns.

Sam was never too busy to be thinking of a gracious gesture in the Latin American traditions of the city. He delighted the Mexican-American population by taking the initiative in planning to move a bronze statue of Fr. Hidalgo, who launched the successful

Mexican Revolution of 1910 against the yoke of Spain, from an obscure park to a place of honor at the Los Angeles Plaza. He rather scandalized the staid fiscal officials of the city by requesting that the City Budget—a formidable document three-quarters of an inch thick—have on its covers a depiction of the restored Plaza, the birthplace of the community. It was a shattering innovation, but it was done; an artistic budget! Sam even included a tribute on the title page to Father Juan Crespi who, in 1769, the year of the Spanish colonizing of California, had given the name "Porciuncula" to the stream later known as the Los Angeles River. Father Crespi, an associate of Father Junipero Serra, California's founder, had felt prophetic about the site of Los Angeles and, on August 2 while camped at the Rio Porciuncula, had written in his dairy: *"Porciuncula River, a large stream, with much good land."*

* * *

Digging out and refurbishing "Pinky" Snyder's portrait, as a matter of fact, led Sam to a new interest in the progression of Los Angeles mayors. He found himself part of a direct governmental chain dating back to the first days of Spanish-Mexican rule. Los Angeles as a pueblo possessed an *alcalde,* or mayor, and an *ayuntamiento,* or city council, even though they might have taken more siestas than is now considered polite under modern Civil Service. These carefree Latin regimes were hardly less casual, though, than the ensuing ones of the Americanos del Norte, who had conquered California during the Mexican War, and set up their own rule after January 1847. Early American-period mayors in Los Angeles were prominent at lynchings and would take time out any day to see a horse thief strung up on the convenient crossbar of a wooden entry gate leading off Main Street to some small adobes on the site of the present Federal Building, only a block or so from the modern City Hall. These early dignitaries were used to threats of horsewhipping and mayhem in a frontier tradition of personal chastisement which later was supposed to have vanished with covered wagons and handlebar mustaches, although Sam in his own feuds sometimes wondered if this conclusion were premature.

Nowhere could Sam find an orderly listing of the successive American mayors with biographical material and pictures. He decided there should be one. On his instructions, the task of compiling and publishing the material was undertaken by the Municipal

Art Department and the new Los Angeles Cultural Heritage Board. Kenneth Ross and Curt Opliger of the art department and W. W. (Bill) Robinson, historian and member of the Cultural Heritage Board prepared a booklet describing, in brief, each mayor since 1850. Four of these had so faded into the misty past that no likeness could be found, and the pages for their pictures necessarily were left blank.

Samuel William Yorty, it was discovered in the research process, was the thirty-sixth individual to have served in the 116-year period from 1850 to 1966, although numerous mayors were re-elected, thus accounting for more terms than persons. The chain had begun with a prominent physician, Alpheus P. Hodges, M.D., who served in 1850–51 as the first mayor.

Each day, as Sam goes to his office to contend with the charter, smog, transit and poverty, the bewhiskered portraits of his predecessors, with "Pinky" Snyder prominent among them, look down at him from their hallway vantage points, as if saying:

"Bear up! We had our troubles too!"

CHAPTER XX

We have learned to be citizens of the world, members of the human community.

FRANKLIN DELANO ROOSEVELT

In becoming the "travelingest" mayor in the history of Los Angeles, Sam Yorty has been fulfilling another aspect of the conjunction between the man and the city. Sam ascribes his global journeys to the increasing importance of Los Angeles in world affairs and the development of jet planes so that no place on earth is more than a few hours away. Yet, in another sense, he has been acting almost as if it were in the carrying out of a predestined role for the community. When Mayor Yorty has gone to France and Germany and Ireland and Hungary and Poland and other countries he has been going to the homelands of many of the early settlers of his city.

A glaring contradiction among the many contradictions of which Los Angeles is made up concerns its vaunted "international character" which originated while it was still a mere pueblo or indolent village.

The evolution of the present cosmopolitan center with innumerable foreign "colonies" dates back to the time when a few merchants were clustered along the muddy little streets around the Plaza. In contrast to such settlements as Boston, Philadelphia, and Williamsburg with their overwhelming Anglo-Saxon population, Los Angeles began to be polyglot almost from the moment it came under American rule at the conclusion of the Mexican War. This was due in part—although Los Angeles now hates to admit it—because of an overflow from San Francisco during the Gold Rush.

Fortune-seekers who came from all over the globe in a frenzied search for gold along the streams of northern California included many who failed to find Golconda. Some of these necessarily turned back to their original professions or trades to exist. Others who migrated to the gold fields were doctors or teachers or dentists or lawyers who immediately utilized their training and talents to become a part of the new civilization springing up on the West Coast. Gradually, a few of them drifted south, lured either by tales of the pleasant climate in contrast to the fog and wind of San Francisco, or simply wandering in the hope of finding a place to settle. Thus, more or less fortuitously, they straggled into Los Angeles.

French, Italian, Hungarian, Scot, Irish, Austrian, German, Swiss, English, Czech, and many other nationalities including some remarkably talented Jews from numerous countries opened businesses along Main or New High streets or on Commercial, Court or Franklin near First Street, to add to the few little Spanish tiendas. The babble of innumerable tongues replaced the once-dominant sound of musical Spanish. Names from many lands were prominent: Hector Alliot, Adelsdorfer Brothers, Syriaco Arza, Domingo Amestoy, Richard Altschul, Louis Vignes, August Wackerbarth, Otto G. Weyse, Isaac Newton Van Nuys, Theophile Vache, Max von Stroble, David Solomon, Harris Newmark, Henry Slotterback, Bergamo Sangiovanni, Louis and Michel Sainsevain and on and on. From these blood strains and from the arrival of innumerable other foreign settlers in ensuing years have come the diverse settlements in Los Angeles, ranging from Russian to Chinese and from Italian to Korean.

All the world these days knows of the international importance of Los Angeles in the realms of aircraft production and space flight research and manufacturing. An institution such as the California Institute of Technology which started out modestly in the last century as Throop Institute in Pasadena now commands universal attention as it directs the procedures for moon flights and planetary explorations. Cal Tech, in fact, began to attain international stature at the time Dr. Robert A. Millikan, Nobel Prize winner in science, became its president.

Sam Yorty's own ability to flit about the world in jet planes from his "international city" was forecast more than half a century ago. It is appropriate today that Los Angeles' principal sky harbor is known as International Airport because the first international air meet in history was held in Los Angeles January 10–21, 1910, at a crude little landing strip known as Dominguez Field in the southwestern area. It could boast a one and one-half mile octagon course, 519.63 feet on each side for the races of the little pusher planes of the period. Such immortal names as Glenn H. Curtiss, Roy Knabenshue, Lincoln Beachy, and Paul Poulhan of the French Signal Corps, electrified crowds totaling 176,466 with their daring feats. Poulhan set a new height record of 4165 feet.

One writer was so awed by the spectacle that he penned exuberantly:

"An indescribable feeling comes over one when an aeroplane begins its flight. It is a feeling of awe and exultation, of joy and fear. One's nerves grow tense; one's heart beats faster and one feels glad in the realization he is living in the wonderful twentieth century."

It is difficult to imagine to what heights this observer might have attained if he had lived to see the Mayor of Los Angeles taking off or receiving visitors in planes travelling a commonplace 600 miles per hour.

Mayor Yorty's interest in increasing the importance of International Airport extended particularly into the effort to make it completely a "going concern" financially. The administration of the airport has, in fact, been so successful that after the initial expenditure of funds from general obligation bonds it now has been able to go onto a revenue bond basis, indicative of the confidence the business world has in its future.

* * *

One busy office in the mayor's suite is devoted to the innumerable duties revolving around "foreign affairs," as if there were a miniature State Department or a small-scale United Nations centered in Los Angeles. This room off one of the long halls where former mayors look down solemnly from their gold frames is where Los Angeles Protocol operates. Everybody, from everywhere, "wants to see the mayor." Some should, some shouldn't. It is Protocol's job to decide.

Presiding over this delicate international hot seat is a suave and handsome young man of Latin-American derivation. He is Sam's liaison with the world of diplomats, Kings, Presidents, Prime Ministers, Consuls, Cabinet officers, tycoons, publishers, corporation heads, union leaders and assorted magnates of every nationality. His name is Edward Martinez. Upon Martinez falls the heavy burden, as the mayor's representative, to coordinate the visits of

all the foreign dignitaries in regard to security, entertainment, transportation and sightseeing. Hollywood Bowl, Olvera Street, and
Disneyland often stand him in good stead. One day he may be
arranging for the arrival of the President of Korea as the city's
guest and the next he may be preparing for flag raisings and
native dances on the City Hall lawn by former residents of Lith-
uania.

The demands upon him are never-ending. It is a pace required
to keep up with the mayor's international activities. Indeed, it is a
cumulative development. People come from abroad to see the
mayor. The mayor goes abroad to see people. In each instance, an
invitation is issued for a reciprocal visit. The circle widens all the
time.

Sam Yorty, in his official capacity as mayor, has entertained
visitors ranging from Prime Minister Nehru of India to President
Chung Hee Park of the Republic of Korea and from Princess
Margaret and her husband, Lord Snowdon, to Shah Mohammed
Reza Pahlevi and Empress Farah of Iran. The mayor always is
giving out keys to the city to ambassadors from many countries.

Each visit involves its own problems in arranging menus and
entertainments for the particular personage involved. An unusually
pleasant occasion was the visit of President Chung Hee Park of
Korea whose visit in May 1965 was returned by Mayor and Mrs.
Yorty in November. The President and his wife were entertained
at the Yorty home.

Included among other notable recent visitors have been Levi
Eshkol, Prime Minister of Israel; Eisaku Sato, Prime Minister of
Japan; Hayato Ikeda, former Prime Minister of Japan; the Crown
Prince and Princess of Japan; President Adolfo Lopez Mateos of
Mexico; Lic. Miguel Aleman, former President of Mexico; President
Diosdado Macapagal of the Philippines; and President Maurice
Yameogo of Upper Volta.

So successful have been the efforts of Mayor Yorty functioning
through Ed Martinez in entertaining foreign visitors that a special
letter of commendation was sent to the mayor by Angier Biddle
Duke, Chief of Protocol of the United States State Department.

Reciprocally, the mayor has gone to Germany, Hungary, Poland,
France, Spain, South America, Mexico, Japan, Korea, Viet Nam,
and way points. On his trips he has tried to show his respect for
the people of the countries he is visiting by communicating with
them in their native tongue.

Sam is willing to try anything in the way of languages in spite of any effects on his own jaw or the ears of his listeners. Since he has been in office he has launched forth in no less than seven different tongues, some with special tutoring and others by sheer doggedness on his own part in an attempt to communicate in the idiom of a particular race.

He shuns phonetics—so often used by public officials when they are attempting to speak in another language—because he finds such a method confusing. Instead, he prefers to learn the basic rules and then to prepare a message according to such guidelines.

In Spanish, he was a smash. In 1963 at the time of the 250th anniversary of the birth of Father Junipero Serra, Franciscan founder of California, Mayor Sam and other officials were invited to the island of Mallorca to the little village of Petra, Father Serra's birthplace. This group included Earl Warren former Governor of California and Chief Justice of the United States Supreme Court, and Lieutenant Governor Glenn Anderson of California.

In Palma, Mallorca, the magnificent port city where Father Serra was a teacher for many years, Sam was a speaker at a great civic banquet in honor of the Americans. In Palma at the time was a Spanish poet-diplomat, Aurelius Valls (now stationed in Athens), who became Sam's tutor in the niceties of Castilian Spanish as differentiated from the variety spoken in Mexico. Sam learned his lessons so well that he was enthusiastically received by the audience for his Castilian lisp.

By contrast, he figuratively fell on his face in Portuguese.

"My worst job was in Brazil," he confesses. "I thought I had mastered Portuguese enough for my few remarks but at one point the audience laughed uncontrollably although good-humoredly. When it was all over I asked what I had done and they said I had put a period in the middle of a word."

He spoke French in Bordeaux and German in Germany, but did not attempt the intricacies of Magyar pronunciation in Hungary. He did greet a Russian track team in Los Angeles in Russian and a Yugoslovian team in San Pedro in their native tongue.

He was quite ambitious in Japan by giving a series of talks in Japanese. In this experience he used not the old-fashioned Japanese symbols but "Romangi," which is Japanese in our alphabet. The big difficulty he encountered was in the vowels which are so different. In the middle of one speech someone on the edge of the crowd yelled out a phrase and Sam, a little startled, covered his confusion with a light-hearted "Hi!" This brought a big cheer from the crowd. Later Sam discovered the remark directed at him had been from a newsman who said in effect, "You're good!" And Sam in replying "Hi" had inadvertently agreed, because "Hi" in Japanese means "Yes."

A real test of his linguistic talents came during a trade mission under the auspices of the Los Angeles Harbor Commission to Korea in November 1965. Mayor Yorty embarked on this trip with a feeling that he could contribute to the goal of people-to-people understanding in the Pacific as well as encouraging more trade with Los Angeles. The Yortys had been so impressed with the friendliness of President Park and his wife, of Korea, on their visit to Los Angeles that they particularly looked forward to their own visit to Seoul.

Naturally Mayor Yorty wished to carry on his usual custom of conveying a greeting in the language of the country, so he practiced in Korean on the way across the Pacific. At the airport in Korea he did speak in Korean, and afterward heard many comments on it from the Korean people.

President and Mrs. Park gave a dinner party for the Yortys to renew the pleasant association they had enjoyed in California. Minister of Defense Kim was host at a luncheon for Mayor Yorty, and the mayor received an honorary Ll.D. degree.

During his Pacific area trip Mayor Yorty took the first steps for formation of an international municipal organization to build "bridges of friendship." He announced plans for COMPACT—the Conference (or Council) of Municipalities Pacific Area Cooperating Together.

"We will try to bring Pacific area municipal officials into friendly contact," Mayor Yorty said. "We have a successful Conference of United States-Japan Mayors, but it is too limited for maximum effect. I hope my idea will have future significance."

Mayor Yorty and Mayor Kyoshi Sugito of Nagoya, Japan, formed the nucleus of an organizing committee which included among its first members Mayor Chi Young Yun of Seoul.

Sam has been impressed by the ready wit and human qualities of many of the outstanding visitors who have come to Los Angeles during his term. Prime Minister Jawaharlal Nehru was hardly off the plane before he was looking around for a conveyance to take him to Disneyland, his primary objective.

"Is Disneyland all you can think about?" Sam inquired facetiously.

Nehru, in effect, replied:

"What else is there?"

Mayor Yorty was entrusted with the job of introducing Nehru at a banquet in Beverly Hills. As they sat together waiting for the program to begin Sam explained that he was not mayor in the particular area where the banquet was being held. To illustrate the point he drew a little sketch on the menu, showing Beverly Hills as a separate city completely surrounded by Los Angeles territory.

"Oh, an enclave!" commented Nehru.

And as a result Sam has called Beverly Hills "the enclave" ever since.

An insight into momentous events in history sometimes is given by visitors whose positions at times of world crisis made their actions of universal importance. Lord Mountbatten who, with General Douglas MacArthur, was engaged in military maneuvers of the greatest significance in the Pacific during World War II described to Sam on a visit in Los Angeles the way history might have been different in the area which has become the scene of the Viet Nam war. It was the firm determination of Lord Mountbatten to occupy the entire region with the troops he had available. In this he was supported by Prime Minister Churchill. But, as the story goes, President Roosevelt insisted upon the northern portion being turned over to Generalissimo Chiang Kai-shek. Chiang was unable to administer the area and left a vacuum for the Communists. This ultimately resulted in the present political complexion of North Viet Nam, and its war against South Viet Nam.

During the visit of Princess Margaret and her husband, the Princess suffered a severe attack of laryngitis in Los Angeles. Despite her discomfort the Princess insisted on continuing her round of activities. One event was an entertainment featuring Bob Hope and Polly Bergen. Mayor Yorty was seated next to the Princess and noticed that she apparently felt worse and worse as the evening progressed. Sam slipped away and asked Hope and Miss Bergen whether they would mind if the Princess, due to illness, were to leave.

"Of course not," they responded.

Sam relayed this word to the Princess but she, with typical British pluck, insisted on remaining to the end so as not to seem to slight the performers.

An indication that the mayor's foreign trips and his activities among the various racial groups in Los Angeles have won an extraordinary position for him in the regard of foreign representatives is contained in an unusual citation. It is a beautifully illuminated parchment bearing the signatures of the Consuls or Consuls General of forty-seven countries, awarded to the mayor in special ceremonies on January 24, 1963. It hangs in a place of honor in Sam Yorty's inner office at the City Hall.

He also has received numerous decorations from individual countries, including high awards from Spain, France and Finland.

Mayor Yorty's enthusiasm and understanding leave an indelible imprint upon the people he encounters in foreign countries. I personally was made aware of this on the island of Mallorca, Spain. My wife and I had gone to visit Petra, the tiny village on Mallorca where Father Junipero Serra the Franciscan founder of California was born in 1713. Sam, Chief Justice Warren, Lieutenant Governor Anderson, and the other notables had been there a short time before on their good-will mission marking the 250th anniversary of Father Serra's birth.

Amid the hospitable reception we were given in Palma, Mallorca, and in Petra by the respective mayors and other leading citizens, we were bombarded with one question. Nobody ever mentioned the Chief Justice or the Lieutenant Governor, but each one said with obvious sincerity:

"When is Sam coming back?"

CHAPTER XXI

From harmony, from heavenly harmony,
This universal frame began.

JOHN DRYDEN

Distressing dissonance was the overwhelming theme of Los Angeles' musical life when Sam Yorty took up the political baton as mayor.

Brahms and Beethoven had been superseded by Brawls and Bellicosity. A Music Center, which in its original intent was to become a leavening cultural influence spreading mellowness and civic unity, had succeeded in stirring up one of the most far-reaching and rancorous battles in the history of Southern California.

The Music Center as a conscious effort to awaken the latent artistic sense of Los Angeles encountered from the start a strange and thwarting obstacle.

Perhaps the outstanding trait of the big, awkward, gawky city trying to grow up and not quite knowing how, had been its inferiority complex in regard to its cultural assets. It had acted as if it were ashamed to suggest it had any. Organizations devoted to promoting the area's climactic and recreational advantages seemingly had shied away from featuring the artistic and mentally stimulating aspects of the region. Orange blossoms and factory sites had had precedence.

Even amid this reticence, though, Los Angeles' residents in recent years had begun to be aware of some of their hitherto-unsuspected cultural attributes because of the interest shown in them by sophisticated visitors. People had come from all over the world to see things entirely apart from Hollywood and Disneyland. A number of the attractions thus brought to light had developed almost unnoticed by the Southern California population, intent upon its own pursuits and more involved with smog, traffic snarls on the freeways, World Series prospects, the antics of film and TV personalities than with "arty" subjects.

The Music Center movement was compelled to combat this indifference of the ordinary citizen manifesting itself in the cultural realm in the same way it had been shown in political affairs, because of the out-of-state origins of so many residents. Its sponsors needed not only to seek to arouse enthusiasm for their own project but also to bring into focus, as a matter of local pride, the outstanding cultural advantages of Southern California, in order to place the Music Center in the position of rounding out a pattern.

This list was a long one. Yet rarely was it viewed as a homogeneous whole, as a unit. The fact of the geographic spread of Southern California was, of course, a factor in this lack of cohesion. Institutions or events associated with a particular locality for a number of years, or decades, were regarded as isolated, not a part of the general picture. Yet as freeways materialized, as the press of population pushed community boundaries together, the metropolitan region actually was becoming, whether it liked it or not, an inseparable unit. Its institutions, in a sense, became common property by proximity and ease of access.

No longer, for instance, was the Henry E. Huntington Library and Art Gallery in San Marino an austere and esoteric gathering place of a few whispering visitors from afar for a few hours in the afternoon. It was recognized as a unique research center for literary delvers and a pulsating working place for students and scholars, while its treasures from Gutenberg Bibles to "The Blue Boy" were viewed by constantly growing throngs of "home folks" as well as tourists.

Scholars—even those from England—discovered that the Huntington Library was the only place they could find some reference material relating to their own country. A. L. Rowse, the biographer of Shakespeare, became a research fellow at the Huntington to pursue his definitive studies on the Shakespeare Sonnets because he could not find the material anywhere else.

Some gathering places such as the Hollywood Bowl were known internationally. Yet even this celebrated home of musical treats had been so neglected by Los Angeles itself that it became necessary for a rehabilitation group headed by Mrs. Norman Chandler to embark in the 1950s on a full-scale campaign to reinvigorate the Bowl. This was accomplished so successfully that Mrs. Chandler was accorded many honors by the city and county for her leadership.

Gradually too around the perimeter of Los Angeles other cultural spots gained local recognition but were never welded into any unified regional pattern. At Claremont Colleges the splendid facilities provided by Bridges' Auditorium drew audiences from a wide area. Redlands' Bowl with its encouragement of local talent emerged as the cradle of starring national talent. The Ramona Pageant, an Indian play by Garnet Holme based on the novel by Helen Hunt Jackson, persisted year after year in its beautiful rocky amphitheater facing Mount San Jacinto at Hemet-San Jacinto, and became an institution itself. Close to the Hollywood Bowl in a hillside theater the Pilgrimage Play, California's version of Oberammergau, earned its own niche with visitors who came back year after year to see its depiction of the story of the Christ. At Laguna Beach an event which had started as a purely local presentation in the "Art Colony" had become internationally celebrated as the "Living Pictures" of the Laguna Art Festival. At Santa Ana the spirit of early California's pastoral era was depicted at the Charles Bowers Memorial Museum. Similarly at Bloomington in San Bernardino County the County Museum caught the spirit of a region which had done much to shape the future of Southern California in its formative years.

In Los Angeles itself some institutions which had been ignored or taken for granted began to assume larger and larger roles in the cultural life of all of Southern California. At the Los Angeles County Museum in Exposition Park, scientists and visitors were privileged to view the greatest array of reconstructed dinosaurs, sabre-toothed tigers, mammoths, and other creatures of past geologic ages due to the fossils yielded by the La Brea tar pits. At the Southwest Museum regional history was evoking an unprecedented picture of aboriginal life and art in the great semi-arid region making up the "Southwest" including part of Mexico. The Casa Adobe, a replica of an early Spanish dwelling, was used by the museum as an adjunct for the entertainment of notable visitors in a traditional atmosphere.

Gaining increasingly greater international attention were the performances of Shakespeare plays during the annual summer festival at the Globe Theater in San Diego. This permanent repertory company with guest stars of the first magnitude presented its offerings in the only authentic replica of the Globe Theater of Shakespeare's day. Critics universally agreed that the plays ranked with those given at the Old Vic in London and at Stratford-upon-Avon itself. Each year the Globe exerted its influence upon an ever-widening circle so that it became necessary to obtain the coveted tickets months in advance.

A recognition for the need for better facilities for the display of masterpieces both traditional and contemporary resulted in the building of the new Art Museum at Hancock Park on Wilshire Boulevard, under the leadership of Edward Carter and many civic-minded individuals.

It had been a rather sore point for Los Angeles for many years that it had no grand opera of its own and had to depend upon San Francisco to send down a company for the "season" in the south. Despite this ignominy, the city could boast of its Philharmonic Orchestra under the baton of such conductors as Otto Klemperer. Of course, too, it was the home of numerous composers whose work in musical comedy or the films had won them international acclaim.

Pre-eminent for many years in the musical comedy field has been Meredith Willson whose *Music Man* and *Unsinkable Molly Brown* merely confirmed the high opinion of his abilities formed by Southern Californians, and dating back to his "Capistrano Suite" of a generation ago.

In motion pictures the talent of composers in the Los Angeles area had been demonstrated all over the globe in compositions by Dimitri Tiomkin, Miklos Rosza, Henry Mancini, Morton Gould, David Rose, Alex North, and others.

Despite the achievements of its orchestra and individual composers, Los Angeles still felt the need for a unifying factor in its musical life such as would be provided by a Music Center.

Even when the Music Center campaign began, however, it went through harrowing difficulties not only of indifference, but of hostility.

In the early summer of 1961 just as Sam took his oath of office the Music Center situation was at a precarious climax due to a citizens suit and lingering rancors. So deep were the wounds of the respective factions in the Music Center fight that the entire project seemed in danger of collapsing.

Only two persons appeared capable of warding off this ultimate ignominy for the community, and they were at opposite political poles in a situation aggravated by the recent bitter mayoralty campaign. One was Mrs. Norman (Buff) Chandler, wife of the president of the Times-Mirror Company, and mother of Otis Chandler, publisher of the *Times,* and the indefatigable principal proponent of a Music Center in downtown Los Angeles. The other was Sam himself, with his newly acquired position and prestige and his innate love of music and abiding ambition to make Los Angeles the cultural envy of the world.

The question was how these two could possibly get together in any common pursuit.

Opposition of the *Times* to Yorty in the mayoralty race had been deep, unrelenting, and bitter. Mrs. Chandler's active participation in the conduct of the *Times* was so well known that most well-wishers of the Music Center considered it impossible that Sam could forgive and forget within any discernible future. Yet she was by far the outstanding figure in support of the Music Center and the mayor's genuine and vigorous backing was, of course, an indispensable necessity for its success even though it was nominally a county project in cooperation with a citizens group.

Under these circumstances, political realists were ready to write off the Music Center as a lost cause.

Reason for their gloom was to be found not only in the apparent present impasse but also in the nature of the struggle which had surrounded the original attempts to create a Music Center. For many years Los Angeles had been compelled to depend upon the old Philharmonic Auditorium at 5th and Olive streets and on the Shrine Auditorium on Jefferson Boulevard, for its concerts, light operas, and grand opera productions. Neither was adequate in the middle of the twentieth century for a metropolis of seven million persons within easy driving distance of downtown Los Angeles.

The Hollywood Bowl and some smaller outdoor amphitheaters filled their own spheres but were not in the Music Center category. The Greek Theater in Los Angeles' Griffith Park was adequate only for Spanish dance troupes, solo recitals and some other productions because of the limitation of seating capacity.

Mrs. Chandler set forth in the mid-1950s to seek support for a genuine Music Center after her successful effort to reactivate and popularize the Hollywood Bowl. This time seemed propitious for launching a Music Center endeavor. The sum involved, however, was so large—around $10,000,000 even at that time for the building —that it seemed imperative to have the cooperation of some governmental unit in the project. It was not strictly for the City of Los

Angeles so the County Board of Supervisors was approached to see whether a working arrangement with a citizens group could be achieved.

Years of futile negotiation ensued. Site and multiple-use surveys were carried out and outside legal opinions were obtained on methods of procedure and financing. Tangles developed on the lengths to which the county should go with the taxpayers' money in the contracts with the private group. County Counsel Harold W. Kennedy became aware of weaknesses in the legal situation and warned of necessary revisions if the plan were to succeed. Some of these changes were not made. As a result, an almost-impossible snarl developed.

At this juncture some outlying newspapers turned their fire on the proposed Music Center and its proposed location in downtown Los Angeles. The *Times* continued its support but eventually the impasse became so hopeless that the private group abandoned its efforts.

A totally new start was necessary if a Music Center were to become a reality. After a breath-catching period, a new campaign was valiantly begun by Mrs. Chandler and a few others who remained undiscouraged by the first failure. The community leaders who took the initiative in carrying on the Music Center effort and in subsequent efforts and donations in its behalf included Mrs. Henry Salvatori, Mrs. George S. Behrendt, Charles Ducommun, Mark Taper, Howard Ahmanson, Mr. Carter, County Counsel Kennedy who performed valiant service throughout, and many others.

This time the base was broadened so that citizen participation would be much greater and the county's role would be, properly, that of an underwriting agent with adequate guarantees to safeguard the eventual pay out.

Even so, with this new approach, great obstacles had developed by the summer of 1961 when Sam Yorty was taking office, and it appeared the entire project was in jeopardy. Mrs. Chandler was fully aware of these difficulties and their importance.

In the complicated legal situation, a test suit had been started to compel Gordon T. Nesvig, Clerk of the County Board of Supervisors, on behalf of the county, the Music Center Lease Company and the Music Center Operating Company to sign papers for the calling of bids for the construction of the $23,000,000 project. A surprise element was injected when a San Francisco lawyer, Harold E. Rogers, Jr., representing Alameda County taxpayers in similar litigation was given permission by Superior Judge Gordon L. Files to appear as a friend of the court. John A. Gay, a Woodland Hills engineer, asked permission to intervene in the case, asserting that taxpayers had been denied the right to challenge the project. He also was represented by a San Francisco attorney, Harlow Rotert.

These rather puzzling developments roused public apprehension over the whole Music Center undertaking, particularly in view of the acrimony displayed in the recent years over the prior project.

Under the stress of these conditions, Mrs. Chandler as the one person most qualified to deal with the situation began to confer with Mayor Yorty. Constraint might have been expected on both sides in view of the bitter feeling engendered by the recent primary. But Mrs. Chandler overcame any qualms about going to Yorty, and Yorty on his part was magnanimous in receiving her cordially. They sat down to talk over something which was of vital importance to the community and in the minds of both transcended passing political differences.

The situation was difficult in several respects. One was that Attorney Phil Silver who had been counsel for Yorty in the $2,200,000 libel action by Yorty against Poulson during the mayoralty campaign now was appearing against the proposed contract between the county and Music Center operating groups.

"I found Mayor Yorty extremely co-operative and fully in accord with our plans for proceeding with the Music Center," Mrs. Chandler said afterward. "Immediately after our first meeting he made it possible for me to confer with friends of his who could assist in trying to remove some of the obstacles. I went to numerous conferences with these emissaries of the mayor and we discussed every phase of the Music Center problem. When it was finally solved and the path was clear for us to proceed I felt that Mayor Yorty deserved tremendous credit for his attitude and his unfailing assistance in helping us reach the goal we all wanted."

The climax came on August 16, 1961.

Mayor Yorty personally accompanied Attorney Phil Silver to court. There, in the presence of the mayor and to the astonishment of some of the on-lookers, Attorney Silver withdrew his opposition to the lease-back financing method which was the crux of the difficulty. He explained he was taking this action at the request of Mayor Yorty.

Under the terms of the decision issued by Judge Files the financing and construction arrangements of the Music Center were upheld as valid. The Supervisors immediately moved by means of instructions to Clerk Nesvig for bids to open November 28, 1961, for the Music Center including a three-building complex made up of the 3250-seat Pavilion, a 2100-seat center theater, a 750-seat Mark Taper Forum and a 2000 car underground garage in the two-block site bounded by First, Hope, and Temple streets and Grand Avenue.

An enormous amount of work remained to be done, however, in raising millions of dollars by subscription to carry out the private contribution phase of the project. It was in this endeavor that Mrs. Chandler manifested an indomitable spirit and extraordinary talent and imagination. She succeeded in arousing the pride of the community in the prospective Music Center to such an extent that with her leadership the necessary funds were raised, despite pessimism of some critics.

*　*　*

Within three years the Music Center was opened with an entire week of performances from December 6 through December 12, 1964. The public was dazzled at that time by the magnificence of the concept which had been carried out under the direction of Architect Welton Becket, FAIA.

"Since it is meant to become a living cultural symbol for future decades, the Pavilion grew to be a contemporary expression of classical architecture," said Becket. "Since the building would be seen from all sides, we did not wish to turn our back on any part of the city. We thus designed the main building as a Pavilion which means that all sides are basically equal. The exterior of the Pavilion is designed with gracefully curving sides directly expressing the functional curve of the auditorium within. The columns which continue around the structure stand free of the building, extending from the plaza level to a soffit beneath the roof overhang. In this way they provide a covered promenade around the building on the mall level and an upper promenade leading off the Grand Hall.

"The Pavilion had to fulfill the function of three major halls—each with its own characteristics. Traditionally a symphony orchestra requires a concert hall with perfect natural acoustics. Grand opera requires a tremendous stage and as large a house as good sight lines permit. Light opera, ballet, and similar presentations require a more intimate type of theater with amplified sound system. Our most precarious task was to design a single auditorium which would combine these three different houses into one hall acceptable to all."

During the week of opening performances Mrs. Chandler put into words her own feelings in regard to the Music Center.

"The Music Center is many things to many people. To some it represents a magnificent addition to our Civic Center, a bright new jewel in the diadem of a great city," she wrote. "To others it heralds a brilliant era in the cultural life of the West with facilities for presentation of the performing arts unexcelled anywhere in the world. To others it is especially significant as a place where exciting new talent—in Music, Drama, Dance—will find expression and fulfillment. It is these things and more. To me the Music Center is important as a challenge—a challenge to the intelligence, imagination and taste of our children and their children and, hopefully, to their children. In a world more immediately imperiled by mediocrity than by intercontinental missiles, the Music Center will stand forever as a symbol of what creative man can accomplish when he sets high his standards and has vision far beyond our present horizons."

The Pavilion was given the name "Dorothy Chandler Pavilion" in recognition of Mrs. Chandler's great civic service in bringing the Music Center to reality.

Mrs. Chandler and Mayor Yorty among the thousands of eager musical enthusiasts at the premiere of the new Music Center with Jascha Heifetz as soloist and Zubin Mehta as conductor could feel a mutual sense of accomplishment. They along with hundreds of other dedicated workers had helped turn dissonance into harmony.

CHAPTER XXII

Men are not superior by the accidents of race or color.

ROBERT G. INGERSOLL

Slightly more than two months after his inauguration Mayor Yorty found himself embroiled publicly in a birthday party fight which for years had been swept under the municipal rug each September 4, anniversary of the founding of Los Angeles. It involved the old persistent controversy over the role of Negroes in the founding of the pueblo of Los Angeles. This time—exactly 180 years later—it was appearing in such explosive form that it could not be ignored. Mayor Sam knew that from a conscientious standpoint he must take sides. He did.

Some Negro leaders, emboldened by the mounting tide of civil rights demonstrations, were demanding from the birthday celebration committee a prominent role in the annual birthday celebration and dinner at the Plaza, normally participated in almost exclusively by descendants of the early Spanish and Mexican families associated with the city's beginnings, and by the historical societies. In 1961 the demands by the Negroes to the celebration group were intensified.

Mayor Yorty said later he did not recall any such demands being made to him but he added that he felt it was the just due of the Negroes to be recognized fully in the celebration so that it might truly reflect the ancestry of the founders. The Negroes themselves said that many of the founders were indeed Negroes and that any birthday observance without their active participation would be an affront and a travesty. Some went so far as to threaten to picket the entire proceedings if they were slighted.

The mayor earlier in the year had been elected in part because of his strong stand for greater recognition of minorities in the city, both Negro and Mexican-American. He had carried out his promises by naming numerous representatives of each to his own staff and to municipal commissions. Now he was confronted with the difficult task of deciding between the two groups who, in this instance, were arrayed against each other. He checked the evidence again before taking his stand.

It was conflicting. The settlers of Los Angeles had been recruited in the northern Mexican States of Sonora and Sinaloa in 1781— many in the charming silver city of Alamos, Sonora—and had been escorted to San Gabriel Mission in Alta California. This was seven miles or so from the site of the prospective pueblo. On the appointed day the 46 persons making up the group of "founders," many of them children, walked from San Gabriel to the spot near the present Plaza where the future city had its center. There they were left by the Spanish soldiers from the Mission.

Exactly who were they?

Their names and descriptions are known due to the Spanish passion for keeping records. But what is the proper interpretation of some of the words? The nuances, the exactitudes?

Many of the adult settlers were identified by Hubert Howe Bancroft, the pre-eminent historian of California, in his translation of eighteenth-century Spanish documents as "Negroes" or mulattoes. Whether this was due to confusion in regard to the exact translation of the Spanish word "negro," meaning "dark" or "black," as applied to the settlers has never been settled. Some modern historians and civic leaders have countered with the assertion that "negro" merely was used in Spanish terminology to identify persons of dark complexion, and carried no connotation of African blood lines. Others cling just as persistently to the viewpoint that they were in actuality African Negroes.

Recognized authorities in their own realms have differed diametrically on the point.

Charles F. Lummis, first City Editor of the Los Angeles *Times*, historian, Los Angeles City Librarian, and the leading spirit in the founding of the Southwest Museum more than half a century ago, was characteristically vigorous in his support of the theory that the pobladores or founders of Los Angeles included a considerable percentage of Negroes in the modern sense. In a specific exposition on the subject in the Los Angeles *Times*, Sunday, April 24, 1927, Lummis listed the Los Angeles founders as: 2 Spaniards with Indian wives; 4 Indian men, 3 of whom had Indian wives and the fourth a mulatto wife; 2 Negroes, each with a mulatto wife; 2 mulattoes with mulatto wives; 1 "Chino"—a mixed breed from Mexico, not a Chinese.

Other authorities have maintained that it is a mistake to attribute African origin to the pobladores. They contend that contemporary Spanish usage in the 1781 period definitely rules out any African connotation and lays stress strictly on the complexion of the various settlers.

A strong adherent of the Lummis viewpoint is Thomas Workman Temple II of San Gabriel. Temple who has spent many years in genealogical and historical research declares that his inquiries have shown why the African strain was so prominent among settlers. When they were recruited in Alamos they were, he contends, either recently freed slaves who had worked in the mines or the relatives of slaves who were willing to take the gamble of "a new life in a new land."

"The mine owners and other well-to-do Spaniards and Spanish-Indian mixtures were well established and 'had it made' so why should they have been tempted to go traipsing off into the wilds of Alta California?" he inquires. "Only the very poorest people, including some Negroes, had nothing to lose and were willing to take a chance in the San Gabriel area. Even they had to be virtually conscripted."

After re-evaluating all the opinions, Mayor Yorty—realizing fully the unpleasant eventualities no matter what he did—came out unequivocally for the Negro position in the 1961 birthday party controversy. His characteristic candor led him to a statement of what he considered to be fair and just. He said that unless the Negroes were granted the full right of participation and were given recognition as equal partners in the founding, he would be compelled to cancel official civic connection with the birthday celebration.

This ultimatum by the mayor created a virtual impasse. Any plans for a re-enactment of the city's founding at the banquet to be held in an old winery in Olvera Street—later the location of the Latin-American Trade Center—were hampered. Threats of picketing of the celebration by the Negroes were circulated.

Mayor Sam stood firm. On the evening of the birthday banquet a few Negroes did hand out leaflets and one or two tried to get into the winery dinner-room uninvited. But the enactment of the founding was merely the arrival of a horseman depicting Gov. de

Neve who was credited with starting the pueblo. No real violence occurred.

Mayor Yorty's strong stand in behalf of the Negroes on this occasion enhanced his reputation as a genuine champion of their rights. When the Watts riots occurred the mayor's long record of friendship for the Negroes placed him in a strong position to take the stand he did in behalf of law enforcement, all responsible Negroes recognizing that he was following his basic beliefs to seek uniform justice for all.

CHAPTER XXIII

Beware
Of entrance to a quarrel; but, being in,
Bear't that the opposed may beware of thee.

Hamlet
SHAKESPEARE

In one major respect, the two principal antagonists in Los Angeles most spectacular running political feud of recent years resembled each other closely. Each was a prodigy in politics. Sam Yorty was twenty-seven when he was elected to the Legislature in 1936. Rosalind Wiener (later Mrs. Eugene Wyman) was twenty-two when she was elected to the Los Angeles City Council in 1953. Sam Yorty, at the time she took office, was serving his second term in Congress, and was forty-four, exactly twice her age. Neither at the time had any inkling, of course, of the controversies in which they would be involved when Sam Yorty became Mayor of Los Angeles almost a decade hence.

Miss Wiener's victory in the 5th District made her the youngest person ever elected to the City Council in Los Angeles and the first woman since 1915 when Estelle Lawton Lindsey served. She was barely out of college when she began her legislative career.

By a strange quirk of fate Sam Yorty was indirectly responsible for Rosalind Wiener's election to the Los Angeles City Council. "Roz" had shown a remarkable aptitude for politics while attending the University of Southern California. She had been a supporter of Representative Yorty because the 5th councilmanic district was in Yorty's 14th Congressional District. It was quite natural that "Roz" should become acquainted with Eleanor Chambers who was Sam's Congressional field respresentative in Los Angeles.

Mrs. Chambers for a long time had wanted to see a woman elected to the Los Angeles City Council, and in fact she herself in her only bid for office had run unsuccessfully for a council seat a number of years before. In the enthusiastic and talented young Rosalind Wiener Mrs. Chambers saw a fine potential candidate for the council. She suggested that Rosalind enter the contest in the 5th District. Rosalind was intrigued by the prospect and after consultation with her family did decide to run.

She went around from door to door during the campaign, vivaciously handing out little cakes of soap "for cleaning up the City Hall." Her persuasiveness and ability to present issues clearly began to win supporters from the start. With the advice and help of Mrs. Chambers, Rosalind Wiener did win.

The stage thus was set, all unwittingly for the Yorty-Wyman feud of the future.

In the City Council Rosalind continued to manifest the enthusiasm and aggressiveness which had marked her campaign efforts. She was one of the leaders in the movement which resulted in the bringing of the Brooklyn Dodgers to Los Angeles in the late 1950s. This effort, in fact, was so energetic that opponents of the plan to provide a site for Walter O'Malley's team in Chavez Ravine near downtown Los Angeles accused her of being part of a municipal "give away" program. The Dodgers won out, and "Roz" Wyman as she was known was acclaimed by baseball fans for her part in bringing them to Los Angeles.

"Roz" at first was the political pet of her district. She was pretty, enthusiastic, imaginative; with an ebullience that won votes.

Following hard work in the City Council Mrs. Wyman who was married not long after her election won, later on, a coveted place in the "Women of the Year" selections by the Los Angeles *Times*.

Up to the time Sam Yorty became mayor in 1961, he and the Wymans were friends through political activities in the Democratic party. Eugene Wyman, a young attorney, worked well as a political teammate with his wife. The Wymans obviously were encouraged in their political ambitions by becoming the "darlings" of the ultra-liberal wing of the Democratic party and were inspired to aim at state and national objectives as well as the narrower goals within the purview of Mrs. Wyman as a councilwoman. These aspirations, of course, involved working intimately with the Democratic structure within the state. This in turn meant that the currents and cross-currents involving Sam Yorty, a perennial figure in California politics, necessarily were encountered by the Wymans. The Wymans from their associations and procedures undoubtedly leaned further left of center than did Sam Yorty. This inevitably meant collisions between their respective political forces. From this larger arena of state politics by the time Sam became mayor the tensions had filtered down to the local level. Hardly had Sam entered office before a breach began to develop.

The mayor was fully aware of the potential conflicts looming ahead.

"My trouble with Rosalind Wyman and her husband Eugene Wyman came about for a very simple reason," Mayor Yorty explains from his standpoint. "They had been very close to Mayor Poulson and were used to having their way in everything. My wife and I had known the Wymans socially and in Democratic party affairs. But when I went in as mayor the Wymans found they could not throw their weight around as they had with Poulson. This set the stage right away for trouble. I saw it shaping up and tried to ward off one phase of the whole thing.

"The Wymans' loss of influence led them almost immediately to efforts to sabotage me. As this was beginning to happen Eugene Wyman was making every effort to become Chairman of the Democratic State Central Committee.

"I told Governor Pat Brown, 'I don't think Wyman ought to be State Chairman. If you name him it's going to cause trouble between you and me.'

"Brown did name him and it did cause trouble. I just didn't approve of the type of operation used by Wyman, but he was an effective money raiser for Brown. I think Brown by now has realized his mistake and wishes he could change it but it's too late.

"Wyman even tried to cause trouble between President Johnson and me. At a big dinner here Wyman was in charge of the arrangements and he failed to invite me, apparently to cause as much embarrassment as possible. Of course the whole thing got in the newspapers and was blown up into a storm.

"Later when I saw LBJ at the White House the subject came up and he said to me:

"'When I come to your city I want you right there.'"

The differences between the new mayor and the Wymans soon came to public notice, although during the first few days of his regime Yorty seemed inclined to "go along" on some of Councilwoman Wyman's proposals. This included notably a suggestion she made for the abolition by charter amendment of all boards and commissions and their replacement with administrative officers appointed by the mayor and approved by the council. This change never materialized. The initial discord among city councilmen actually revolved more around hurt feelings over internal reorganization than any outright clashes between the mayor and the Wymans. Mrs. Wyman had supported John S. Gibson, Jr., as Council President, but Harold A. Henry was chosen in his place. In the subsequent reshuffling Mrs. Wyman indicated she felt she had been slighted and declared angrily in regard to her appointments on committees, "I'm sure if they could have found some worse committees I'd have been named to them."

In the midst of mounting political fires in the fall of 1961 Los Angeles and Mrs. Wyman's councilmanic district in particular were staggered by the devastating Bel Air fire in the real, and not the figurative, sense. This catastrophe placed heavy burdens on the city in the wake of the suffering and losses caused by the sweep of the flames which razed many homes and some of the most beautiful building lot property in the area. Mayor Yorty and the City Council immediately were confronted with serious problems involving rehabilitation, reseeding of denuded acreage and assistance for homeowners who had lost their houses in the blaze. As soon as some of these pressing matters had been resolved, however, the struggle and the acrimony in the council resumed.

Oil—distinctly not the kind used for pouring on troubled waters —stirred a fierce exchange. This was the same oil under the sea at Los Angeles Harbor which had figured in the 1961 campaign. The 1956 lease for prospective oil development there had drawn the criticism of Mayor Yorty because of the alleged lack of proper competitive bidding.

In explaining how he feels such public matters should be handled, Mayor Yorty said:

"Although oil was first discovered in Los Angeles Harbor Department properties in 1936, no positive action was taken fully to explore the outer ocean area under Harbor control until the Board of Harbor Commissioners, during this administration, authorized seismic surveys to test the existence of a potentially productive oil field and followed through to seek qualified bidders after reports indicated that there was an excellent possibility of a considerable oil pool in the Outer Harbor area involved.

"Now it should be understood that we are talking about property north of and inside the breakwater which is under Harbor Department control. I want to make this distinction because I was never pleased with the lease entered into between the city and the Los Angeles Harbor Oil Development Company in 1956 for proposed development of oil outside the breakwater in ocean area under the control of the City of Los Angeles but not under the Harbor Department.

"This lease was awarded on the basis of an application to the council from the Los Angeles Harbor Oil Development Company, a paper corporation, over the protest of some established oil companies who alleged that they were given no chance to bid or make an offer for this lease.

"I determined that I would do everything in my power to prevent a repetition of a similar incident and made my position quite clear on the matter.

"The Harbor Commission of this administration moved rapidly ahead to authorize seismic surveys and to analyze the data made available. I carefully chose the most practical approach to oil development in the area and then proposed a drilling plan which was approved by the California State Lands Commission in September 1964.

"Ample notice to potential bidders was assured. The Board published their resolution of intent to lease the land for oil prospecting for four weeks. Scores of potential bidders were sent copies of the proposed contract.

"I was present at the public meeting on December 9, 1964, when five responsible bids were opened and an award was made on the joint bid of Standard Oil Company of California and Pauley Petroleum, Inc., who offered an amount equal to slightly in excess of 75 percent of net proceeds in addition to a basic royalty of 16 and two-thirds percent of the gross proceeds from the venture.

"This is a very satisfactory arrangement from the standpoint of the City of Los Angeles and I invite a comparison of the manner in which this case was entered into and the manner in which the LAHODCO lease was carried off during the former administration.

"The current Harbor Department lease, accomplished in the light of full publicity with an intensive effort to secure qualified bidders so that Los Angeles citizens may receive the benefit of the best possible offer illustrates the way I think City business should be contracted."

During this fight over the Harbor Oil Development Company lease the mayor's feud with Mrs. Wyman began to assume more dramatic proportions. The mayor accused Councilman L. E. Timberlake of being the "architect" of the 1956 lease, which the mayor termed "a give away." Immediately Mrs. Wyman accused Mayor Yorty of indulging in "character assassination."

"I resent very much the personal attack on a member of our council," said Mrs. Wyman.

In the midst of these purely local controversies the nation was shocked on November 22, 1963, by the assassination of President Kennedy in Dallas. For the moment all antagonisms were forgotten in the mutual feeling of horror and revulsion at the assassination. Even this event, however, was translated within a month into another clash between mayor and the council. The City Council arranged a memorial service for the late President at the City Hall. Mrs. Wyman was chairman of the event. The invitation to the mayor asked him to be a platform guest. This form of invitation stirred Sam Yorty to such an extent that he sent Mrs. Wyman a letter saying:

"I consider it insulting for you to inform the mayor that he can be a 'platform guest' at such a civic ceremony as a memorial to our deceased President instead of following accepted protocol. I am amazed that you will carry your petty politics to such extremes. The ceremony should be above such politics in view of its purpose. Is there no limit to your lack of respect for normal courtesy and protocol?"

Mrs. Wyman immediately replied:

"I am physically sick that the mayor would use this occasion to launch another attack on members of the City Council who have put this ceremony together."

Exchanges of this kind did not add to the stature of either the mayor's office or the council. To Sam it was obvious the stalemate on many important matters was hurting him with the people even though, under the charter's restrictions, he was powerless to take positive action to bring definitive results. He decided he must gain new supporters in the council to make the carrying out of his program possible. The mayor consequently began in the 1963 campaign supporting a slate of candidates against councilmen who had consistently opposed him. As the climax to the campaign Mrs.

Wyman charged that the mayor's forces would spend at least $50,000 in the last few days before the election.

"What favors, if any, have been promised?" Mrs. Wyman asked. "The stakes must be higher than any of us have ever realized if in one week he can spend this much money."

She professed to be "shocked" by the mayor's announced intention to oppose the re-election of certain councilmen on Monday night TV programs prior to the election.

"I know he wants a rubber-stamp council," she said, "but I didn't know that anyone would go to such lengths to get one."

So bitter had become the feelings of the antagonists that by the time of the April primary the monthly luncheons which had been held by the mayor and the councilmen were cancelled. During the final days of the campaign following the April primary and leading up to the general election the Yorty forces concentrated their fire principally on Lemoyne Blanchard and Joe Hollingsworth.

In the showdown vote Mayor Yorty gained only two victories when his supporters Tom Bradley and James B. Potter, Jr., succeeded in unseating the incumbents Hollingsworth and Blanchard, with other returns more or less indecisive. Then, because the mayor obviously had failed to score any sort of decisive victory the council took its revenge. It held a secret caucus and elected Timberlake president and Mrs. Wyman president pro-tempore.

Amid the reorganization ceremonies it became necessary for Mayor Yorty to enter the council chambers and "congratulate" his inveterate foes, Timberlake and Mrs. Wyman.

President Timberlake did not hesitate to fire a volley at the mayor:

"Those who would attempt to divide us should recognize that they have a losing battle on their hands. We have not fully used the entire powers given to us by the City Charter."

Not to be outdone Sam immediately replied pointedly:

"We must remember the powers granted by the people can also be taken away by the people."

Then as an additional barb Yorty said in regard to the departure of his five field secretaries who had been forced out the day before by the elimination by the council of their salaries from the budget:

"I'm surprised that you could find anybody in my office to deliver your message to because you have stripped it of employees."

On this querulous note the second half of the mayor's first term began.

186

* * *

    The election of the new councilmen in 1963 provided an object-lesson for Los Angeles citizens. A pattern of behavior began to emerge amid the clamor of the conflicts which still continued despite the new line-ups. The mayor was pressing ahead below the surface for major objectives of his administration which had been gradually shaping during the first two tempestuous years of his regime. It appeared that perhaps little had been accomplished, yet many undertakings were beginning to take some form.

    Mayor Yorty's insistence on cooperation among department heads and greater liaison between the various commissions had begun to have its leavening effect. The fact that various commissioners and department heads were becoming acquainted with city government as a whole rather than with merely one small facet as in the past, was in itself a major gain. At first it was not at all spectacular. Still, it was a phenomenon which never before had been observed in City Hall government in Los Angeles.

    The mayor was intensifying his campaign against spot zoning in residential areas, an evil which he felt had been carried to extremes by persons who were ready to go into any area no matter what the consequences merely to make money with shopping centers or similar enterprises. He was stepping up his efforts for consolidation of the City and County Health Departments in the interest of better administration. He was making great attempts to bring about the creation of a Civic Auditorium and Convention Center, one of the matters which he felt to be of primary importance for the city. He had been urging a law for the registration of municipal lobbyists and their control. He was watching with appreciation the progress of the Music Center project which had been carried forward with his help. He was striving mightily to hold down city taxes on real property.

    In order to further all these aims the mayor began peace overtures with the council a couple of months after the election. He announced that he would resume the monthly luncheons which had been interrupted in the heat of the campaign. He also prepared to meet privately with Council President Timberlake and in fact commended him for taking a more moderate stand. The mayor said Timberlake had stopped "the long indignation sessions" in the council where attacks were made against the mayor's office. But the underlying animosity could not be bridged so easily even in the midst of the "peace" negotiations. The mayor planned a trip to Germany so that it would coincide with a schedule under which Council President Timberlake would be in the city all the time. This was to prevent Mrs. Wyman, the president pro-tem, from becoming mayor as she would do under the city's charter if the mayor and the president of the City Council both were out of town at once.

"I don't want to be gone when Mrs. Wyman could be in the driver's seat," the mayor candidly admitted.

Strangely enough, though, by November 9, 1963, this very contingency had arisen. Sam and Betty Yorty flew down to Baja California to the little fishing village of Mulege on the Gulf of California for a few days rest. President Timberlake became acting mayor, but he then went to Hemet for a four-day vacation. This left Rosalind Wyman as the first woman Mayor of Los Angeles in its history.

Even prior to this occurrence, however, the "war" between the mayor and the council had flared anew, again this time on the question of municipal lobbyists. The mayor had been urging for some time an ordinance curbing lobbying activities, one proposed ordinance before the council had been described as virtually meaningless because there were wholesale exemptions. Mrs. Wyman then introduced a stronger measure and challenged the mayor to support it. The strong law was exactly what Sam Yorty wanted so he of course gave his support to it.

"If the Wyman-Rundberg team has decided in response to public opinion that it's willing to back a really effective lobbying ordinance, that's good news," the mayor said. He was referring to Karl Rundberg, the councilman who along with Mrs. Wyman had been one of his severest critics.

As a matter of fact, despite all the mayor's efforts the anti-lobbying measure did not pass. Bitterness mounted on a variety of subjects ranging from the Health Department mergers to the temporary blocking of Yorty's appointment of his executive assistant, Raymond G. Parker, who served as his liaison to the Police Department.

A proposal came from a City Council committee headed by Mrs. Wyman that a $6,000,000 underground convention exhibit center be built in Exposition Park where the Los Angeles Coliseum and the Los Angeles County Museum are located instead of on city property in Elysian Park near the Los Angeles River as Mayor Yorty favored.

Mayor Yorty immediately labeled the underground proposal as a "mole hole" and stirred up new cries from his antagonists. This form of feuding was carried over into a proposed $25-a-plate testimonial dinner for the City Council in August 1964. Joseph W. Hawthorne, general manager of the city's Civil Service Department, who was coordinator of the event, which had been planned for September 28 at the Hollywood Palladium, finally announced a postponement to "satisfy all participants that there is no partisanship involved."

This action stemmed in part from a statement by Mayor Yorty which hinted that the proceeds from the banquet might be used as a "slush fund" for Hawthorne, a possible opponent in the 1965 mayoralty race. The mayor added that it might be part of a "plot" by the old Poulson crowd to return to power. In the exchanges Yorty referred directly to the Wymans as possible participants in the plotting against him, a natural assumption under the circumstances of the feud which had been becoming progressively more violent.

From then on as the 1965 campaign approached the charges back and forth became more and more furious. Mrs. Wyman blasted the proposed establishment of a New York office of the City Economic Development Board aimed at obtaining additional business and industry for the Los Angeles area, a long-time project of the mayor. Sam was convinced of the necessity of keeping Southern California's economy stable through the addition of industries which could be advantageously located in the area. The industrial development idea, however, was only one of many subjects on which the infighting raged back and forth.

Even the issue of combined rubbish collection system as favored by Sam echoed anew as Mrs. Wyman warned that the cost might add to the city tax rate. The combined pick up had been a triumph for the mayor, who had been working for it for nearly two years. It had been approved finally on the basis that it would represent a saving of $91,000 a year over the previous separate pick up of tin cans and combustible rubbish. Mrs. Wyman's objections arose out of appropriations for overtime for the Bureau of Sanitation which she contended represented an increase in the cost under the new system.

Amid such bickering the prospective 1965 race for mayor began to have its effect upon everything which took place in city government. As early as September 2, 1964, Mayor Yorty charged that Governor Brown and the Wymans were trying to push James Roosevelt, son of FDR, into the mayor's race. Yorty said that the candidacy of Roosevelt, U. S. Representative from the 26th District, would be designed to "assist a lot of Democrats who would like to see me removed from office so that I no longer would be a 'threat' for other elective office," presumably, later on, the governorship or United States senatorship.

Representative Roosevelt in commenting on the matter said that he hadn't even felt a "nudge" in regard to the matter although he was non-committal on the question of his actual candidacy.

As the election year, 1965, rolled around Mrs. Wyman began to indicate some trepidation about her own contest in the 5th District. She charged the mayor was "recruiting candidates to oppose me and building a slush fund for their use." She said the mayor has "built a political machine inside City Hall unequalled in the history of this state. He has assigned at least three commissioners to my district for the sole purpose of defeating me. These commissioners in urging candidates to run have assured them of huge financial support."

This statement was made January 7 as she and Karl Rundberg filed for re-election. She and Rundberg, because of having teamed up on so many occasions to oppose the mayor's program, realized keenly that their candidacies would be tests in the forthcoming showdown.

Great state-wide interest was aroused in the contest for council because, aside from the mayor's own race, it would provide the best indication whether Yorty or the Wymans were gaining the ear of the people for future elections for higher offices than that of Mayor of Los Angeles.

CHAPTER XXIV

. . . Like dull narcotics numbing pain.

In Memoriam
SHAKESPEARE

In the brick and stone caverns of East Fifth Street in Los Angeles, glutted with human derelicts who have drifted by a kind of mass instinct of misery to its ugly confines, the pushers of narcotics ply their trade among thieves, pimps, prostitutes, and desperate penniless addicts. Around schools in good neighborhoods, too, the purveyors of heroin, cocaine, opium, marijuana, and "brand-name" drugs seek to find new prey to draw into their clutches. It is a fearful problem with which Los Angeles always is contending.

The Mexican border, stretching for about two hundred miles from Yuma on the Colorado River to the Pacific shore just below San Diego, is the boundary only 135 miles from Los Angeles across which large dealers in narcotics continually seek to smuggle their illegal wares by all manner of devices. It is believed that 80 percent of the illicit drugs coming into Southern California come in across this border. Every sort of ingenious trick is employed: drugs under hub caps, hidden in spare tires, under false bottoms in brief cases, concealed in hairbrushes, stuck in jeep cans, beneath brassieres, behind automobile headlights.

Those amounts of heroin, in particular, which succeed in penetrating the defenses of border guards contribute to crime and disorder in the whole Los Angeles area. Public officials and peace officers have grown more and more concerned about the problem in recent years. Their worry has manifest itself not only in efforts to stamp out the illegal traffic but also in the passage of laws to prevent the indiscriminate dispensing of harmful drugs to addicts or potential addicts from normally legitimate sources in California pharmacies. The result has been the creation of a system of triple-prescription rules to help doctors curb abuse of medical prescriptions.

Amid the multiplicity of pressing problems which faced him when he came into office, the drug situation concerned Sam Yorty deeply.

He was intent upon maintaining and enhancing the world-famous reputation of the Los Angeles Police force under renowned Chief William H. Parker, and this objective involved reducing the drug traffic in all its forms. Violent crime flowed directly from narcotics of many kinds. Addiction to the "milder" drugs often resulted in the victims turning to stronger and stronger forms of stimulants, so the suppression of the so-called "milder" forms was an inherent part of the over-all problem.

Mayor Yorty conducted an examination into all phases of drug addiction, and its contributing causes in whatever form. Prominent in the discoveries of his investigators was the growing role played by Percodan, an opium derivative, in the California drug market. This product, long used to provide relief from pain in some surgical and dental procedures, was increasing rapidly in sales during the 1950s and early 1960s as a result of an advertising campaign by its producers, Endo Laboratories, Inc., of New York.

In the definitive Merck "Index of Chemicals and Drugs" (7th edition, 1960)—the Merck Manual—known as "The Doctors' Bible" Percodan, described technically as Dihydrohydroxycodeinone, is listed as a narcotic sedative used locally as a myotic, and at the end is appended the notation:

"Causes true addiction!"

It was obtainable by a simple, single prescription, and was not subject to the triple-prescription safeguards of other opium-derived drugs. The effectiveness of the triple-prescription method had been proved beyond doubt in connection with such pain-killers as morphine, Dilaudid, and Demerol, which all were being used safely in California by physicians in hospitals and private practice. Abuses were rendered extremely difficult under this routine because one copy of the prescription was retained by the prescribing physician, another was taken by the patient and given to the pharmacist, and the third was filed with the State Bureau of Narcotic Enforcement. It was hardly worth the while of anyone to attempt counterfeiting of prescriptions under this plan because of the probability of immediate detection.

In the course of Mayor Yorty's study he discovered that in 1962—the first full year after he took office—more than 35,000,000 units of Percodan were sold in California. Los Angeles as the largest city in the state with a population within the municipality of more than 2,500,000 persons was known to be a tremendous market for Percodan, although under single-prescription dispensation it was virtually impossible to trace individual sales to addicts. Even to gain an idea of abuses it was necessary to conduct spot checks of drugstores. These checks were made by state investigators.

The disclosures were startling. For four weeks a survey was made in 174 drugstores in Los Angeles to discover if possible how extensive the misuse of Percodan might be. At the end of the check period the agents had discovered more than 300 prescription violations involving 131 of the drugstores. To state officials and to Mayor Yorty this was additional specific proof of the seriousness of the situation. By this time many important organizations were combining in efforts to suppress the growing danger represented by uncurbed Percodan sales. California Attorney General Stanley Mosk included triple-prescription for Percodan in his 1963 program of dangerous drug legislation. This program had been accelerated during the immediately preceding years as the result of a series of articles by Gene Sherman in the Los Angeles *Times* in 1959 exposing ramifications of the illicit drug traffic across the Mexican border. This series subsequently had won for the *Times* and Sherman the Pulitzer Prize in Journalism for Community Service.

Supporting the Attorney General's 1963 control bill on Percodan were the California Medical Association, the California Pharmaceutical Association, the State Bureau of Narcotic Enforcement, and Mayor Yorty's administration.

The measure went to an Assembly committee, where it bogged down. The Assembly committee amid charges by Attorney General Mosk that $300,000 was being spent in lobbying against the bill failed to report out the measure to the Assembly, and it died in so far as the 1963 session was concerned.

An attempt later was made to have Governor Brown place the matter on the Agenda for subsequent extraordinary sessions of the Legislature but he declined to do so. The governor stated that legislative leaders had decided the Percodan matter was not an emergency and that it would have to wait for the regular session of the Legislature in 1965.

Apprehension in regard to Percodan itself, though, had grown to such proportions that in December of 1963 the Federal Bureau of Narcotics listed Percodan as a Class "A" narcotic. This left the drug in a peculiar category. It was listed Federally as of sufficient danger to warrant triple-prescription to make it more difficult for drug addicts to obtain, and yet it was the only Federally classified Class "A" narcotic not required to have triplicate prescription in California.

Public sentiment had been aroused to such an extent at this point that many civic organizations and the Los Angeles City Council and the Los Angeles County Board of Supervisors joined in the fight to require triple-prescription for Percodan. So obvious was the sentiment that Endo Laboratories ended its opposition to triplicate prescription control. The Legislature moved inexorably toward closer control of the drug. The Assembly by a 71-0 vote approved triple-prescription of Percodan April 5. The measure went to Governor Brown May 4, and was signed into law.

One more source of drugs for California's addicts had been dried up, with Sam's help.

CHAPTER XXV

I cast my first vote for FDR, and then I had to beat his son.

SAM YORTY

In the ninety days between January 6, 1965, and April 6, 1965, Los Angeles was invited to watch U. S. Representative James Roosevelt spend $150 an hour, or $3609 a day, in what was described as "running" for mayor against Sam Yorty. Many considered it a slow jog. It all was billed as a "spectacular" but it turned out to be a penny peep show despite the prominence of the cast. The voters displayed a frenzy of apathy. The charges, countercharges, thrusts, parries, accusations, and rebuttals were as dramatic as a knitting needle duel.

Even the fact that Roosevelt had spent $324,779 did not emerge, of course, until after the so-called campaign had closed and the reports of expenses, as required by law, were filed. Mayor Yorty reported spending $198,016.18. Roosevelt commuted from Washington to Los Angeles to carry on his effort to unseat Mayor Yorty. He engaged in a series of expensive and carefully directed TV and radio appearances.

From the start Sam displayed an air of assurance which apparently was more galling to his chief opponent than any direct frontal attack could have been. The two candidates filed within two hours of each other on January 6 by paying their $500 filing fee. Roosevelt appeared first and then a little later Mayor Yorty went to the City Clerk's office and declared:

"In my own heart and conscience I know I have given this City good government."

A few days later the mayor said he expected to run a "relaxed" campaign because he felt sure his opponents could not find any issues on which to present a good case.

"I have great faith in the people," said Mayor Yorty, and then added that Roosevelt and some other candidates were "thrashing around to find some kind of campaign issue."

Perhaps the only bright moment of the whole campaign came when Roosevelt issued his classic statement that:

"Los Angeles must not be subjected to government by tantrum."

Before long the mayor was saying that his opponent was dredging up "petty little things" in an attempt to find a talking point. From the headlines during the campaign it appeared that there was indeed little of great public moment involved. The mayor was accused of permitting campaign solicitations in the City Hall on his behalf, of belonging to the Jonathan Club despite the fact it allegedly barred Negroes from its membership, of having worked mistakenly for the consolidation of city and county departments, of making a "deal" with Police Chief William H. Parker, of having mishandled the Bunker Hill Redevelopment Project, and of having gone too fast with some projects and too slow on others, of trying to destroy the public parks movement, and of contempt for taxpayers.

Roosevelt's billboards, itemized at $41,605, appeared all over the city. The Roosevelt message was purveyed in $38,640 worth of newspaper advertisements. But still the voters remained seemingly uninterested. It was a remarkable contrast to the heated nature of the campaign of 1961 in which Sam Yorty had been the underdog and had taken to television to put over his own message. This time the mayor was spending far less money than Roosevelt and was depending upon press conferences and TV appearances to hammer away at his theme that he had given the city a competent administration and had actually reduced the property tax rate.

The Los Angeles *Times,* faced with a difficult decision because of the virulence of its 1961 campaign against Sam Yorty, now did the gracious and sporting thing and came out editorially in support of his candidacy.

Four days before the primary the Los Angeles *Times* ran an editorial with the heading WHY YORTY, NOT ROOSEVELT? in which it said:

"The Times has endorsed Mayor Yorty as best fitted to lead this fast-growing metropolis for the next four years.

"Our choice stems from the fact that Yorty has demonstrated

during his first term an ability to grow on the job, that he has learned the complexities of governing the nation's third largest city, that he has gained a practical appreciation of its fiscal problems . . . voters are confronted with a known quantity in their present Mayor, and an unknown quantity in Roosevelt."

This was in startling contrast to the editorial the *Times* ran June 2, 1961, immediately after Yorty's election. At that time under the heading THERE'S NOTHING LEFT BUT HOPE the *Times* commented:

"We fear they [the voters] will be sorry they took this chance. We said again and again before the election that Mr. Yorty is a threat to good city government. His victory brings the threat closer. There is no comfort for Los Angeles in the new mayor's public record, in his private associations, in his campaign pronouncements, in the scurrillity of some of his television supporters. Whatever he may be, the colors he carries are the mark of a political privateer."

Coincident with the mayor race, several other contests developed which in a sense were more of a test of the mayor than his own race with Roosevelt. These involved in particular two of the city councilmen who had been consistent opponents of the mayor's programs, sometimes allegedly without regard for their basic importance or value. The most conspicuous of these were the contests between Rosalind Wyman and a young attorney, Edmund D. Edelman and between Karl Rundberg and Marvin Braude. As the most consistent and vitriolic of Mayor Yorty's foes in the City Council, Mrs. Wyman and Rundberg were doing all they could to get themselves re-elected as an indication of the mayor's unpopularity. Mrs. Wyman's race especially became much more of a public spectacle than any other single contest, including that for mayor. As primary election day, April 6, neared, Yorty's confidence increased. The polls showed him well ahead of Roosevelt and Patrick D. McGee, Republican candidate, with all indications pointing to his election at the primary.

These predictions were borne out. Mayor Yorty was swept in with a total vote far outnumbering that of all his opponents put together. The vote count was 392,775 for Yorty and 247,313 for Roosevelt.

At the same time Mrs. Wyman was forced into a run-off contest with Edelman.

✿ ✿ ✿

Several months before the councilmanic election, just at the start of the campaign, a remarkable incident changed the complexion of Mayor Yorty's future relations with one of his two principal antagonists. This involved Councilman Rundberg. As Mayor Yorty recounts it Rundberg came to him and forthrightly said he has been misled, and that he wished to make amends. The mayor accepted the overture and agreed to let the past be forgotten. Subsequently when Rundberg had in fact been defeated in his bid for re-election Mayor Yorty demonstrated his own good faith by appointing Rundberg to the Los Angeles Harbor Commission.

✿ ✿ ✿

On the day of the run-off election public interest was centered on the Wyman-Edelman contest. When the returns were in Edelman had snowed under Mrs. Wyman by a vote of 37,291 to 12,201, a ratio of three to one. Braude defeated Rundberg 22,023 to 18,976.

This result was considered by many to be more of a vindication of Yorty policies and support for his future operations than had been his own victory over Roosevelt in the lackluster campaign for mayor. The road ahead appeared much clearer for the major objectives which Yorty had outlined for his city.

CHAPTER XXVI

Whoever hears of fat men heading a riot, or herding together in turbulent mobs?—no—no, 'tis your lean, hungry men who are continually worrying society, and setting the whole community by the ears.

WASHINGTON IRVING

Los Angeles and other large American cities may ultimately be torn apart in violent collisions between the thwarted poor and rebellious taxpayers if demagogues are encouraged or permitted to organize the poverty-stricken through programs of no lasting merit.

This is the warning of Mayor Yorty to the United States as the aftermath of the bloody rioting which raged among Negroes in the Watts district of Los Angeles on the hot sultry days of mid-August 1965, as the mayor was launching efforts to aid the needy and to carry out the major aims of his new administration following his defeat of Roosevelt, and the enforced retirement of Mrs. Wyman from the City Council. Contemplating the fearful toll of thirty-four dead, more than a thousand injured, and property damage in excess of $40,000,000 due to arson and looting, the mayor has devoted the ensuing months amid a variety of investigations and analyses to studies of remedies based on the lessons learned in the holocaust. He spoke out irrevocably against any kind of so-called anti-poverty procedures giving false hopes of immediate "money to the poor."

In the aftermath, the mayor stressed that state officers had participated in the incidents which touched off the riots and not Los Angeles officers trained in the technique of arrest in the Negro district. He also emphasized that state officials had been remiss in not providing the vitally needed National Guard assistance to halt the riots in their early stages by a massive demonstration of force.

Mayor Yorty and Police Chief Parker had demonstrated their realization of the grim potentialities of the situation in the Negro colony by starting the move for purchase of riot helmets for the police years before the outbreak occurred. On October 12, 1962, a request for three thousand riot helmets was made by the mayor and Police Chief Parker. In the budget for 1963–64 an item of $50,930 was included and approved for the purchase. These helmets then were kept in readiness in the event of necessity. Both Yorty and Parker knew such an eruption was possible and Parker had discussed it with Governor Brown. Their energies were devoted to preventing it. The individual police officers were carefully trained in handling the delicate situations involved in making arrests in the Watts area and neighboring regions. Little was feared from that standpoint. The constant danger was that some spark might be touched off by a criminal element or outside agitation, igniting the emotion-ladened situation.

Detailed preparations were made in case such an outbreak should occur.

Governor Brown's participation in the planning for possible calling out of the National Guard in Los Angeles in case of emergency grew out of warnings sounded by Chief Parker in an address to the National Conference of Police Associations at the Marina Hotel in Los Angeles on July 20, 1964. This was at the time of the Harlem riots. Chief Parker spoke of the necessity of being prepared for any such occurrence in Los Angeles. This in turn led to discussions with Governor Brown on procedures for calling out the Guard should the need arise. Mayor Yorty was participating through Chief Parker in these joint preparations of the city and the state. On this basis Mayor Yorty felt everything possible had been done to prepare for any eventuality. Meanwhile he was exerting every effort and influence to bring about a betterment of economic and social conditions among the Negroes in an effort to prevent violence. He expressed the view that misguided outside influences and unwise trends were making it more difficult for big cities to cope with the basic difficulty: the problems of the poor.

"Federal officials should not set time bombs in our big cities," he declared later. "It is a very dangerous thing to raise expectations beyond ability to fulfill. The anti-poverty program is a recognition of the problem, it is true. But some of the poor expect actual money; they do not realize that the benefits, on the contrary, are to be primarily long-range in the fields of education, job training, and improved economic opportunity. There is no overnight solution!

"The people who expect immediate cash hand-outs in the anti-poverty effort may feel incensed if they don't get it and be inclined to resort to violence in their anger. At the same time local taxpayers will be driven toward revolt, too. It has not been made clear enough that local taxpayers—program sponsors—in our cities soon will be called upon to pay a full 50 percent share of the 'anti-poverty' bill instead of the mere 10 percent they are paying now as contrasted with the 90 percent put up by the Federal government. In the midst of this situation the Office of Economic Opportunity—as set forth in its own shocking 'Work Book No. 3'— encouraged organization of pressure groups of the poor for benefits which include, as we see proposed in San Francisco, everything from divorces to dance lessons. When the overburdened local taxpayers and sponsors awaken, as they are bound to do before long, to the fact they are being called upon to pay for half of these expenses, there is bound to be adverse reaction.

"If demagogues organize the poor for expensive programs of no lasting merit, local taxpayers will revolt and at the same time the disappointed recipients may march on city halls and tear our cities apart."

His feeling in regard to the necessity of acquainting both the recipients and the taxpayers with the complete truth regarding the administration of the "anti-poverty" program resulted in the mayor's own head-on clash with Sargent Shriver, Federal administrator of the program. Mayor Yorty insisted all during the formative period of the anti-poverty program as applied to Los Angeles that the board in charge of distribution of the funds must include a majority of taxpayers' representatives rather than being completely dominated by the recipients.

"You can't turn this thing, including the purse strings, over to the people who are going to get the benefits," he contends. "We must learn to live and work together in these matters and not attempt something impossible by granting complete control of such a costly program to the people who are going to receive the aid."

Outbreak of the violence did come at a time when controversies were going on between Federal officials and municipal leaders, like Mayor Yorty, over handling of anti-poverty programs. Evidence was lacking that this factor in itself was a dominant or even a

relatively important reason for the specific occurrence in Los
Angeles.

The heat smothering the city, the recent inciting to violence by
some civil rights advocates, liquor, asserted ineptness in arrest
procedures by state officers all were elements. Together, they
created spontaneous combustion.

The riots lasted for five days. Strangely, they were intermittent.
Peaks and lulls puzzled police officers familiar with normal riot
patterns. The greatest death toll occurred after the second day,
leading Mayor Yorty to contend later that if the plea of himself
and Chief Parker for 15,000 National Guardsmen on the third day
of the rioting had been granted immediately, the ensuing deaths
and holocausts might have been contained or greatly minimized.
As it was, the surging death toll came during the period when the
National Guard was being assembled in the city and brought up to
full strength—approximately the 15,000 originally requested by the
mayor—and this led to charges the state assistance came too late
and too slowly.

The original incident which precipitated the riot was participated
in by California Highway Patrol officers. In an official account of
the event as contained in a report of an investigating commission
headed by John McCone, it was stated:

"On August 11, 1965, California Highway Patrolman Lee W.
Minikus, a Caucasian, was riding his motorcycle along 122nd
Street, just south of the Los Angeles city boundary, when a passing Negro motorist told him he had just seen a car that was being
driven recklessly. Minikus gave chase and pulled the car over at
116th and Avalon Boulevard, in a predominately Negro neighborhood, near but not in Watts. It was 7 p.m.

"The driver was Marquette Frye, a 21-year-old Negro, and his
older brother, Ronald, 22, was a passenger. Minikus asked
Marquette to get out and take the standard Highway Patrol
sobriety test. Frye failed the test, and at 7:05 p.m., Minikus told
him he was under arrest. He radioed for his motorcycle partner,
for a car to take Marquette to jail, and a tow truck to take the car
away.

"They were two blocks from the Frye home, in an area of two-
story apartment buildings and numerous small family residences.
Because it was a very warm evening, many of the residents were
outside.

"Ronald Frye, having been told he could not take the car when

Marquette was taken to jail, went to get their mother so that she could claim the car. They returned to the scene about 7:15 p.m. as the second motorcycle patrolman, the patrol car, and tow truck arrived. The original group of 25 to 50 curious spectators had grown to 250 to 300 persons.

"Mrs. Frye approached Marquette and scolded him for drinking. Marquette, who until then had been peaceful and co-operative, pushed her away and moved toward the crowd, cursing and shouting at the officers that they would have to kill him to take him to jail. The patrolmen pursued Marquette and he resisted.

"The watching crowd became hostile, and one of the patrolmen radioed for more help. Within minutes, three more highway patrolmen arrived. Minikus and his partner were now struggling with both Frye brothers. Mrs. Frye, now belligerent, jumped on the back of one of the officers and ripped his shirt. In an attempt to subdue Marquette, one officer swung at his shoulder with a night stick, missed, and struck him on the forehead, inflicting a minor cut. By 7:23 p.m., all three of the Fryes were under arrest, and other California Highway Patrolmen and, for the first time, Los Angeles police officers had arrived in response to the call for help.

"Officers on the scene said there were now more than 1000 persons in the crowd. About 7:25 p.m., the patrol car with the prisoners, and the tow truck pulling the Frye car, left the scene. At 7:31 p.m., the Fryes arrived at a nearby sheriff's substation."

As the Highway Patrol officers were preparing to leave the scene someone in the crowd spat upon one of them. At this point a strange misunderstanding occurred. Miss Joyce Ann Gaines, a young Negro woman barber wearing a barber's gown, was seized by the officers as being responsible for the spitting. When she was placed under arrest the crowd, mistakenly thinking her barber gown was a maternity smock, was aroused to fury by the supposed rough handling of a pregnant woman. The cursing and screaming became louder.

By the time Miss Gaines had been arrested a few more minutes had elapsed, so that it was 7:40 P.M. as the last law-enforcement car left the scene, and it was stoned by the mob.

It was a hot stifling evening. Tempers continued to mount. The crowd, radiating outward, began to throw rocks, bricks, and bottles at passing cars. More and more Los Angeles officers were called. Within two hours a widespread riot was in progress. An attempt was made by the police to seal off an eight-block area in the neighborhood of San Pedro Street, Imperial Highway, Stanford Street, and 118th Street. By 9:30 P.M. barricades had been set up.

Residents of Los Angeles, listening to the radio and watching television during the riot period, were horrified and benumbed to hear and see familiar street names and locations in the midst of shooting, assaults, and fires that lighted the skies for miles.

"Why, I was just there yesterday!" someone would exclaim as a place figuring in the violence was mentioned.

After the outbreak of the disturbance the harried police actually borrowed a technique from "covered wagon" days. A circle of patrol cars was set up to guard the command post at Imperial Highway and Avalon Boulevard, reminiscent of the protective ring of pioneers on the plains warding off Indian attacks.

Deputy Police Chief Roger Murdock, in charge of the police squads, was directing his main efforts toward containing the trouble within as small area as possible. But hour by hour the radius of the rioting enlarged.

All during the tense night the rioting, or uneasy interludes, kept the officers constantly on the alert. The situation at this point still was considered to be sufficiently within recognized patterns for the Los Angeles police force to be able to suppress it. This hope prevailed to such an extent that a report was not made to Mayor Yorty, who had gone on a courtesy visit to a Mexican trade fair in Tijuana and to San Diego for a speech Thursday noon, until the middle of the morning Thursday. This lapse in time in notifying the mayor was due to the unusual pattern of the rioting itself.

In almost all riots there is a peak of violence and then a repressive measure of such magnitude by law-enforcement authorities that it is crushed, and does not break out again. In Los Angeles, however, the riot came in successive waves rather than as one continuous build-up with a sudden termination. These peaks and interludes continued until Friday, August 13, when there was a continual mounting toward the most violent climax.

During Thursday, August 12, the temperature was still in the 90s and apparently contributing to the inflaming of the rioters and looters, there was disorder in a wider and wider area throughout Watts and Willowbrook. Friday morning, however, there appeared to be another quieter period, although by this time Mayor Yorty and Chief Parker were making an all-out effort to obtain National Guard assistance in force.

On Thursday the number of participants in the outbreak had

risen to approximately seven thousand. Fires were set in markets and liquor stores along Avalon Boulevard from Imperial Highway to 120th Street. Windows were smashed and wholesale looting started. Molotov cocktails apparently prepared in advance were being thrown along with the rocks, bricks, and bottles. White people, both pedestrians and motorists, were being set upon by the Negro mobs. Many victims were badly beaten. Police were fired upon from apartment houses at Parmelee Avenue and Imperial Highway. The law enforcement officers now numbered at 350 were made up of Los Angeles police, Los Angeles County Deputy Sheriffs and members of the California Highway Patrol.

Many of these were needed to help protect firemen who were set upon and beaten or shot at as they responded to alarms.

Major General Charles A. Ott, Jr., Commander of the 40th Armored Division of the National Guard made up of 10,500 men, said they had been alerted (they were already mobilizing for training at camp) and that five hundred were on stand-by orders to move in if so ordered.

By this time the toll of injured was seven police officers, two firemen, and forty civilians. By the following night, Friday, this toll had risen to more than one hundred, including thirty police and the fire damage had mounted to an estimated $10,000,000.

It was during a lull early Friday that Mayor Yorty was confronted with a difficult decision, whether to fly to San Francisco for a scheduled conference with Mayor Jack Shelley and a long-scheduled speech to the Commonwealth Club. He was keeping in close touch with Police Chief Parker and finally decided that he should make the flight north and keep his commitments and hurry back in early afternoon.

During the late morning, acting at the mayor's request, Police Chief Parker began the series of calls to the staff of Lieutenant Governor Glenn Anderson who was Acting Governor in the absence of Governor Brown in Greece, asking for the immediate bringing in of 15,000 National Guardsmen to halt the rioting with an overwhelming show of force. From the events of the ensuing hours grew the prolonged controversy between Mayor Yorty and Chief Parker on one hand and Lieutenant Governor Anderson and Governor Brown on the other.

As Mayor Yorty returned to Los Angeles from San Francisco in mid-afternoon Friday, the efforts were being intensified to hasten Lieutenant Governor Anderson's sending in of the Guardsmen. So tense was this waiting period that at one point during the five hours of uncertainty Chief Parker threatened to ask President Johnson for military help if it was not forthcoming from the state.

Whatever the reasons, the order for use of the National Guard was not signed by Lieutenant Governor Anderson until 5:05 P.M. Friday, August 13, more than five hours after the Lieutenant Governor's staff had been informed of the official request from Mayor Yorty and Chief Parker for the National Guard. The first of the Guardsmen under the command of Colonel Irving J. Taylor began arriving at 9:45 P.M. Friday, with 2000 standing by for duty. Colonel Taylor set up his headquarters at Walter Riis High School in the riot area with Guardsmen from units in Burbank, Inglewood, Glendale, Long Beach, and Santa Ana. These Guardsmen supplemented the 560 local officers who by now were in the trouble zone.

Even with the presence of the initial contingent of the Guard, the shooting and looting went on unabated or actually increased. The first officer to meet death in the rioting, Deputy Sheriff Ronald Ernest Ludlow, twenty-seven, was shot in the stomach while he was at Imperial Highway and Wilmington Avenue at 9 P.M. Friday, just before the Guardsmen began arriving and died at St. Francis Hospital in Lynwood. Three Negroes were killed Friday.

At last on Saturday the Guardsmen began arriving in force and by nightfall there were approximately 15,000 on duty including 8000 soldiers from the 49th Infantry at Camp Roberts. Lieutenant Governor Anderson signed a Disaster Proclamation and invoked an 8 P.M. curfew in a 50-square-mile area. By late Saturday night 23 persons had been killed; 63 policemen, 17 firemen, two members of the military, and 512 civilians were injured. Arrests had risen to 1701, fire and looting damage was placed at more than $40,000,000.

The disorders had spread to other regions. Molotov cocktails were thrown along Fair Oaks Avenue in Pasadena where there is a large Negro population. Fire bombs were used by Negroes against other Negroes in Monrovia and Police Chief Ray Blair ordered suppression of the violence and for his men to protect themselves in the process. Negro ministers in Monrovia offered the services of themselves and their congregations to help preserve order.

Los Angeles County Sheriff Peter Pitchess asked a stand-by of officers in Orange, San Diego, Riverside, San Bernardino, and Ventura counties, to come in if called.

The entire world was watching the outbreak.

Mexican newspapers gave the story top bannerlines. A dispatch from Gene Sherman of the Los Angeles *Times* reported London worried because of its own mounting problem over racial difficulties. The controlled Communist press indicated the riots were a revolt of the masses against their capitalistic masters in America.

As a hot dawn arrived on Sunday, August 15, the charred and bloody Watts region was, at last, adequately patrolled by the National Guardsmen and the law-enforcement officers. Even this late, however, when the restoration of relative calm was only a few hours away, Governor Brown encountered trouble when he tried to tour the area. He reportedly had been requested by police not to enter the danger zone and divert needed officers for his protection, but he proceeded nevertheless. Despite the efforts of law-enforcement agencies to protect him, sniping broke out at 103rd Street and Success Avenue and caused him to turn back and hasten to the State Building for a conference with fifty Negro leaders.

During the day, Sunday, the outbreaks spread for a short time to Long Beach and San Diego. By nighttime Sunday the major force of the rioting definitely had been halted in the curfew area which included eleven square miles of county territory. The death toll at this point stood at thirty-one.

By Monday, August 16, it was obvious the National Guard and the police were in control and that the riot period had ended. Immediately thereafter there ensued the series of charges, counter-charges, accusations, recriminations, and rebuttals in regard to primary responsibility for the outbreak and the blame for delays in getting the rioting under control.

Mayor Yorty, by chance, was out of the city the evening the trouble started. Later, he described his actions during the riot period.

He had flown to San Diego Wednesday a few hours before the chase and arrest of the Frye brothers and the incidents which grew into the riot. He was accepting an invitation to repeat a pleasant experience of the year before in his cordial relationship with the Mexican people and their leaders. He was to attend the Feria del Hogar, or Home Show, of Mexico in Tijuana. In 1964 he had flown to Mexico City at the invitation of the Feria to see it in its beautiful setting in Chapultepec Park; the Mexico City version being described as the largest trade fair in the world. Now, in Tijuana, the 1965 Feria was about 70 percent the size of that in Mexico City and in itself represented a major accomplishment for the state of Baja California. The Mexican officials in charge of the Feria were looking forward particularly to the attendance of Mayor Yorty because it was known that he was *simpatico* with the Mexican people. President Lopez Mateos had visited in Los Angeles. Mayor Yorty had been one of the few American mayors participating as a guest in the inauguration of new President Diaz Ordaz and he also was an *embrazo* friend of former President Miguel Aleman, who had taken over the promotion of tourism in Mexico. Mayor Yorty in fact had worked with Aleman on a "package deal" of tourism for visitors from South America who were encouraged to include both Mexico City and Los Angeles on their itineraries.

On his arrival in San Diego Mayor Yorty was guest of honor at a reception at the Cuyamaca Club atop a tall downtown building. His party then drove to Tijuana and saw the Home Fair including the artisans from all parts of Mexico and the folklorico entertainment. He returned to San Diego from Tijuana unaware of the Watts incident. The mayor after a scheduled speech to the San Diego Rotary Club Thursday noon was booked to fly directly from San Diego to San Francisco where he was to speak Friday noon to the Commonwealth Club on "The World of the Cities."

Between 9 and 10 A.M. Thursday, August 12, Mayor Yorty received a call from Ray Parker, his press relations officer who also was in charge of liaison with the police, and was informed that there had been a disturbance in Watts but that it seemingly had abated somewhat. Yorty immediately canceled his flight to San Francisco and after making his talk to the San Diego Rotary Club flew back directly to Los Angeles. He at once went into conference with Chief of Police Parker who informed him of the circumstances surrounding the incident precipitated when the state officers made their multiple arrests.

"Chief Parker told me that if the rioting continued we should consider calling in the National Guard, Friday, the next day," the mayor relates. "I felt that we should not wait if the situation became worse. Chief Parker and I were agreed that if it were necessary to call the National Guard we should ask for an overwhelming force of 15,000 men to suppress it immediately. Chief Parker told me that an extraordinary pattern was visible in the situation because it was peculiar for riots to start and stop as these had done so far.

"The latest disorder which threatened to become of such proportions that it would be beyond the power of local police control

[10] *At right,* the Mayor welcomes President Chung Hee Park of the Republic of Korea on Los Angeles visit. (*H. Reigl photo*)

[11] *Below left,* greeting Prime Minister Nehru of India. (*Los Angeles City School Districts photo*)

[12] *Below right,* Betty and Sam receive an old friend, President Adolfo Lopez Mateos of Mexico. (*H. Reigl photo*)

[13] *Above,* this freeway interchange near Civic Center, while an engineering triumph, can also be a motorist's nightmare during peak hours. *(Los Angeles Times photo)*

[14] *Below left,* making harmony on the Johnny Carson show. Actor James Stewart, comedienne Phyllis Diller, Yorty and Carson. Mayor Sam, who once had his own dance band in Nebraska days is a talented banjoist. *(NBC photo by Paul W. Bailey)*

[15] *Below right,* rain or shine the day begins with a dip at the hilltop home in Studio City section of San Fernando Valley. *(Bill Bridges photo)*

[16] *Above,* over thirty lives were lost and damage ran into millions in the tragic Watts riots in August, 1965. This is 103rd Street near Wilmington Avenue showing Negro looters in action while incendiary fires rage. Firemen, stoned and shot at, had to withdraw from area. *(Los Angeles Times photo by Larry Sharkey)*

[17] *At right,* capable, blunt and controversial, Police Chief William H. Parker has had the foursquare backing of Mayor Yorty before, during and after the Watts rioting. *(Los Angeles Times photo)*

[18] *Below,* military and law enforcement officers move into action in burned and looted section of Avalon Boulevard during riot. *(Los Angeles Times photo by Don Cormier)*

[19] *Above,* Los Angeles contrasts. A Fourth of July celebration in 1871. The site is near the Plaza where the first three story building, the Pico House, a hotel, had been built only two years before close to the present site of the City Hall. *(Los Angeles Times photo)*

[20] *Below,* the developing Civic Center and Mall. At right is the City Hall and directly in front of it, at an angle, is the old Hall of Records which will be removed to permit completion of the Mall. At the opposite end is the huge Department of Water and Power Building, with the celebrated Music Center, identified by its tall columns, just southeast of it. *(Los Angeles Times photo)*

had come shortly after a meeting which was intended to be a peace session but in actuality developed into an inflammatory gathering. This was a meeting in Athens Park which at first was reported to have been called by County Supervisor Kenneth Hahn and the County Human Relations Committee, but which later was disavowed by both. This session participated in by the Reverend H. H. Brookings and both whites and Negroes had been set for 2 P.M. Thursday and was widely publicized and then televised. This was the occasion on which a sixteen-year-old Negro boy said in substance on TV:

"We're going to burn tonight!"

"The incidents growing out of this no doubt well-intentioned meeting were, in my opinion, a factor in starting the riots again. At this time I talked to Chief Parker about the advisability of me going into the riot district and he pleaded against it.

"'Please don't go down there,' Chief Parker urged me. 'We need every man on the job and if we had to divert them for your protection it would be a serious handicap to us. We do not want to be responsible for your safety under these circumstances.'

"At his urging I remained away from the affected district and kept in close touch with the situation during Thursday night. Friday morning I was faced with a dilemma of whether to go to San Francisco for my long-standing engagement with the Commonwealth Club which had been made months before. I talked to Chief Parker again about the procedure of calling the Guard through Lieutenant Governor Anderson who was Acting Governor in the absence of Governor Brown in Europe. The situation at this moment was temporarily quiet but uncertain. I talked to the Negroes on my staff and obtained their opinion and also to a Negro minister in the Watts area in whom I had great confidence. He told me that in his opinion the situation was dangerous but that he believed the riots were over. A disturbing factor was a report which had come in that Communists were going to seize upon the tense atmosphere and attempt to get the riots going again.

"At the last moment I decided it would be possible for me to make the trip to San Francisco and deliver my speech and return by around 3 P.M., while keeping in touch with the whole situation on the plane and at the Palace Hotel in San Francisco. I therefore drove to the airport and flew to San Francisco and immediately went in to conference at the Palace with Mayor Jack Shelley. We discussed the riots and the anti-poverty program which was closely tied in with the Negro problem and the civil rights movement. Our discussion lasted until it was time for me to give my talk to the Commonwealth Club and I went directly there and spoke without eating lunch. In my speech I dwelt with particular emphasis upon the necessity of law enforcement and the suppression of riots regardless of the color of the rioters. Then I was given a motorcycle escort by the Mayor to hurry to my plane and flew back to Los Angeles, arriving about 3 P.M. after an absence of only a few hours.

"I went immediately to the Command Headquarters in the 'War Room' of the Police Building close to the City Hall. By this time due to the new outbreak of violence every effort was being made to reach Lieutenant Governor Anderson to induce him to call out the National Guard to assist the police and Los Angeles County Deputy Sheriffs."

In the light of subsequent disagreement over the sequence of events, Mayor Yorty ordered the preparation of a chronology of the telephone calls relating to the calling out of the National Guard.

Ray Parker submitted this memorandum on the chronology to the mayor August 18 on the basis of his own observations and from the records:

HERE IS THE TIMETABLE OF MAJOR PHONE CALLS TO AND FROM POLICE CHIEF PARKER'S OFFICE REGARDING THE ALERTING OF THE NATIONAL GUARD, THE NOTIFICATION OF THE GOVERNOR'S OFFICE AND THE EVENTUAL SIGNING OF THE ORDER BY LT. GOV. ANDERSON. (I WAS PRESENT IN THE CHIEF'S OFFICE WHEN MOST OF THESE CALLS WERE MADE. IN ADDITION, DURING SPECIFIC TIMES I HAVE DEFINITE KNOWLEDGE THAT THERE WERE ONE OR MORE MEMBERS OF THE PRESS WHO WERE INTERVIEWING THE CHIEF WHEN THE CALLS WERE MADE OR RECEIVED.)

AS YOU KNOW, THE INITIAL PLAN TO USE THE NATIONAL GUARD IN DISORDER SITUATIONS WAS FIRST DISCUSSED, ACCORDING TO CHIEF PARKER AND GOV. BROWN, A LITTLE OVER A YEAR AGO. SUBSEQUENTLY, CHIEF PARKER TALKED TO LT. GEN. RODERIC L. HILL, ADJUTANT GENERAL OF THE CALIFORNIA NATIONAL GUARD, AND VARIOUS MEETINGS HAVE BEEN HELD BETWEEN LOS ANGELES POLICE OFFICIALS AND NATIONAL GUARD OFFICIALS. THE FIRST NIGHT OF RIOTING WAS WEDNESDAY NIGHT.

THURSDAY: (AUGUST 12)

4:52 P.M.—CHIEF PARKER CALLED LT. GEN. HILL AND TOLD HIM THAT BECAUSE OF THE RIOTING IT MIGHT BE NECESSARY TO

CALL OUT THE GUARD. IT WAS THE CHIEF'S UNDERSTANDING THAT GEN. HILL WOULD DO ALL THE CLEARING WITH THE GOVERNOR.

5:30 P.M.—GEN. ELDER, OF THE NATIONAL GUARD, WAS ALSO TALKED TO BY THE CHIEF'S OFFICE.

5:38 P.M.—MAYOR YORTY CAME TO THE CHIEF'S OFFICE WITH MRS. CHAMBERS (THE LOG INDICATES THAT I WAS ALSO THERE HAVING COME IN AT 4:20 P.M. I HAD BEEN THERE SEVERAL TIMES EARLIER IN THE DAY.) ALSO PRESENT AT THIS TIME WERE DEPUTY CHIEF ROGER MURDOCK, COMMANDING THE PATROL BUREAU, AND INSPECTOR GATES, ONE OF THE FIELD COMMANDERS. THE CHIEF OUTLINED THE SITUATION AS OF THE PREVIOUS NIGHT, THE PLANS THAT WERE TO GO INTO EFFECT IN THE FIELD THURSDAY NIGHT AND HIS CONVERSATIONS WITH THE NATIONAL GUARD COMMANDERS. ALSO DISCUSSED WAS THE ATHENS PARK MEETING REPORTEDLY CALLED BY SUPERVISOR KENNETH HAHN, AT WHICH YOUNG TEENAGERS WERE ALLOWED TO MAKE INFLAMMATORY REMARKS ABOUT INVADING WHITE NEIGHBORHOODS, WHICH WERE TELEVISED. A POLICEWOMAN WHO HAD ATTENDED THE MEETING WAS CALLED IN TO GIVE YOU AND THE CHIEF A REPORT OF WHAT HAD HAPPENED AT THE ATHENS PARK MEETING. TO THE BEST OF MY KNOWLEDGE YOUR MEETING WITH THE CHIEF MAY HAVE LASTED OVER AN HOUR.

SOMETIME EARLY THURSDAY EVENING I SAW COL. QUICK, OF THE CALIFORNIA NATIONAL GUARD, AT THE EMERGENCY COMMAND CENTER. COL. QUICK WAS LATER ASSIGNED TO COORDINATE LOGISTICS, ETC., WITH INSPECTOR (JOHN) KINSLING. (THE ECC RECORDS SHOW THE EXACT TIME.) COL. QUICK SPENT MOST OF THE NIGHT, IF NOT ALL OF IT, IN THE EMERGENCY COMMAND CENTER. I SPENT A CONSIDERABLE AMOUNT OF TIME THURSDAY EVENING AND EARLY FRIDAY MORNING IN THE ECC AND LATER AT THE FIELD COMMAND HEADQUARTERS WHICH WAS THEN AT THE 77TH STREET DIVISION.

FRIDAY: (AUGUST 13)

BEFORE LEAVING MY HOME FRIDAY MORNING, IT MUST HAVE BEEN ABOUT 8 OR 8:15 A.M., I CALLED YOU AND AT YOUR DIRECTION I WENT TO THE CHIEF'S OFFICE. APPROXIMATELY 9:15 OR 9:20 A.M. THE CHIEF CALLED YOU. I WAS PRESENT IN HIS OFFICE. AT THE COMPLETION OF THE CALL THE CHIEF TOLD HIS STAFF THAT THE MAYOR HAD AUTHORIZED HIM ON BEHALF OF THE CITY TO CALL OUT THE NATIONAL GUARD. INSPECTOR KINSLING WAS TOLD TO NOTIFY THE NATIONAL GUARD. HOWARD HERTEL, REPORTER FROM THE TIMES, WAS IN THE OUTER OFFICE. HE TOLD ME HE HAD BEEN SENT OVER TO CHECK OUT REPORTS THAT THE NATIONAL GUARD HAD ALREADY BEEN ALERTED. I TOLD HIM THAT

THE MAYOR HAD JUST TALKED TO THE CHIEF AND THERE WOULD PROBABLY BE SOME SORT OF AN ANNOUNCEMENT SHORTLY.

9:50 A.M.—A CALL WAS RECEIVED IN THE CHIEF'S OFFICE FROM A MR. HAAS IN THE GOVERNOR'S OFFICE. THE CHIEF WAITED ON THE LINE, SEVERAL REPORTERS, HOWARD HERTEL OF THE TIMES, GENE BARNS OF NBC, AND PAUL PIERCE OF KMPC, WERE IN THE CHIEF'S OFFICE OR CAME IN SHORTLY AFTER. THE CHIEF HELD ON THE PHONE FOR QUITE A WHILE BUT THE CALL WAS NEVER COMPLETED.

SOMEWHERE WITHIN THE NEXT HALF-HOUR INSPECTOR KINSLING, AND I BELIEVE THAT COL. QUICK WAS WITH HIM AT THE TIME, REPORTED THAT IT WAS NECESSARY FOR THE CHIEF TO MAKE A FORMAL REQUEST FOR THE GUARD TO THE GOVERNOR. THE CHIEF INSTRUCTED THE CALL TO BE PLACED TO ANYONE IN THE GOVERNOR'S OFFICE FOR THIS PURPOSE.

10:50 A.M.—A MR. CHRISTIAN OF THE GOVERNOR'S OFFICE CALLED AND THE CHIEF TOLD HIM, IN THE PRESENCE OF NEWSMEN, THE SITUATION IN LOS ANGELES WAS OUT OF CONTROL AND THAT HE HAD BEEN AUTHORIZED BY THE MAYOR ON BEHALF OF THE CITY TO REQUEST THAT NATIONAL GUARD TROOPS BE AUTHORIZED. THE CHIEF THEN TOLD NEWSMEN THAT CHRISTIAN HAD TOLD HIM THAT HE WOULD TRY TO GET HOLD OF LT. GOV. ANDERSON AS SOON AS POSSIBLE.

AT APPROXIMATELY 11:45 A.M. I WALKED ACROSS THE HALL TO WHERE COL. QUICK WAS TEMPORARILY OFFICED WITH INSPECTOR KINSLING. WE DISCUSSED THE URGENCY OF GETTING THE PROCLAMATION ISSUED. I GAVE COL. QUICK THE PLACE WHERE YOU WERE SPEAKING IN SAN FRANCISCO AND THE TELEPHONE NUMBER AND HE IN TURN, IMMEDIATELY IN MY PRESENCE, PHONED, I BELIEVE IT WAS SACRAMENTO, AND URGED THAT IT BE GIVEN TO LT. GOV. ANDERSON WITH THE REQUEST THAT IF HE HAD ANY DOUBTS ABOUT THE SITUATION TO GET IN TOUCH WITH YOU AS SOON AS POSSIBLE. (VARIOUS NEWS MEDIA WERE THEN GETTING REPORTS THAT GOV. ANDERSON WAS IN BERKELEY, OAKLAND OR ENROUTE TO MCCLELLAN FIELD.)

SOMEWHERE AROUND 12 NOON MR. KLEIN OF THE GOVERNOR'S LOS ANGELES OFFICE CALLED AND SAID THAT LT. GOV. ANDERSON WAS COMING DOWN HERE TO SEE FOR HIMSELF AND THAT HE WANTED SHERIFF PITCHESS, CHIEF PARKER, THE MAYOR AND NEGRO COMMUNITY LEADERS TO MEET IN THE STATE BUILDING AT 4 P.M. THE CHIEF REITERATED STRONGLY THE SITUATION WAS OUT OF CONTROL AND THAT HE WANTED THE NATIONAL GUARD. HE FURTHER SAID HE COULD SEE NO PURPOSE OF THE MEETING IN THE MIDDLE OF A RIOT. HE FURTHER SAID SOMETHING RELA-

TIVE TO WHETHER OR NOT THERE WAS ANY NEGRO LEADERSHIP
WHICH COULD NEGOTIATE WITH A MOB.

1:40 P.M.—KLEIN OF THE GOVERNOR'S OFFICE (LOS ANGELES)
ASKED THAT LT. GOV. ANDERSON BE PROVIDED WITH A SITUATION
REPORT.

CHIEF PARKER TOLD HIM AGAIN THAT THE SITUATION WAS OUT
OF CONTROL AND THAT THE GOVERNOR COULD COME TO THE
EMERGENCY COMMAND CENTER WHERE ALL THE INFORMATION
WAS AVAILABLE.

3:50 P.M.—THE CHIEF WAS NOTIFIED THAT LT. GOV. ANDERSON
HAD ARRIVED AT THE AIRPORT IN VAN NUYS. (THE PRESS RE-
PORTED THAT ANDERSON GOT OUT OF THE AIRPLANE AND SAID
THAT HE WOULD SIGN THE PROCLAMATION.)

AS YOU WILL RECALL ABOUT THAT TIME I MET YOU WITH
POLICE COMMISSIONER MIKE KOHN AT THE CITY HALL HELIPAD
AND WE WENT DIRECTLY TO THE CHIEF'S OFFICE WHERE THE
CHIEF WAS BEING INTERVIEWED BY THE PRESS AND TELEVISION.
YOU WILL RECALL THAT A HERALD-EXAMINER REPORTER, NOR-
MAN JACOBY, REPORTED THAT THE PROCLAMATION HAD BEEN
SIGNED. HOWEVER, AT THE SAME TIME JOHN BELLIT OF THE GOV-
ERNOR'S OFFICE CAME OVER AND SHOWED YOU AND THE CHIEF
A PROCLAMATION THAT CALLED FOR NATIONAL GUARD TROOPS
BUT HE SAID IT WAS AWAITING THE GOVERNOR'S ARRIVAL AT THE
STATE BUILDING FOR SIGNATURE.

ACCOMPANIED BY SUPERVISOR DORN, COUNCILMEN MILLS AND
GIBSON, WHO WERE WITH YOU AT THE CHIEF'S OFFICE, WE THEN
WENT TO THE GOVERNOR'S OFFICE AND WERE MET BY MEMBERS
OF HIS STAFF INCLUDING TOM LYNCH, HALE CHAMPION AND
BRAD CRITTENDEN. CHAMPION SAID THAT ANDERSON WAS EN-
ROUTE FROM THE VAN NUYS AIRPORT. FIFTEEN OR TWENTY MIN-
UTES AFTER WE HAD ARRIVED OUR GROUP RETURNED TO THE CITY
HALL WHERE WE FOUND OUT THAT THE LT. GOVERNOR HAD FI-
NALLY ARRIVED AT THE STATE BUILDING AND SIGNED THE PROC-
LAMATION (WE MUST HAVE CROSSED IN THE ELEVATORS). I
BELIEVE THIS WAS 5:05 P.M.

AT NO TIME DURING THE HOURS I HAVE JUST RECOUNTED DID
LT. GOV. ANDERSON PERSONALLY EVER TALK TO THE CHIEF OR
CONTACT HIM.

As a sequel to the riots, Governor Brown had named the Riot
Investigation Commission headed by Mr. McCone, former chairman
of the Atomic Energy Commission and former director of the
Central Intelligence Agency. In a letter to Mr. McCone, Mayor
Yorty stressed that mass migrations to urban centers such as Los

Angeles have "brought large numbers of unskilled and uneducated people to areas where they are unable either to adjust to urban life or compete for available jobs. An atmosphere of lawlessness has been created in an unsatisfactory environment. It is my belief that the Federal government over the years has been slow in recognizing its responsibilities to alleviate the problems arising from this national phenomenon of immigration to cities from other areas, particularly the South. The State has not accepted sufficient responsibility for helping the urban areas in meeting this problem. There is a clear and immediate need to augment the resources available on the local level if this problem is to be overcome."

Mayor Yorty's firm and unyielding stand for law enforcement was accented, by reiteration, on a CBS television program, "Face the Nation" just a week after the riots ended, on Sunday August 22. He unhesitatingly challenged statements by Chester L. Washington, editor of the *Sentinel,* Negro newspaper in Los Angeles, which tended to cast aspersion on the police.

"Upholding the morale of the police is my aim," the Mayor said. "You call an officer, not a politician when trouble comes."

To Martin Agronsky and other newsmen on the panel, Yorty pointed out that "the white community did not attack Negroes," but relied on the proper arm of society, law-enforcement officers, rather than taking the law in their own hands.

At one point involving an alleged instance of the much-mentioned "police brutality," Mayor Yorty with great emphasis said directly to Washington:

"You asked me to call off a hearing on two little girls allegedly being dragged out of class by police" because, as the mayor added, it was not true. "Why not go ahead and tell the real story," he challenged Washington. "I want the public to know the truth."

He added that, in reality, the arrested girls were not taken from the classroom, and had been handcuffed in the police car only to keep them from trying to jump out and possibly harming themselves.

On a basic point regarding efforts to aid the poor, the mayor pointed out that a city program which he originated in April 1962 —the Youth Opportunities Board—had been given Federal funds and had worked smoothly until it had been thrown into confusion by an effort to merge it into the "War on Poverty."

In the wake of the disorders, figures were compiled showing that 3438 adults and 514 juveniles had been arrested on a variety of

214

charges ranging from assault to looting. The records disclosed that of these adults a total of 2057, or more than 50 percent, had been born in Southern States.

Mrs. Frye, the mother of the two brothers, Marquette and Ronald Frye, whose arrest touched off the original incident leading to the riots, was sentenced December 2 to pay a fine of $250, in $10 monthly installments, or twenty-five days in jail. The sentence meted out by Municipal Judge George M. Dell followed Mrs. Frye's conviction by a jury November 1 on a charge of obstructing an officer in the performance of his duty.

* * *

Mayor Yorty in the period following the riots devoted his time to the primary aim of finding solutions for aiding the poor, rather than to futile attempts to place the blame in the disorders. He worked steadily on plans for placing Los Angeles in a stronger position to combat the forces which he recognized as constantly pushing the jobless and the underprivileged toward outbreaks of violence. These objectives included both greater emphasis on state participation in some realms of activity and greater local self-reliance in others. Education and employment must be fostered, he stressed, as the initial steps to meet fundamental economic needs, and respect for law in Los Angeles had to be emphasized by responsible leaders.

"The big cities are the economic building blocks of the United States," the mayor stated. "Without healthy cities no healthy economy can exist in the nation as a whole. So the recognition of the expanding and increasingly important role of cities is absolutely necessary for solutions of the pressing problems of poverty and unemployment within them. Los Angeles and Southern California because of the delay of reapportionment to end rural domination and unfairness have been shortchanged for a long time on their share of gasoline tax money and state funds for schools. The state does not help our big population centers on things like airports and convention centers, as do some other states such as New York and Illinois. This reduces our cities' economic potential. In these realms we could use more State assistance. I'm hoping that it will take place under the just and equitable reapportionment—for which I battled for so many years—which went into effect on October 27, 1965, under a plan finally approved by the Legislature as ordered by the Supreme Court.

"In some other spheres we in Los Angeles are perfectly capable of carrying on our own activities and applying remedies if we have cooperation and understanding at the state and Federal levels. This applies particularly to our Police Department. I gave strong support to Chief Parker during the Watts rioting, in contrast to Governor Brown who vacillated and did vast harm to the situation by blowing hot and cold in regard to Chief Parker.

"We must recognize one stark fact. We come in direct contact on the city level with the lawless, the transients, and new arrivals because we are the entry corridor for most of these people swarming to Southern California. Many Negroes from the South bring with them their long-abiding resentments, their lack of skills, and their poverty inherited from generations of economic and social maladjustment. Some get in trouble out here and of course when they do that they meet the police. It is on the law-enforcement level that Los Angeles must contend with these frustrated or maladjusted people. The city then bears the brunt because the police are called adverse to the Negroes. We shouldn't have criticism from other officials on our legitimate handling of these inevitable collisions with the lawless, but genuine understanding and help and all-out support of fair and just law enforcement.

"That was one of the fundamental facts emerging from the Watts riots. Harm was done to the entire cause of law enforcement and the preservation of our American society under the Constitution by Reverend Martin Luther King and others who, for no good reason except expediency, demanded the removal of Chief Parker in the aftermath of anarchy. Then Governor Brown contributed to the confusion by setting up a corps of press agents in a hotel instead of using his own offices in the State Building across the street from mine in the City Hall where we could have conferred, and issuing misguided press releases. In Rome on his way back home from Greece after the riots broke out he had called our situation here 'war.' But after his arrival in California he wavered on his support of Chief Parker at a time when we needed unqualified support of law enforcement. Governor Brown caused untold trouble by insisting upon going into the riot zone at a time when desperately needed officers had to be diverted in an attempt to protect him, and he was finally compelled to turn back because of the very violence about which he had been warned. I heeded the urgent pleas of Chief Parker not to hamper the police by drawing off patrol forces for my protection, and I did not attempt to go in the area on the ground. My inspections were by helicopter which did not require pulling officers off their jobs to protect me.

"My four-hour interview with Reverend Mr. King in my office revolved around his impossible demands for us to undermine Chief Parker and the police by agreeing to conditions which would have degraded them in the minds of the public and rendered future law enforcement more difficult. These demands included the creation of a so-called Civilian Police Review Board. This supposedly would have given the Negroes and other minorities a better chance against what Communists, dupes, and demagogues have for decades called 'police brutality.' I pointed out repeatedly that under the system of government in Los Angeles the police already are under the direction of a civilian board, the Los Angeles Police Commission. Formation of a new civilian board merely would have been a device to harm the police and bring about an intolerable overlapping of jurisdiction and consequent total confusion.

"Rev. Mr. King fully understood my position in favor of law enforcement against any anarchy group of any color—and that it was not directed against the Negroes as such in the riot area or at any other time—and yet he went out from my office and made an inflammatory and unjustified attack upon Chief Parker. It was then that I was compelled to answer him forcefully."

Mayor Yorty has made it plain many times during the investigations and discussions following the riots that although the placing of blame for the specific outbreak is important, the greater goal is to create conditions which will prevent a repetition. To this end he has redoubled his efforts to obtain what he considers a vital preventive procedure which he had previously sought in vain. This was a comprehensive "community analysis"—or data bank—on the physical assets and liabilities of Los Angeles, of a kind successfully used in other American metropolitan centers. Such an analysis, consisting of detailed studies and filing by computers of the information on all aspects of life in the community, could have been used he feels as a barometer to indicate impending trouble such as that causing the riots. If these signs were detected in time, he has contended, the remedies might be applied in time at specific places to prevent social and economic explosions.

"Community analysis could have helped, but my efforts to get the Federal funds for it were defeated," Mayor Yorty says. "Certain interests in Los Angeles opposed the program because it did involve Federal help, although some of them now have realized that it is of such major importance that we should proceed as quickly as possible to create such a fund of information for use to prevent future crises."

Both the mayor's office and the business community, in particular the Chamber of Commerce headed by F. M. Banks, began devising practical methods of assisting residents of the Watts area. The Chamber of Commerce through a committee headed by Chad Mc-Clellan set to work to "aid the entire curfew area by getting business back on its feet and operating again." One step was to persuade the State Insurance Commission to define the trouble in Watts as "rioting" rather than "insurrection."

"Next," said McClellan, "we went to the financial institutions who agreed that if a business could qualify for a loan in another area, it would be able to get it in the Watts area. If a man could get insurance or financing in Glendale he could get it in Watts."

Special attention was paid to relieving unemployment. In a test period of three months the McClellan Committee succeeded in finding new jobs for 900 unemployed in Watts. As a result of this success the Chamber's Board of Directors approved expansion of the test program into a full-scale continuing activity.

Mayor Yorty gave his support to a specific program for job training which he describes as "the most hopeful I have seen to reach the great mass of frustrated individuals who are unemployed and need encouragement to seek jobs." This is an adaptation of a plan which has been acclaimed for its success originating in Philadelphia. In essence it involves "pre-apprentice training" in fundamentals which untrained job seekers have lacked. It is designed for individuals who are not even up to the Job Corps level. It includes such basic things as attention to simple reading and writing, manners and personal grooming.

After these elemental courses the job seekers are taught how to get along with people and trained for jobs in accordance with their abilities.

Responsible for the program in Philadelphia has been Reverend Leon Sullivan, a Negro minister, who began devoting his efforts to train the poor in his home city. He was so successful that officials of other large cities began watching his achievements. He eventually was given a Ford Foundation grant to acquire equipment for the Philadelphia training program.

Reverend Mr. Sullivan came to Los Angeles to give the benefit of his experience to Mayor Yorty and members of city administration trying to evolve new approaches to job training in the riot region. Reverend E. V. Hill, another Negro minister, became the leader of the effort in Los Angeles.

"The reason this program is so encouraging to me is that it emanates from the people themselves," said Mayor Yorty, "and thus has the benefit of being spontaneous rather than imposed artificially from outside. Reverend Mr. Sullivan's efforts now have the aid of the Office of Economic Opportunity."

Such techniques as setting up a supermarket and giving instruction in the handling of groceries have proved highly valuable in the training effort.

Mayor Yorty encouraged Opportunity Industries Centers as a major facet in a many-sided approach to the solution of unemployment and disquiet in the riot region.

Subsequent to the riots, officials of the Los Angeles Chamber of Commerce decided that Mayor Yorty should have in permanent form some of the thousands of commendatory letters he received during and immediately after the Watts crisis, praising him for his unyielding stand for law enforcement. Under the leadership of J. Don Hanauer of the Chamber a beautifully bound book was prepared containing representative letters.

A typical one read:

"Your support of Chief Parker will be, I believe, a potent factor in the continued maintenance of law and order in this community. Although irresponsible individuals and groups may call for your political demise, responsible elements in this city should unite in support of your continued public service."

Continuingly explosive aspects of the Watts riot situation dominated the report of the McCone Commission, which was made public December 6, 1965, after 100 days of investigation.

Governor Brown and Mayor Yorty acted a few days after the issuance of the report to implement its recommendations. They met harmoniously at a luncheon December 10, and after announcing jointly that the remedial procedures necessarily would be expensive, appointed personal representatives to work on the program. The governor named Winslow Christian, his executive secretary, and Mayor Yorty selected Robert L. Goe, executive assistant.

Immediately afterward, the governor announced he would call a special session of the Legislature to consider educational reforms in Watts and other poverty areas. The commission report had strongly urged sweeping educational changes.

One public official—Lieutant Governor Anderson—was the only individual singled out in the report for criticism in connection with conduct during the riot period. Lieutant Governor Anderson, the report declared in connection with the delay in calling out the National Guard as requested by Mayor Yorty and Police Chief Parker, "hesitated when he should have acted."

In regard to the contention that the California Highway Patrol officers had delayed too long at the scene of the arrests, the McCone report stated:

"Considering the undisputed facts, the Commission finds that the arrest of the Fryes was handled efficiently and expeditiously. The sobriety test administered by the California Highway Patrol and its use of a transportation vehicle for the prisoner and a tow truck to remove his car are in accordance with the practices of other law enforcement agencies, including the Los Angeles Police Department. . . .

"Although the wisdom of stopping the withdrawal to make these arrests (persons in the crowd, for allegedly spitting on the officers) has been questioned, the Commission finds no basis for criticizing the judgment of the officers on the scene."

In its analyses and recommendations, the commission rejected the idea of a new police review board in Los Angeles as had been urged by some Negroes and a few other persons, but it did urge strengthening of the present civilian Police Commission. It also recommended an independent inspector general under the authority of the Chief of Police to investigate citizen complaints, and an expanded community relations program by the police department. Mayor Yorty soon afterward did propose the appointment of an inspector general, in line with the recommendation.

A Federal program involving an outlay of $4,500,000 for three job skill centers in the Los Angeles area—in Watts, East Los Angeles and Pacoima—was set up late in January 1966 with funds from the U. S. Department of Labor and the Department of Health, Education and Welfare. It, too, was designed to carry out the recommendations of the McCone Commission. The California State Employment Service was listed as the sponsor of the project, which was designed to be carried out in cooperation with a job placement task force of the Los Angeles Chamber of Commerce.

The commission laid great stress on increased efforts to provide jobs, including training and placement centers.

A grave warning was issued about the continuing tensions between the general community and the "disadvantaged area." If allowed to persist, the commission declared, these tensions:

"Could in time split our society irretrievably. So serious and so explosive is the situation that, unless it is checked, the August riots may seem by comparison to be only a curtain-raiser for what could blow up one day in the future."

This was, in substance, exactly what Mayor Yorty had already declared about future dangers. Action which he had taken prior to the issuance of the report was designed to help accomplish in Los Angeles the goals set by the McCone Commission to improve the lives of the poor and ward off repetitions of violence.

CHAPTER XXVII

. . . fated always to disagree.

ERNEST DOWSON

In California, picking a political fight is the simplest of procedures, particularly when, as in 1965–66, a race for governor is
in the offing.

Sam Yorty, a Democrat who on occasion has not hesitated to turn
his back on his party, and Governor Edmund G. (Pat) Brown, a
Republican turned Democrat, have managed to focus more attention on themselves than anyone else in this situation hurling
challenges from opposite sides of the lists in California's political
arena. The causes which projected Mayor Yorty into one camp and
Governor Brown into another trace to such unexpected sources as
an unpredictable Republican Senator and to the husband of a defeated councilwoman. Political feuds sometimes have simple causes;
on other occasions they are obscured by a host of tiny contributing
factors. The Yorty-Brown antagonism stems from circumstances
displaying the inevitability of a Greek tragedy. Yet on occasion the
jousting has had something of a Sancho Panza touch.

Most important of the basic causes was a decision taken in
Washington, D.C., regarding the 1958 race for governor of California by the then-Republican leader of the U. S. Senate, William
F. Knowland of Oakland. Apparently without telling anyone—even
his family, it was reputed at the time—he announced his candidacy
for governor. Consternation and confusion ensued in the GOP. The
governor at the time, Republican Goodwin J. (Goody) Knight, was
contemplating running again, and was considered to be a virtual
certainty for re-election during that Eisenhower era. The Knowland
announcement, however, upset everything. Knight at first refused to
abandon his own race for governor; but, after all sorts of manipu-

lations including the personal intervention of Vice-President Nixon, Knight fumingly entered the Senatorial race, giving up his governorship candidacy to the unabashed Knowland.

The outcome was inevitable from the outset. The Republicans were so shattered by the Knowland move and the realignment of candidacies made necessary by it that they fell easy prey to the Democrats. Brown, as the Democratic candidate for governor, was elected not so much through his own efforts as through the disaffection and intra-party strife of the Republicans. Knowland not only was overwhelmingly beaten by Brown but Knight was carried down in the Republican debacle and snowed under by Democratic Senator Clair Engle.

Pat Brown, originally a Republican who had become a Democrat in 1934, because, as he said, of his admiration for Franklin Delano Roosevelt, thus fell heir by indirection to the governorship through the mistake of a leader in his own former party.

Brown was born in San Francisco in 1905. He obtained his law degree at San Francisco College of Law at the age of twenty-two. By the time he was thirty-six he had been elected District Attorney of San Francisco County and then in 1950 he became State Attorney General. He used this office as a steppingstone to the governorship, as had Earl Warren.

By the time Sam Yorty was elected mayor, Brown was approaching the end of his first term and was preparing for the 1962 contest which eventually developed between him and former Vice-President Nixon. Brown did win the governorship again over Nixon. Even while this contest was in progress the rift between Brown and Yorty was widening over the influence of Eugene and Rosalind Wyman in state political affairs. At this point Councilwoman Wyman's ambitions were running high and she was reputed to be preparing to run for some state or national office. Her husband in his position as State Democratic Chairman meanwhile was working hard for Brown and in so doing was creating greater tensions between Brown and Yorty.

It was not until 1965, however, that the proportions of the looming conflict between the mayor and the governor began to be apparent. Wyman and Brown, according to political observers, had seen in the James Roosevelt candidacy against Sam Yorty their opportunity to dispose of the mayor politically. Their calculations went awry. Instead of Roosevelt emerging as Mayor of Los Angeles and an ally of the Wyman-Brown faction in Southern California,

Yorty won so overwhelmingly that he instantly became a menace on the state level to the ambitions of the governor, and Council-woman Wyman herself was defeated.

This situation involving Yorty stirred national discussion just as the rising political star of Representative John V. Lindsay, the Republican who was moving toward the office of Mayor of New York, was winning the attention of Americans in all areas.

Russell Kirk, the columnist, in a discussion of Sam Yorty's new position after the 1965 elections wrote:

"Mrs. Wyman had flirted with the possibility of becoming United States Senator, Congresswoman, or Governor.

"But now the Wymans are political handicaps to their ally, Governor Pat Brown, and the leftward-moving faction of California Democrats is harder hit by this blow than it was even by the election of Republican George Murphy to the Senate, or the re-election of Mayor Yorty by a walloping majority.

"Ever since Samuel Yorty became Mayor of Los Angeles, the Wymans have attempted to undo him. That battle is ended now, with Mr. Yorty the best-entrenched mayor in this country.

"And California Democrats are likely to shift toward the moderate views of Mayor Yorty and Speaker Jesse Unruh."

When the Watts riots occurred the serious political confrontations of the mayor and the governor began to assume an even more inflexible form. The tempestuous events of the rioting period—not only the maiming, looting, burning and killing—but the political accompaniment plunged California into a maelstrom of contentions and stresses.

Within less than a month after the riots the Associated Press had condensed the feelings of many political observers into a dispatch from Sacramento:

"Rioting in Los Angeles' Negro slums has converted next year's California elections into 'a new ball game,' says Hale Champion, chief political adviser to Democratic Governor Edmund G. Brown . . .

"Many Democrats believe the eruption in the slums of Watts has posed a deep problem for Democrats already worried about holding the loyalty of white residents of the suburbs.

"The riots have given a boost, they say, to Los Angeles Mayor Samuel W. Yorty, who is considering running against Brown in the Democratic primary next June. He has steadfastly defended the city's Police Chief, William H. Parker, against Negro accusations of police brutality.

"Even before the riots, Democratic strategists expressed fear of voter rebellion in Los Angeles county's nominally Democratic white suburbs.

"Don Bradley, who will help run Brown's re-election campaign, recalled that the registered Democrats in the 'predominantly white low-income areas' rejected party civil rights leadership last year (1964) and voted for an initiative nullifying anti-discrimination housing laws. The measure won in Los Angeles County by almost a million votes."

Just before he took off for Japan, Korea, and Viet Nam on a trade promotion visit in November 1965, Mayor Yorty was honored at a $100-a-plate testimonial dinner at the Hollywood Palladium. More than 1800 persons turned out for the event which brought in more than $100,000. Mayor Yorty had said the funds would go for "voter education" but he did not rule out the possibility of their utilization as campaign financing. Gene Autry and the mayor's long-time supporter George Putnam TV news commentator were at the mayor's table.

Mixed in with these serious issues and political maneuverings there came the seemingly inevitable concomitant of irrelevant or frivolous exchanges between the principals. Governor Brown failed to greet Princess Margaret and Lord Snowdon in his home city of San Francisco on their visit to the United States in the fall of 1965. He went to Los Angeles instead to greet the Princess there as if it were an attempt to supersede the functions of the mayor. Mayor Yorty, though, happened to get in a position so that when a newsphoto was taken for the front page of the Los Angeles Times the Yorty visage was full-face to the camera, and Governor Brown's was a second-best profile.

Governor Brown signed a bill reapportioning the Legislature at the exact hour in Los Angeles when Mayor Yorty's weekly press conference was always conducted, so the mayor who had long advocated reapportionment could not attend.

Needling back and forth went on from day to day. The governor, obviously with tongue in cheek, wrote a "Dear Sam" letter offering to relieve Los Angeles city police officers from duty on the freeways by replacing them with California Highway Patrol officers. This drew an immediate rejoinder from Sam Yorty that it was just another "political move," and that in previous discussions the idea had been rejected. Still it was typical of the mounting antagonism, presaging a showdown.

In Los Angeles after the Watts riots, the Yorty-Brown disagreements became a predominant topic because of the impending election for Governor of California in 1966. I heard expressions of opinion about Sam on all levels.

A woman checker in a supermarket volunteered:

"Sam Yorty says and does the kind of things I believe in."

Meredith (Music Man) Willson, the composer and a canny observer who meets all sorts of people, remarked to me:

"Sam can go all the way."

Perhaps the most impressive summary came from a man unique in Los Angeles business circles. Walter Braunschweiger, executive vice-president of the Bank of America, retired—and the "retired" must be in quotes—has been president or chairman of the four major downtown groups in the city: the Chamber of Commerce, the All-Year Club, the Downtown Business Men's Association, and the Community Chest. He remained after "retirement" in advisory capacities to the bank's board.

"As a banker who has known Sam Yorty thirty years, I have been impressed always by his integrity and honesty in all affairs," Braunschweiger told me. "He has the stamina and courage to fight for what is right, and he has never resorted to the usual political procedure of trying to evade issues. His conduct always has been that if you are right, let nothing stop you. Diplomacy has had to take second place sometimes when he has refused to compromise on principles. My feeling always has been that Sam Yorty because of the combination of these qualities of courage and integrity is qualified to hold high political offices."

CHAPTER XXVIII

Tell the people you are going to do something, then do it, then tell them you've done it.

SAM YORTY

Sam was determined not to go off on exultant tangents because of a "mandate from the people" in his double victory, the personal triumph over James Roosevelt and the subsequent repudiation of Mrs. Wyman by the voters. His chief aim, instead, was to seek to put into practical effect the long-range objectives with which he had entered office, many of which had been sidetracked because of turmoil involving the City Council and the mayor. Coupled with this program he embarked upon another designed to provide new blood for the commissions in Los Angeles.

With the newly acquired asset of a more cooperative council, many of the basic improvements in city government which had been almost overlooked in the bickering between mayor and council now began to emerge and move toward realization. Part of this advance was due to citizen participation which formed so great a part of the Yorty political creed. By this time six or seven thousand members of advisory groups named by the mayor were participating in neighborhood activities aimed at keeping the people closely in touch with what was going on at the City Hall. These advisory groups deliberately were set up geographically so they would not coincide with council districts and thus possibly become local political pressure groups. Rather, they were created along the lines of neighborhood interests. The mayor met at regular intervals with the chairmen of these advisory groups so as to keep in close touch with the sentiments of people in various regions.

Great emphasis was placed, too, on the participation of women in planning and accomplishment. The Women's Division of the Los

Angeles Chamber of Commerce and the League of Women Voters were encouraged to keep up with current developments in the City Hall. For the benefit of citizens at both ends of the age bracket, a series of Town Hall meetings on all manner of political subjects was held once a month on a Saturday, with speakers and moderators at group sessions. Both senior citizens and teenagers were included. These attracted as many as three thousand persons who met at the City Hall Annex and the Police Facility and indulged at noon in an old-fashioned box lunch. Often Sam himself talked to them and listened to the ideas of individuals. The subjects ranged all the way from the theory of city government to specific beautification projects.

"All these things have resulted in the greatest participation in local government we have ever had in Los Angeles," said Deputy Mayor Joe Quinn. "The communication within the City Hall family and outside is unprecedented. Sam Yorty has demonstrated his deep belief in keeping the people informed on all levels of government and to do this he has kept his staff on the job finding out all about what is going on at the county, state, and Federal levels as well as the municipal one."

Los Angeles has so many suburbs and so many celebrities that it has combined the two situations and come up with an enormous number of "Honorary Mayors." This dates back to the days of the late Al Jolson who was an honorary mayor himself, but it has flowered and proliferated during the Yorty regime. Sam Yorty, always an organizer, has gone a step further than his predecessors and encouraged the formation of the "Association of Honorary Mayors." This group has been headed by Francis Lederer, longtime film leading man, and honorary mayor of Canoga Park who is an enthusiastic participant in Yorty gatherings.

Among those who have won the honor of being named honorary mayors and are included in the association are Mr. and Mrs. Roy Rogers of Chatsworth, Michael Landon of Encino, Frank Wilcox of Granada Hills, Bill Vileta of Highland Park, Steve Allen of Hollywood, Allin Slate of Magnolia, Miss Merry Anders of Mission Hills, Miss Verna Felton of North Hollywood, Monty Montana of Northridge, Jerry Paris of Pacific Palisades, Ed Nelson of Pacoima, Bror E. (Ben) Nelson of Palms, Philip Ahn of Panorama City, Miss Amanda Blake of Reseda, Ray Crash Corrigan of Sepulveda, Harve Presnell of Sherman Oaks, Dale Robertson of Studio City, Max (Alibi) Terhune of Sylmar, Don Reed of Tarzana, Wendell Niles of Toluca

Lake, James R. Kemper of Tujunga and Sunland, Miss Joan Staley of Universal City, "Aladdin" of Van Nuys, Scott E. Miller of Westchester, William Deemer of West Hollywood, Joseph C. Valentine of Westwood, A. N. Albright of Wilmington, Miss Frances O'Farrell of Winnetka, and Gary Owens of Woodland Hills.

Mayor Yorty undoubtedly has a schedule of more meetings with councilmen, the City Attorney, department managers, commissioners, the women's groups, the advisory boards, the editorial boards of the newspapers, radio and TV executives, his "advisory cabinet" of a hundred businessmen and union leaders, and his active staff than any previous mayor. In addition he conducts his long-established "catch-as-catch-can" press conferences every Wednesday as he has done since taking office.

It was in this atmosphere of citizen participation that he launched in the summer of 1965, after his re-election, the drive to make a reality of the goals as yet unattained because of previous disruptions in the council-mayor brawlings. At the top of the list was the objective of creating a genuine Master Plan for Los Angeles, something which hitherto had never been accomplished. Along with this he set his sights on a comprehensive revision of the City Charter on scientific lines.

Stubborn, underlying opposition to charter reform existed among powerful groups. Prominent among these were city employees who, through gradual accretion over the years had built up pay increases actually favorable to them as contrasted with the nominal barometer, the outside scale in private industry. This was due largely to the fact that the criteria used for figuring the periodic increases given city employees provided an opportunity for fractional gains above those prevailing elsewhere in the community, according to a government analyst. These gains, the employees feared, might be jeopardized by revision of the charter which would establish new standards of procedure on equating municipal pay with that in industry.

Inertia and outright opposition have been apparent, too, in some major facets of business. Many business people were quoted as saying that, "We have good city government now—very little petty larceny, not many shakedowns. Let's not jump overboard on charter revisions and maybe get something worse than we have."

Between the inertia and the sometimes-outspoken hostility, the charter remained its old piecemeal self, patched and re-patched but not rehabilitated.

Other Yorty goals included the long-cherished hope of eliminating city property taxes, of determining the proper kind of long-range mass transportation system needed by the Los Angeles metropolitan area, of providing greater economic and job opportunities for minorities such as Negroes and Mexican-Americans, of stamping out disruptive spot zoning in established residential areas, of aiding the elderly, of creating a giant auditorium and convention center in Elysian Park, of getting a new main zoo open in Griffith Park to round out the activities of the Children's Zoo, and, always, of working toward a solution of the menace of air pollution.

The inequity of the school aid situation was disclosed in detail in a report from City Administrative Officer Piper to Mayor Yorty.

"The figures concerning State aid to schools show that Los Angeles City Schools have not received nearly as much revenue from the State on a per-pupil basis as the average school district." Piper's report said, "It is also clear that the trend has been toward reduced State support for City Schools since the portion of the total budget financed through State aid has decreased from 38 percent in 1954–55 to 28.1 percent in 1962–63. This means that the proportion of local financing compared to State aid has increased from 1.63:1 ten years ago to 2.56:1. In the latest year for which data was available to the City Schools Budget Division (1963–64), the percentage of State Financing of Los Angeles City Schools was 10 percent less than the percentage of State financing of other school district budgets."

In his endeavor to bring fresh blood and new vigor into these efforts he took a step which resulted for a time in such clamor that some observers wondered whether the new "peace era" was going to survive. As he departed for Europe soon after his second inauguration, on a combined study of air routes beneficial to Los Angeles and a glimpse behind the iron curtain in Poland and Hungary, he announced a policy of City Commissioners serving only one five-year term. This sudden and unexpected action, even though Sam had made it clear from the outset of his first term that in his concept commissioners served at the pleasure of the mayor, created an uproar. By the time of his return from Europe the furor had subsided sufficiently for an orderly reorganization of the commissions. As a matter of fact, it was not a total obliteration of all members but rather the changing about of a few from one commission to another and the naming of many new appointees for the blood transfusion.

In the shuffle there was an indication of the progress Sam had made in public estimation and of his success in efforts to heal old municipal wounds. This was illustrated in the appointment of Dr. Reynaldo J. Carreon, eye, ear, nose and throat specialist and a native of El Paso, who had been a leader in Mexican-American affairs in Los Angeles for a generation. Dr. Carreon had served as the confidential emissary of Sam's predecessor Mayor Poulson on many Latin-American missions, and also had been adviser to mayors as far back as George Cryer who was in office when Sam arrived in Los Angeles as a boy. Dr. Carreon accepted from Sam an appointment on the vital Police Commission where another notable Mexican-American, Francisco Bravo, M.D., had rendered distinguished service during the preceding term. The appointment of Dr. Carreon seemed emblematic of the spirit of amity Sam Yorty was trying to inject into municipal affairs.

By way of contrast to the selection of these older civic leaders, Sam also made some appointments emphasizing youth. The youngest of the commissioners in this category was Robert N. Starr, thirty-two, a microbiologist of Sherman Oaks in the San Fernando Valley. At the time of the shuffling he was serving on the Building and Safety Commission, and Sam moved him up to a more important post on the Harbor Commission. Starr had won a wide reputation for his civic activities in the San Fernando Valley.

Among the aggravations besetting the mayor during the long period of the Wyman feuds until the defeat of Councilwoman Wyman was the issue of the use of funds from the local bed or motel and hotel tax, which had been considered originally for a reserve for the proposed Los Angeles auditorium and convention center. Mrs. Wyman had succeeded in having this money diverted into the general fund where it was not earmarked for auditorium purposes. It was necessary for the mayor to begin all over again and to attempt to have at least one-half of the money expressly designated for the improvement fund.

Mayor Yorty had succeeded in his objective of having the City and County Health Departments merge, and now he was aiming at some sort of system which would permit the same thing to happen to the police and fire departments. For this he had considerabe precedent but always on a smaller scale as far as the cities were concerned. Ever since the "Lakewood plan" had gone into effect a decade before there had been a number of cooperative arrangements between the county and municipal police, fire, health and sanitation departments. It was more difficult to contemplate the fusing of such gigantic organizations as the offices of the Los Angeles County Sheriff and of the Los Angeles Police Department. One of the real questions was whether tax rates under such a system would actually be less. It had been pointed out in regard to the Health Departments' merger that although a nominal saving of $5,000,000 a year—the cost of operating the Los Angeles department—was involved, there were other factors which reduced this amount as a net saving. Fees and other charges had brought in a considerable amount. Under the new system larger numbers of employees were bound to be needed than the number required for only the county or the city.

Among the efforts to which Sam Yorty gave top priority was that for a community analysis program, which he so far had been unable to get. He kept harking back to this over and over again. His contention was that with the city seriously undertaking a cohesive master plan for the first time it must provide a more scientific diagnosis of the community's physical aspects and its needs.

Los Angeles by this time had gone out and, after a national search for the best man, had hired Calvin S. Hamilton of Pittsburgh as director of the Planning Department. Prior to going to Pittsburgh he had been Planning Director of Indianapolis for six years and had won a wide reputation for his achievements there and for his imaginative approach to the whole subject of putting cities in their proper grooves for the future. His academic training had included work or degrees at the University of Illinois, Harvard, Massachusetts Institute of Technology, and London University, with time in Sweden and in Florence, Italy, for particularized delving into European municipal development.

At Mayor Yorty's request, Hamilton summed up in the fall of 1965 the aims of the Community Analysis Program for Los Angeles, which involves a total cost of $3,700,000 over a three-year period. The study involves two-thirds in Federal grants and one-third from local contributions. The city's contribution would be in the form of salaries of existing employees, services and equipment. Hamilton prepared the application which was approved by the City Planning Commission, and also was authorized by vote of the City Coordinating Board composed of the heads of municipal agencies concerned with the physical development of the city.

The mayor referred to the Watts riots as one good reason for initiating a CAP program.

"Of particular concern at the present time, the Community Analysis Program would provide the most practical and effective means of spotting underlying causes of social and racial unrest," he said. "While not a study of racial relations itself, the program would nevertheless provide public and private agencies with an early awareness of the many physical, economic and social factors which contribute to the problem.

"Here is the opportunity for the city to examine itself and inventory its situation in a comprehensive manner. Too often decisions are made with insufficient facts on the city's development. Through the availability of comprehensive data available for computer processing, we will be in a better position to know our city. This CAP will be helpful not only to the city government but to private business in making decisions on private investments.

"The City of Los Angeles is the third largest city in the United States with an April 1965 population of 2,731,700 and a housing inventory of 1,047,560. The growth rate since April 1960 is 4163 persons per month and 2266 housing units. The rapid growth of the city, together with obsolescence and decay has presented a challenge which the City Planning Commission is finding itself unable to meet.

"Because the same problem faces all the major cities in the United States, the Federal government has made funds available on a matching basis to study the problems. At least a hundred cities have taken advantage of this program in order to make the first step toward solving their problems. That step is gathering information."

The Community Analysis Program would assist in the Master Plan to set Los Angeles on the path of the future with scientific assurance. But coupled with the "computer era" techniques would be all possible human counsel and guidance too. Mayor Yorty and Planning Director Hamilton initiated a long-range effort to set up community goals, so that the analyses and other technical devices could then become the implementing tools for the endeavor. For this purpose, they called on the latent talents of churches of all denominations to aid in fixing goals.

Los Angeles "provides a speeded-up version of a process of urbanization that is imminent for every city of the nation," Hamilton said. "If this is true, it is important that the churches not only observe and reflect on what is happening in Los Angeles but more than that, they have a responsibility to participate with other segments of society in the shaping of the growing city and its style of life. We need and we want the input of the religious community to help determine what kind of region and what kind of city Los Angeles is to become. We have the golden opportunity. We can make our future environment what we want it to be. But we must decide what we want it to be! The religious community of Los Angeles can make tremendous contributions to humanity, for what we do in Los Angeles will be carefully watched. Probably imitated. The pattern that emerges may well be the forerunner of the urban world of tomorrow.

"To develop such a goals-setting program for the Los Angeles region, we must answer some basic questions about its quality of life and the types of policies that should be developed to create a satisfying life for the people who are here today, those thousands who are arriving each week, and the vast multitude who will reside here in the future.

"This Goals Project is oriented toward answering those questions. It proposes to utilize the resources of that portion of the community that is naturally contemplative of the moral and philosophical needs of man coupled with those resources in the community capable of contributing to the substance of this future civilization by anticipating and delineating both needs and solutions arising out of future advances in science and technology. This project also proposes to use public planning agency responsibilities as a catalyst in bringing together the knowledge of these varied groups to bear on finding direction for Los Angeles and its region, and to use the results of this thinking process in providing public policy guides for the future development of the region."

Sam Yorty well realized that in many cases he could only initiate; he could not hope to see full materialization of his programs during his terms in office. The Master Plan itself, even with the expected aid of mathematical models and every advanced technique, could not be expected to be a reality until 1970, a year beyond the end of his current term. Even after that, it would be constantly unfolding, constantly adapting itself to changes in social forces, population pressures, new building materials, advanced architecture and citizens artistic aspirations. He could only help start the movement.

Some things he could see coming to fruition. The new municipal Junior Art Center at Barnsdall Park had been started as a 1965

Christmas present to the children of Los Angeles. The zoo was under way in Griffith Park. The Civic Center was progressing.

Mayor Yorty's determination to have the Plaza restoration project resumed did in fact come to a successful culmination late in 1965. Under an agreement entered into by the state, the county, and the city, funds provided by the Legislature were released for continuation of the work on the old Pico House (hotel), the Masonic Hall, the Mercedes Theater, and other structures which for years had presented an unsightly appearance due to the bogging down of the work.

It represented another instance of the persistence of Mayor Yorty having broken through official inertia to accomplish a specific objective for the benefit of the city, although he was the first to give credit to many others in reaching this goal. The Plaza restoration was, in actuality, a continuation of the work done by one remarkable woman, in particular, and other dedicated civic leaders in creating Olvera Street, the Mexican thoroughfare adjacent to the Plaza. This colorful street was rescued from its former condition of abandonment and degradation by Mrs. Christine Sterling, with the aid of Harry Chandler, late publisher of the Los Angeles *Times*, and John Steven McGroarty, *Times* columnist and Representative in Congress. Olvera Street with its typical Mexican shops and restaurants became, in time, the leading tourist attraction in Los Angeles.

The proceeds from Olvera Street, channeled through an organization known as El Pueblo de Los Angeles headed by Superior Court Judge McIntyre Faries, aided in the Plaza restoration fund. Consuelo de Bonzo, owner of La Golondrina Cafe in the street; Mario Valdez who became manager of the street after Mrs. Sterling's death; Bill Gaskin, manager of the Latin-American Trade Center and many other historically minded citizens aided in creating public interest in the Plaza region.

The Music Center, although a citizen-county project, had been aided by Sam's own efforts and was gaining new international recognition every day. The Cultural Heritage Board was bringing a new awareness to Los Angeles of its place in history, and the opportunity to introduce traditions of the past graciously into the present. City government was gaining in orderliness and efficiency. New attention was being given to the needs of the underprivileged.

Planners throughout the world, stirred by intimations of great things to come, were looking toward Los Angeles and saying:

"Watch! The megalopolis begins to have a soul."

CHAPTER XXIX

A civilization begins to manifest itself when men and women have begun to take thought about what it is that they construct, and why, and to what end. It begins to be a living whole when the idea of beauty has found its place alongside the pressure of utility and the spur of need.

AUGUST HECKSCHER

Of all the things he has learned trying to aid in creation of a better city, Sam Yorty knows the most important is thinking in the present tense about future accomplishments, without getting sidetracked or discouraged. He suffers like his contemporaries in high political office from an occupational hazard. General Dwight D. Eisenhower when he was President voiced the common plaint: "I'm so busy I never have time to think."

Sam works, as it were, in a hydraulic world. All things are fluid, flowing, changing, shifting, subject to the slightest pressure, defying containment, everlastingly elusive. He must seek to make decisions *now* for a hypothetical *then*. It is a world tending to cause pessimism. Nothing ever seems really accomplished. The social order backslides like poor mortal sinners who have hit the sawdust trail and then fallen from grace. Contending with the intangible backsliders, Sam has attempted to handle multifarious subjects simultaneously; to move his city forward, not just materially but on many fronts. He has tried to get buildings built while seeking jobs for the poor. His thoughts on a Master Plan are interrupted by the need to combat a riot. He goes from greeting a Princess to negotiate a tax reform. He is diverted momentarily from plans for a Children's Zoo to serious thoughts on the crime rate. He turns from a letter to the mayor of a sister city of Los Angeles to nullify a Communist thrust at the needy.

Amid the press of these and a thousand other questions thrusting in upon him, Sam Yorty depends each morning upon a period of meditation during which he thinks of the larger aspect of his responsibilities and asks spiritual guidance. He excludes details from his mind, dwells upon directions, trends, goals, fruitions, determinations, conclusions. From these he then shapes his conduct in regard to specifics when he enters upon the hurly-burly of his daily tasks.

It is from these meditations that he draws the strength for contending with all his problems.

His conduct is directed toward achieving many accomplishments for the benefit of Los Angeles. He is working on crime statistics not for their own sake but for a definite aim:

"We must make our cities safe."

He considers that a Master Plan for a city, any city—but particularly Los Angeles in his own case—must be concerned not only with buildings, freeways, transit, zoning, height limit, drainage, construction materials, and geography but with the way people live, how they are protected, what their freedoms are, how they can express themselves.

In this, he agrees with the statement of City Planning Director Hamilton that:

"We need a philosophy of planning before we can do a responsible job of planning for the citizens of a 'great City.'

"Pending technological changes forecast one area within which planning must anticipate change and for which planning must determine goals. In order to arrive at the physical expression of city development it is equally necessary to know what the human values and individual desires are that are the basic ingredients of a community.

"Physical form results from human activity and in varying degrees responds to the individual decisions that ultimately produce the structure of the city. Facilities for movement, structures for shelter, business, production, and recreation—these are what we see and these are the factors that give substance to the city, but each element was the result of basic human desire and need. Within the city, and particularly within the context of contemporary human urban civilization, human desires far outstrip the physical shell that past generations have constructed to house human activities. This in a large measure is the cause of blight and slums and creates the necessity constantly to renew the antiquated city—antiquated in the sense of the lag between human desire and technology on the one hand and urban capital investment and lack of flexibility on the other."

For people to enjoy their physical city, it is necessary that they be safe. That is why Mayor Yorty has been taking the lead in collecting material to show that the courts, in his opinion, are sacrificing the law-abiding citizen in some cases to the criminal— through technicality. He has been making up a montage, or compendium, of notable cases in which convicted murderers and sex criminals have been released from prison because of technical trivialities.

"The individual's right of fair trial is and will always remain as one of the foundation stones of our system," he says. "But the right of each individual to be protected from crime is equally basic and should be guarded with at least equal zeal. Unless it is, if the criminal offender is afforded more protection than those who obey the law, the meaning of all individual rights can disappear."

Law enforcement, to the mayor, means the carrying forward of the process of justice from the patrolman on the beat, doing his job for society amid constant personal peril, right through the courts so that just punishment is meted where merited. Otherwise, he contends, the failure of the judicial system to implement the efforts of the law-enforcement officers creates disillusionment and discouragement among the police, and frustration and bewilderment among the people.

Constantly, he stresses law enforcement as the keystone to all progress in the city.

*　*　*

Occasionally, by way of relief, Mayor Sam permits himself a half-fanciful look into the future, made up of technical projection, science fiction, the dreams of city planners, and his own aspirations. He puts it in the present tense as if the years had rolled away and he himself were seeing the Los Angeles-that-Is-to-Be.

*　*　*

He will be looking at this city from the symbolic white tower of the City Hall, his vantage point for both physical observations and mental scannings of far horizons. It will be a clear day; by all means, a clear day. Gone will be the obliterating menace of man-made smog choking the inhabitants with the wastes of their own scientific creations. Smog will be gone in Los Angeles in that happy day of the future—say in a generation, in 1996 or some such date—because men will have been forced by circumstance to learn that to live at all there must be some practical appliance of helping others to survive too.

So, first of all, it will be a clear day. From the City Hall tower the pristine landscape, long obscured by noxious vapors, will stand forth once more under the brilliance of a sun welcomed back to its old haunts. Up there on Mount Wilson, clothed again in emerald reforestation covering the black scabs of old fire wounds, astronomers in the observatory tower no doubt will be peering at moon travelers as well as comets, at planet voyagers as well as galaxies.

Excursions into Space, however, will have failed to divert the ordinary mortal's primary attention from the affairs of Planet Earth. Automation, ten-hour work weeks, convertible helicopter-cars, computer kitchens, robot-nurse hospitals, greater longevity and almost-intolerable crowding will be providing their own crop of current problems. Science will not, in any material degree, have changed the physical appearance of the Los Angeles Basin.

Besides the mountains there will also be the sea. From the City Hall tower, the view of distant San Pedro, Wilmington, and Long Beach harbors likewise will be uninterrupted by the erstwhile air pollutants. At the harbor, atomic ships will be visible as mechanical stevedores swiftly load and unload them. Giant submarines will be bringing raw materials from the new "granary of the sea" to provide quick protein food in wholesale quantities. Electronic and atomic devices still will be extracting petroleum from far beneath the ocean floor, but not for fuel, only for the proteins to be obtained from it, too.

Back and forth from rejuvenated Santa Catalina Island, transformed by face-lifting into a seaward suburb, huge air-steam hovering barges will skim above the surface of the waves at an elevation of four or five feet, carrying commuters. Water supplies will have ceased to be a problem on the island and elsewhere along the coast due to new techniques in sea water conversion. Sam Yorty will find Catalina far different from the sleepy retreat it was when he went there to rest after his first campaign way back—when was it?—in 1936.

Primarily, though, in the Los Angeles of the Future, Sam will be interested as he always has been in how ordinary people get along in their ordinary lives, every day. The appearance of the megalopolis is bound to provide some clues just by a glance from the City Hall tower.

As a revised Biblical phrase might say:

". . . And the streets shall be paved with grass; and the people shall rejoice thereon."

Nearly all the main streets will be lawn from curb to curb as a radical extension of the "green belt" idea to provide a glimpse of rural atmosphere in urban areas. Paved streets will be unnecessary because public transportation will have taken several pleasant new forms. In particular, the main arteries will have their own fleet of hover-craft borne along gently by air propulsion, carrying anyone who wishes to go a considerable distance. Their use will permit the aesthetic use of the streets for long, green parks.

Around the perimeter of principal business and shopping centers a transformed mode of public conveyance is to be noted. This consists of immense flying cranes of the type developed a generation before—in 1966—by the Sikorsky Corporation. At huge parking lots—"community corrals"—for the new-type small electric and atomic vehicles owned in common by all the residents of the various municipalities making up the megalopolis there will be pick ups by the flying cranes. These are supplementary to the hover-craft and have different routes.

Surface travel on pneumatic tracks is the third main device for mass transportation in addition to the hover-craft and the flying cranes. The tracks are for use by the small swift autotype machines, all of which are equipped with reverse magnetism to prevent collisions. These handy little everyday transport machines are purchased out of tax funds and belong to everybody. A housewife going to the store takes a machine from the sidewalk, drives to her market, and leaves it there in the common pool. When she comes out she selects another handy atom cart and goes home in it.

Fleets of roaming repairmen in Automobile Club uniforms constantly patrol the passageways designated for the carts and immediately take in tow any which have broken down. For long trips into the suburbs where it is inconvenient for a passenger to reach a hover-craft or flying crane, the cart which is adaptable to tracks is put on the line headed in the desired direction and shunted on to the line of its destination at various switching yards. Attendants at these yards expertly take care of the switching which is controlled

240

by computers after the passengers in the individual machines push a destination button.

Guided by a Master Plan under constant technical improvement, the physical megalopolis stretching from San Diego through Santa Barbara is divided by intent into a comprehensive pattern of centers and connecting corridors. The business centers are nodes with radiating spokes so as to permit all types of living within each area. The Master Plan has provided that with high-rise buildings in the nodes there are spaces for normal-sized apartments, duplexes and individual homes so as to avoid long stretches of uniformity devoted to any one type of habitation. In the same way opportunity is divided for people of every taste to have a cool climate at the beach, a warm dry climate in the San Fernando Valley or at Tujunga, and flatland in the valleys or view lots in the mountains. Developments in building materials have made it possible for such cheap construction that less affluent people can enjoy hillside or hilltop living as well as the rich.

A complete choice is available under these circumstances in perimeter regions around Westwood, Hollywood, Topanga, Van Nuys, the airports, the downtown area, San Gabriel Valley, Orange County and elsewhere.

Density of population in the far-flung regions of the megalopolis is the determining factor in the particular mode of transportation most adaptable to its needs. The handicaps of Los Angeles in the old days of 1966 have been overcome. At that time there was never enough density for economic use of subways and even conventional monorails and the most improved types of surface vehicles were unable to cope with the distances involved and the spread out nature of the population. Elevated railways likewise were ruled out because of their unsavory reputation for noise and quick obsolescence. The clogged freeways also proved inadequate for automobiles, although they became useful for the routing of electronic and atom vehicles when they materialized to supplant gasoline-driven automobiles.

Transition of the petroleum industry into the production of protein has been carried out in an orderly fashion to avoid economic collapse of that segment of the business world.

Predominant in the thinking of community leaders in the 1996 era is the objective of providing adequate space for wholesome recreational and cultural activities. In this the presence of the

2,870,000-acre Angeles National Park on the very edge of the mega-lopolis has proved of overwhelming importance. The discovery of new seeding techniques and efficient fire-resistant plants in scientific studies at the Los Angeles State and County Arboretum in Arcadia, the Santa Ana Botanic Garden at Claremont and in National Forest experiment areas at Glendora and Riverside has made possible the unprecedentedly green appearance of the mountains. Cheaply operated air-propelled hover-craft have made watering simple during periods of drought. The fire-resistant chaparral belt has proved so efficient that even blazes started by lightning have been reduced to a minimum and quickly extinguished by the use of flying cranes.

In the vast leafy parklands so provided wilderness areas have been carefully preserved. Yet at the same time innumerable amphitheaters and auditoriums have been provided for specialized activities in woodcraft, the drama, and musical presentations.

Even in the midst of the areas bisected by grassy streets new park areas have been set up as cities and counties have cooperated more intelligently under the arrangement provided by the Southern California Association of Governments established in October 1965. This splendid organization permitted governmental units to cooperate on a voluntary basis among themselves as contrasted with the coercion attempted under some "metropolitan government" plans advocated by the State of California and resisted resolutely by cities and counties intent upon preserving their independence. Along the beaches too this procedure has enabled the utilization of all strands still available for the public.

Everywhere, there is visible the constant fluidity of the population: helicopters dotting the sky and finding convenient heliports on all major buildings, flying autos carrying suburbanites to subdivisions designed especially for "the air set," a ground-level scurrying to shopping and amusement centers.

Flying classrooms convey children every day to places of historic interest for firsthand views: the Los Angeles Plaza with its restored buildings and period costumes, San Juan Capistrano Mission, where the white pigeons and the famous swallows have become accustomed to their giant hovering rivals, the site of the signing of the Treaty of Cahuenga near Hollywood Bowl, the scene of pirate raids by freebooter Hippolyte Bouchard in 1818, the spot where San Gabriel was founded and then washed away, the location of the first power plant in Southern California, the Old Spanish Trail, and the First Navel Orange Tree, among many others.

* * *

His task, as Sam Yorty keeps telling himself, is to evaluate daily the constant blending of Past, Present, and Future, of which history always has been compounded. His hope is that on the Los Angeles of the Future there will be the impress of his own wishes for it, in better living for all.

Looking out from the City Hall tower on that distant day, with the mountains glistening and the sea sparkling as they encompass the swarming millions of inhabitants in their endless pursuits, Sam knows what he would like to see. It would be not only a physical scene. It would be a culmination of mental and spiritual forces set in motion long before. Sam would want to see enthusiasm, zest for work, a constant widening of knowledge, an appreciation of life as an opportunity for creativeness, a passion for individual rights; not total leisure, apathy, continual ease, refusal to look ahead, creature comforts to the exclusion of all else.

Fantasy? Idle dream? Sam cannot say for sure. He is positive of only one thing, that if there is to be a bright Tomorrow he has to keep working for it Today.

CHAPTER XXX

They shall sit every man under his vine and his fig tree.

MICAH IV, 4

One Saturday morning the lower driveway of Mayor Yorty was piled high with bush trimmings and all manner of trash from a job of driveway widening at his hilltop home in Studio City. It looked almost like a symbol of "trash barrel Sam" in the first campaign slugging it out with "the tin can monopoly" for the kind of combined trash collection most housewives wanted. It was a mess. Cars could hardly get in and out of the narrow passageway beside the trash to go up the inclined drive to the house.

At about 11:30 A.M. Betty Yorty came in where Sam was being interviewed and remarked, "Well, the trash man missed us today. What shall we do?"

Sam's reaction was instantaneous.

"Don't call them back!" he admonished. "Just phone and ask them to get it on the next regular round."

It was a typical and spontaneous reflex of a man whose home, in his own estimation, is not only his refuge from public life but also in the same category as that of every other citizen in regard to "special service" on Saturdays or any other day. Later in the day, though, the trash was gone. Somebody evidently had realized the error of his ways.

The Yorty house sits on a knoll looking out in three directions over the San Fernando Valley. It is presided over by Jet, a Dalmatian female acquired when Bill, the Yorty's only child, now twenty, was a small boy. Jet isn't worth shucks as a watchdog but she is a privileged member of the Yorty family. She greets guests with dignity and affection although the Yortys believe she would cer-

244

tainly lavish the same attention on a burglar. Jet's main failing is her gluttony. Just prior to her last birthday anniversary on October 14 when she was going to be thirteen, Jet tried to advance the date of the celebration. On the drainboard of the sink when Betty had gone to the store, Jet spotted an eight-inch chocolate cake in a bakery box. Jet nuzzled it off the drainboard, ate one-half of the box to get inside, and then consumed the entire cake. By the time Betty got home Jet was writhing with acute indigestion and had to be rushed to the veterinary hospital. She did recover, but she missed her own birthday party.

Sam just naturally likes dogs, and always has.

"My first dog—a mongrel—I bought for a penny and named her 'Penny,'" Sam remembers. "I must have been about four years old. She was about the size of a terrier, maybe fifteen inches tall, brown with black stripes. I loved the dog and she followed me everywhere except to school. When my mother's Irish temper inclined her to give me physical punishment—an old-fashioned whipping—I kept the dog near as she would not permit anyone to touch me in anger. I got a dog book and looked up all the dogs in it—I decided my little pal was a Great Dane—of all things! She was so smart she used to take a football by the strings and run through a line of kids as we tried to tackle her. When she got through she would stop and come dodging back through the other way.

"We have had Jet since Bill was a small boy. She is our first Dalmatian and is a full-fledged and privileged member of our family. She has never growled or shown any sign of temper except once when a poodle seemed to annoy her. She is the most gentle dog I have ever seen, and very intelligent. She has watched us so long and so intently she can predict some of our actions. The sight of a suitcase being packed puts an end to her otherwise perpetual-motion tail wagging, and she is so intent she looks like a statue."

The present Yorty home containing lovely furniture and paintings, many of them by Betty herself, is large enough for official entertainment but it shows no sign of ostentation. It has something definitely in common with the two other homes which have been owned by Sam and Betty since their marriage almost thirty years ago. This concerns Sam's penchant for providing surprises. Each home has been acquired under these circumstances.

"I'll never forget our first house and the way I got it," Sam likes to recall. "We hadn't been married very long and I was hardly making enough to get along on. I was in the Legislature but the salary was so small and I had just gotten my law degree and was going into practice. My friend, Sam Green of Inglewood who was a former Assemblyman, was going to get married and he wanted to sell a little house he owned in the southwest part of Los Angeles. He offered it to me for a very small down payment. Betts and I went to look at it. There was a sign out front saying it was for sale but I didn't let on that there was much chance we could get it. We looked it over and both fell in love with it, but I kept saying I didn't think we could scrape up a down payment.

"Betts was completely fooled. She just about gave up hope of getting it although it was exactly what she wanted, but she tried to be brave about it and not let on to me. I went ahead and made the deal with Sam Green and then one day said to Betts, 'Let's go see if that house has been sold yet. I don't think we can afford it but I'd like to see if the for sale sign is still there.' We drove up to the house but the sign was down and I said in a real disappointed voice, 'Oh, somebody must have grabbed it. Let's just go up to the door and ask, anyway.' I had Betts' brother Norman hidden out in the house with a bottle of champagne. Betts didn't catch on that the house was ours until we opened the door and Norman handed her a champagne glass.

"Later on when I got elected to Congress in 1950 I flew back ahead to get a little idea of what I was supposed to do and to arrange for a hotel where we could live. I think one of the great thrills of my life was as we flew into Washington and I looked down at the great dome of the Capitol thinking I was going to be a Representative there. I wondered, too, how to go about finding a place to live. I really didn't want to stay in any hotel. As soon as I could I hunted around and found a house on 32nd Street and made a down payment. I located furniture by answering ads and taking a taxi to the residences of Congressmen who had been beaten and were going to have to move away. When Betts arrived we stayed at first at the hotel and then I said, 'Why don't we at least try a little house hunting.' We wandered around and finally came up to this house on 32nd Street and she thought it looked pretty nice and we ought to try to get inside. Once more she didn't suspect a thing. I took her up to the door and it wasn't until she actually got inside that she realized that we had another house.

"It was the same way out here in Studio City. We had looked at this house which once belonged to Mickey Rooney but it had been empty and had gotten real rundown. It was a mess. The pool and the yard and the house all looked neglected. Betts and Bill and I looked it over and I could tell it was basically sound if it could be bought at a proper price. This was right after I was elected mayor for the first time and we had all been over in Catalina resting up.

"I came back first and went to the foreclosure sale on the place and was lucky enough to get it. It's on a great lot with a tremendous view and I knew the house and yard could be fixed up. When Betts came home I said, 'Let's go up on that hill and take another look at that old rundown house.' As we arrived a lot of friends came streaming out carrying 'Welcome Home' signs and it wasn't till then that Betts realized we'd got ourselves another home."

Sam at home likes to slouch around unshaven and in an old robe early in the morning or on Saturday when he has a few minutes away from official duties. He will sit out beside the pool with a cup of coffee and glance appreciatively at the view in between reading the newspapers. Sometimes the previous day will have been so hectic that he gets his first news happenings in the council from an account in the press. This was the way he learned on a Saturday of the decision finally reached by the City Council—as he had urged long ago—to install automatic and simultaneous electrical voting apparatus.

"They should have done it way back," he commented, "because the old system of voting alphabetically gave people down at the end of the line such as Rosalind Wyman the chance to evaluate all the other votes and go along if it seemed advisable or make some maneuver which wouldn't have been possible with this simultaneous voting."

Sam's passion for reading dates back so far it fades into the shadows of earliest childhood.

"I don't remember when I started reading to myself but I loved Andersen's tales," he recalls. "Very early I liked biographies better than fiction because I liked the sense of reality and I gained inspiration from the accomplishments of others. I read some Horatio Alger books when I was young. I have read the biographies of people from many walks of life—Washington, Lincoln, Jackson, Sam Houston, Caruso, Chaliapin, Wagner, Bizet, Beethoven, and many others. I have read the works of many philosophers and many religious writers. In my early quest for truth I read Robert Ingersoll and later completely rejected his views.

"Much of my knowledge of history since around 1919 or so is the result of avid attention to current events as reported in the press.

I still read several newspapers a day and enjoy seeing the same events described as if they were quite different."

Among his mementos is a slightly tattered copy of a song dating back to the musical era in Sam's life. It is "Takea Me Backa Tony" with the credit line "Lyrics by Sam W. Yorty." It was published in 1930, with music by Marini. The fact that his composing efforts had not been forgotten over the years was made clear to Sam in 1965 when a letter from the Music Mart in Los Angeles disclosed that a copy of the song had just turned up there. The music store wanted to know whether the "Sam W. Yorty" on the cover was the present Mayor Yorty of Los Angeles. Sam cheerfully admitted it was.

Betts and Sam Yorty work in the closest unity in the home on everything that affects the family and particularly their son, Bill, a college student.

While he was still in high school at Harvard School in Los Angeles, Bill won an award for the best poem in a state-wide contest conducted at the University of California at Davis. Sam and Betts thereafter, in bringing out the poem for perusal by family friends, showed as much pride in it as if Bill had made a 90-yard run in a championship football game.

When the Dodgers won the 1965 National League Pennant race and went up to Minneapolis-St. Paul to play the first two games of the World Series there, Sam had to do a lot of adjusting to schedules. A few weeks before when the Dodgers were four and a half games behind the Giants he had felt free to make commitments for speeches and other appearances. Then all of a sudden he found it necessary as the Chief Executive of the contending city in the World Series to represent Los Angeles at the two first games. Then as a reciprocal courtesy he entertained not one mayor, but two—those of Minneapolis and St. Paul, Arthur Naftalin and George Vavoulis—because the Twins wanted every rooter they could get.

Somebody had told Sam when the Dodgers were trounced twice in a row in Minnesota despite the efforts of both Don Drysdale and Sandy Koufax that he should have gone in as a relief pitcher. Instead of doing this he had the confidence to wait and see the Dodgers redeem themselves with the homefolks by winning three straight with the pitching prowess of Claude Osteen and the re-generated Drysdale and Koufax, and then go on to take the Series.

On the walls of the Yorty home are innumerable pictures of Sam in all sorts of political and social situations. One of his favorites is of a jam session on the TV show of another Nebraskan, Johnny Carson. Jimmy Stewart the actor is on accordion, Phyllis Diller on sax, Carson is on drums, and Sam Yorty is on banjo.

"We were hot that night. I'd like to do it all over again," Sam exclaims.

He gets little opportunity because of the press of his obligations to indulge his taste for personal participation in music. At one time Betty played the piano but she has been too busy of recent years to keep it up. Sam and Bill have to provide the music.

On the walls of the living room and dining room are examples of Betty's oil paintings ranging from portraits of Jet the Dalmatian to Paris scenes in the impressionist tradition. She has felt an urge to be a painter ever since she was a girl but the main trouble nowadays is that she so rarely finds time for lessons. She has progressed beyond the point of mere amateur canvases and needs professional guidance to advance her art.

"I got time for a lesson yesterday!" she will exclaim to her mother, Mrs. Hensel, when she sees her, as if she had stolen away for a Caribbean vacation.

Betty is active in social and money-raising affairs for Harvard School from which Bill graduated, and where he was active in football and track, including the 100-yard dash. Bill spent his first year at Occidental College in Los Angeles, then went to the University of California at Berkeley and, in 1965 entered Grenoble School near the Swiss border in France.

Sam when possible permits himself the luxury of watching a football game on Saturdays. He is a rabid fan for USC against Notre Dame, even though Betty was with the Notre Dame contingent when they met in Palm Springs. She forgives him for this.

Betty does all her own housework and cooking in the same way she did when they were first married except on the occasion of an official party or reception at the house. Then she has professional help. Otherwise she depends only on a cleaning woman who comes in twice a week. She appears always to be filling up the coffeepot for friends who drop in or for the "regulars" who come over in the evenings for a game of paddle tennis on the court by the garage to help keep Sam in condition physically. The demands on Sam are so sudden and unexpected that the paddle tennis friends keep themselves "on call" in case he gets a few minutes of free time for a game. They feel it is part of their contribution to maintain his remarkable state of fitness. The members of the team include Myrna

Dell, Lorraine Erickson, Rhonda Fleming, Angela (Green) Martin, Marie Hupp (Marie Windsor), Eileen Kenyon, Tippi (Hedron) Marshall and Noel Marshall, Rudy Ralston, Mel Erickson, C. B. Jordan, Stewart Martin, Jack Hupp, Dr. Keith Kenyon, Irv Edelstein, Louis Gill, and Tony Jackson.

Most of all, though, Sam depends on the swimming pool to keep him feeling in trim. He goes in every morning. It is as much a ritual as his brief period for meditation. Even if it is raining he has his swim, or swims, because if it is warm in late afternoon when he gets home he will take time for another dip.

Closeness of family ties is an important factor in Yorty family life. Sentiment in the Irish tradition always prevails. When he first went to Congress in 1951 Sam took Betty to a big family reunion at the old "Yordy" farm in Lancaster County, Pennsylvania, where there were uncles, aunts, cousins, and assorted children from all over the country. The following year Sam and Betty went on a little pilgrimage to Clonmel, his mother's birthplace in Ireland.

On a recent trip to Lincoln Sam went to see his favorite teacher whom he remembered from his ninth-grade days, and found Mrs. Grubb apparently as glad to see him as he was to see her. He reminded her of her comment advising him to try to be a "statesman" and she indicated she felt he was on the right road. Later, on the occasion of Mrs. Grubb's eighty-ninth birthday in the fall of 1965, he sent her special greetings.

It was one of the great disappointments of Sam's life that his mother did not know of his election as Mayor of Los Angeles. She was so ill that she was in a coma. Few people knew it but Mayor Sam Yorty went every day to the hospital during the many months from the early part of 1961 until the early part of 1962 when his mother died. Then, soon after, his stepfather also became mortally ill and Sam also visited him every day in the hospital until his death.

The vivid personality of Sam's mother still remains alive in the Yorty household. Sam speaks often of her great courage, her capacity for work, her Irish intuition. He firmly believes he himself has extrasensory perception, a "sixth sense" which occasionally manifests itself.

"I once had a friend in Lincoln, a boy named Gene Erisman who came out to Los Angeles and became an auditor," Sam recounts. "For a while we saw a lot of each other. Then he got married and was divorced and somehow we drifted apart. I hadn't seen him for years. Then one evening I got the strangest feeling I should get in touch with him. I started phoning around to see if I could locate him but didn't have any luck. My sister Enid was with me, and she could see how strong this feeling of mine was. 'Keep on trying,' she told me. Finally I phoned a family friend from Lincoln.

"When she answered, she was crying. 'How did you know to call?' she asked. 'I just got word Gene was killed in a crash in Santa Paula and my daughter who was with him was injured.'

"I arranged Gene's funeral."

When Sam's mother was still alive she and Betty's mother were frequent visitors at the Yorty home. Mrs. Hensel still drops by at frequent intervals and helps to dissipate the loneliness occasioned by Bill's absence in Europe. The Yortys frequently see Sam's sister Enid who lives in Los Angeles. His other sister, Kathleen or Kitty (Mrs. Leslie J. Seacrest), lives in Lincoln. On a recent visit there, Sam and Kitty took Betts to see all the places Sam lived as a boy, including a little tower which was his room in the former governor's mansion which had become an apartment house operated by Sam's mother. At another house, Sam looked for the screenporch where he slept but it had been turned into a room.

"Too much progress!" he commented wryly. "The snow used to drift in when I slept there."

On trips "back home" in Nebraska and elsewhere, Sam guards against eating too much. The temptation at barbecues and banquets is great but he resists manfully because he is determined to keep his weight down. When he went into office in 1961 he weighed almost 180 pounds, and he figured it was too much for anyone of his medium height. He started dieting. The worst problem was cutting out pies and pancakes, which he loves. But he not only did this but eliminated bread, potatoes, and every kind of dessert, and compelled himself to eat all other foods in moderation. As a result he got his weight down to 155, and there it stays. Fortunately, he is fond of simple foods such as sauerkraut, in fact cabbage in all forms; and of turnips. He prefers fish and chicken to other meats, and hence can be happy on the "luncheon circuit" where he eats most of his mid-day meals.

"If I've managed to work my way down under 155 with a game of paddle tennis on Sunday, I let myself go and have a big dinner," he confesses.

In the executive dining room at the City Hall, outside guests are invited to have a luncheon cocktail if they wish. Sam takes a glass too.

"But I have apple juice in it," he says. "It's the same color as whisky, and I'm appearing sociable—without many calories or getting sleepy in the afternoon!"

At home, Betty takes care of innumerable phone messages for Sam, although lately she has necessarily had to get secretarial help for one day a week. One big task is keeping up with Sam's scrapbooks. He has dozens of them with thousands of clippings about his political activities dating back to his first campaign in 1936.

One whole book is filled with clippings from the *People's World*, denouncing Sam in the most vicious terms. He treasures this.

A favorite item from the past was written by Sam's friend, Joe Longfellow, an Indian who was editor of the Westlake *Post* at the time Sam first went to the Assembly. It has the flavor of American journalism of another day:

FLASH
Off to Washington

Last week we ran a story about Sam Yorty, our Assemblyman, and closed the story by saying "Yorty Goes to Town" or is it "Washington?" Well, the answer is Sam has been made a delegate at an important national conference in Washington this month. This is Sam's first trip to the East. Don't forget your red flannels, Sam.

Of all the thousands of letters that come in to Sam at the office and at home, only a few touch the heart. One of these arrived shortly after Sam's re-election as mayor over James Roosevelt. For Sam it evoked memories of himself as a tiny boy on the streets of Lincoln looking up at a figure in frock coat, who was talking to his father. That figure, later idolized when Sam was old enough, was long since dead, but the letter was from his son.

It read:

June 23, 1965

Dear Sam:

I can't see well enough to drive any more so I seldom get into Los Angeles—but I read the newspapers. Wish I could have been there for your inauguration, for you are still one of my favorite people in public life.

More power to you Sam— My hearty congratulations and every good wish for a long and successful administration.

Sincerely yours,
(*signed*) Wm. Jennings Bryan, Jr.

Along with the clippings and letters, Sam has scores of family pictures taken in Lincoln, in Pennsylvania, in Ireland. He is a rank sentimentalist about them, and knows great-aunts and great-uncles by their first names.

The ornate family Bible contains a genealogical record down to Bill Yorty. Sam looks at it with a memory covering more than half a century. In it the latest listing is of his mother's death. Now it awaits the happier listing of more marriages and births. Sam says firmly about the entries:

"We must keep them up."

Inevitably, on the comforting eminence of his home hilltop with Betts, Sam thinks of his mother's oft-repeated story of the flood on Salt Creek before he was born, and her determination amid those horrors to find a place of safety and refuge. She longed for the mountains and high places, away from the dangers of the flatlands. To her, it became an abiding hope not only for herself but for her children, too. Sam was sure she and Betts both wanted him to stand on the high places, yearning to attain the challenging horizon of the Future. . . .

BIBLIOGRAPHY

BOOKS

Ainsworth, Edward M., *Eagles Fly West*, New York: Macmillan, 1946.

Ainsworth, Edward M., *Leo Carrillo's The Calfornia I Love*, New York: Prentice-Hall, 1961.

Allen, Robert S., editor, *Our Fair City*, New York: The Vanguard Press, Inc., 1947.

Altamira, Rafael (translated by Muna Lee), *A History of Spain*, Toronto, New York and London: D. Van Nostrand Company, Inc., 1949.

Bancroft, Hubert Howe, *History of California*, Vol. I, II, III, IV, and V, San Francisco: The History Company, 1886.

Bartlett, John, *Bartlett's Familiar Quotations*, Boston and Toronto: Little, Brown and Company, 1955.

Burke, Robert E., *Olson's New Deal for California*, Berkeley and Los Angeles: University of California Press, 1953.

Carr, Donald E., *Breath of Life*, New York: Norton, 1965.

Crouch, Winston W. and Dinerman, Beatrice, *Southern California Metropolis*, Berkeley and Los Angeles: University of California Press, 1963.

Cunningham, Glenn, editor, *Day Tours: Geographical Journeys in the Los Angeles Area*, Palo Alto: Pacific Books, 1964.

The First Los Angeles City and County Directory: 1872, Los Angeles: The Ward Ritchie Press, 1963.

Graves, J. A., *My Seventy Years in California*, Los Angeles: Times Mirror, 1928.

Harris, Joseph P., *California Politics*, Stanford: Stanford University Press, 1961.

Hill, Laurance L., *La Reina: Los Angeles in Three Centuries*, Los Angeles: Security-First National Bank, 1931.

Mann, Dean E., *The Politics of Water in Arizona*, Tucson: University of Arizona Press, 1963.

Newmark, Marco R., *Jottings in Southern California History*, Los Angeles: The Ward Ritchie Press, 1955.

Newmark, Harris, *Sixty Years in Southern California: 1853–1913*, New York: The Knickerbocker Press, 1926.

Nolting, Orin F. and Arnold, David S., editors, *The Municipal Year Book 1965*, Chicago: The International City Managers' Association, 1965.

Schlesinger, Arthur M., Jr., *The Politics of Upheaval: The Age of Roosevelt*, Boston: Houghton Mifflin Co., 1960.

Steffens, Lincoln, *The Autobiography of Lincoln Steffens*, New York: Harcourt, Brace and Co., 1931.

Stone, Adolf, editor, *California Information Almanac* (1966) Garden City, N.Y.: Doubleday & Company, Inc., 1965.

Stone, Irving, *Men to Match My Mountains: The Opening of the Far West 1840–1900*, Garden City, N.Y.: Doubleday & Company, Inc., 1956.

Weinberg, Arthur and Lila, *The Muckrakers: 1902–1912*, New York: Simon and Schuster, 1961.

Workman, Boyle, *The City That Grew*, Los Angeles: The Southland Publishing Co., 1935.

Yorty, Samuel William, *Report to the People*, Los Angeles: Citizens for Mayor Yorty, 1964.

PERIODICALS

Ebony, The White Problem in America, Vol. XX: No. 10, Aug. '65.

Fortune, Los Angeles Prototype of Supercity, by Richard Austin Smith, 98 to 212, Mar. '65.

Newsweek, Upset, 57:38, Je. 12 '61.

Newsweek, Wins by Ins, 65:26–27, Apr. 19 '65.

Time, After Sam's Scalp, 84:15, Dec. 25 '64.

Time, Renegade's Triumph, 77:15, Je. 9 '61.

U.S. News, Candidates Size up to the Election, Interview 37:79, Nov. 12 '54.

NEWSPAPERS

Hollywood Citizen News covering period from 1936 to date.

Lincoln Star (Nebr.) covering period from 1936 to date.

Long Beach Press Telegram covering period from 1936 to date.

Los Angeles Examiner covering period from 1936 to date.

Los Angeles Herald covering period from 1936 to date.

Los Angeles Herald-Examiner covering period to date.

Los Angeles Times covering period from 1936 to date.

New York Times covering period from 1936 to date.
Omaha World-Herald (Nebr.) covering period from 1936 to date.
Pasadena Star News covering period from 1936 to date.
People's World covering period to date.
Sacramento Bee covering period from 1936 to date.
Sacramento Union covering period from 1936 to date.
San Fernando Valley Times covering period from 1936 to date.
San Francisco Chronicle covering period from 1936 to date.
San Francisco Examiner covering period from 1936 to date.
Westlake Post covering period from 1936 to date.

MANUSCRIPT MATERIAL

Yorty, Samuel William, Personal Correspondence, covering period from 1927–1965.

Yorty, Samuel William, Personal Scrapbooks, covering period from 1936–1965.